Conflicting Landscapes

American Schooling/Alaska Natives

By

Clifton Bates & Michael J. Oleksa

Library of Congress Control Number: 2008923337

ISBN: 978-1-57833-396-7

First Edition

10 9 8 7 6 5 4 3 2 1

Printed March 2008

Printed by Everbest Printing Co., Ltd., Nansha, China
through **Alaska Print Brokers**, Anchorage, Alaska

Book design: Vered R. Mares, **Todd Communications**
Cover Art: Watercolor Painting by Xenia Oleksa
Photographs: From the personal collection of the authors
Clifton Bates & Michael J. Oleksa

This book was typeset in 12 point Adobe Garamond Pro.

Published by

4300 B Street, Suite 207
Anchorage, Alaska 99503
(907) 243-2944
www.kuskokwim.com • info@kuskokwim.com

Distributed by:
Todd Communications
611 E. 12th Ave.
Anchorage, Alaska 99501-4603
(907) 274-8633 (TODD) Fax: (907) 929-5550
sales@toddcom.com • **WWW.ALASKABOOKSANDCALENDARS.COM**

ACKNOWLEDGEMENTS

For their comments, suggestions and support, the authors would like to acknowledge and thank sincerely Sarah Scanlon, Dr. Ted Mala, Dr. Richard Dauenhauer, Dr. Judith Kleinfeld, Joyce Gardella, Doreen Brown, Maver Carey, Leo Morgan, Anu Wysocki, The Kuskokwim Corporation, our friends at the Thai Village Restaurant, and all our students, past and present who have taught us so much and challenged us to expand our own vision of the world.

— *Clifton Bates & Michael J. Oleksa*

The sections of this book bracketed by this symbol, created by Xenia Oleksa, often relate authentic incidents whose locations and personalities have been changed to protect the identities of the real people whose privacy we have sought to respect.

DEDICATIONS & SPECIAL THANKS

For My Mother and Byron
&
To My Daughter, Ara Jaren
In Memory of Her Mother, My Wife
Pia

Special thanks to my students past (including Gary Pete), to my late father, to Thomas Bate, Pat Shepley, Fred Pickering, Greg Clark, Sean O'Leary, Jack Campbell, Ann Pham, Alex Hagler, Leo Morgan, Jim MacDiarmid, Phramaha Boonnet and, of course, Father Michael J. Oleksa.

— ***Clifton Bates***

In gratitude for the love, support and encouragement of my Aunts, Alice Oleska, Mary Radio, and Kathryn Solan, my Uncles, Metro Oleska, John Radio and Dr. John Solan and fifteen extraordinary teachers

Jean Gernert, Neil Moyer (in Pennsylvania)
Walter Giles and Carroll Quigley (Georgetown University)
Irene Reed and Lydia T. Black (University of Alaska)
Nicholas Arseniev, Alexandra Chetvertikova
Lydia and Veselin Kesich
Sophie Koulomzin
John Meyendorff, Alexander Schmemann
Sergei Verhovskoy, and my beloved sister

JoAnn Oleksa

— ***Michael J. Oleksa***

ABOUT THE AUTHORS

Clifton Bates

Clifton Bates was born in Seattle, Washington and educated at the University of Washington, earning a B.A. in Art, B.A. in English and a Master Degree in Education, Curriculum and Instruction with an emphasis on cross-cultural education. He also acquired a teaching certificate with endorsements in K-12 art, English/language arts and social studies and an administration certificate with endorsements as K-12 principal, program administrator and curriculum supervisor. He has been involved in Alaska Native education since 1977 as a teacher, school district administrator, and full time university professor. In 1991 Mr. Bates was presented the Sallie Mae/Newsweek Teacher Tribute Award. The Alaska Department of Education requested his participation on various committees such as developing the English/language arts State Standards, creating the Science and Math Frameworks, and reviewing State achievement tests. He was also selected as a member of the Writing Assessment Advisory Board and as presenter at Alaska Bilingual/Multicultural Conferences. He has had various poetry, short stories, and articles on Alaska Native education published over the years. In 1984 he wrote and produced with Alaska Public Television *Somebody's Taking Pictures*, an historical documentary aired statewide dedicated to the people of the Yukon-Kuskokwim Delta. His one act play, *Witnesses*, concerning indigenous cultures in transition, was one of 25 plays selected from 21 states and presented in 2005 at the Playwrights Showcase of the Western Region in Denver. He is a widower living in Chugiak, Alaska.

Michael James Oleksa

The Very Reverend Michael James Oleksa, Th. D., was born in Allentown, Pennsylvania and educated at Georgetown University (B.A. History, 1969) and St. Vladimir's Orthodox Theological Seminary, (M. Div. Cum laud, 1973) before completing his doctoral work at the Pravoslavna Bohoslovecka Fakuta of Prague, in Presov, Slovakia (D. Th., 1988). His first publications were written in Yup'ik Eskimo, a "hymnal" containing the fixed hymns for Orthodox Vespers, Matins and the Divine Liturgy, and a short biography of SS. Innocent Veniaminov and Jacob Netsvetov. He has taught Alaska Native History and Cross Cultural Communications at Alaska Pacific University and all three main campus of the University of Alaska's system, and has offered training to teachers, lawyers, judges, federal and state as well as corporate leaders in these fields for over three decades. His four-part Public Television series, *Communicating Across Cultures*, has been widely acclaimed. The author of several books, including ***Alaskan Missionary Spirituality, Orthodox Alaska,*** and ***Another Culture/ Another World***, Father Michael has received the Alaskan of the Year Denali Award, the First Alaskans Award from the Alaska Federation of Natives, and citations from the Alaska State Legislature and the National Governors' Association as well as the Board of Regents of the University of Alaska. Father Oleksa continues to offer courses and workshops across the USA and abroad to promote intercultural understanding and interracial harmony, while residing with his Yup'ik wife, Xenia, and serving as adjunct faculty at Alaska Pacific University in Anchorage.

In addition to their professional work, the co-authors have lived a marital commitment to the success of cross-cultural communication. Fr. Michael's wife, Xenia, is Yup'ik from the village of Kwethluk; Clif's late wife was from Thailand, and Clif continues his involvement with the immigrant Buddhist community in Anchorage.

— *Dr. Richard Dauenhuer*

TABLE OF CONTENTS

SECTION I: AS IT IS AND HAS BEEN
Part One by Michael J. Oleksa
A Personalized View of Native Schooling: The Historical, Social, and Cultural Context

Examples of Training Curricula
by Michael J. Oleksa

Chapter 11
by Clifton Bates

FROM THE PUBLISHER

The Kuskokwim Corporation is proud to publish ***Conflicting Landscapes***, a book we hope will spark discussion and debate on educational issues in rural Alaska. I encourage Alaska Native parents, school board members, rural teachers and school administrators, as well as university professors, state officials and legislators to read and consider seriously the message of this book.

Few Alaskans realize that in the 1800's, multi-lingual, multicultural schools graduated Alaska Native leaders who not only founded churches, but operated trading posts, built and sailed ships, mapped our coasts, and spoke, read and wrote two, three and four languages. Whenever we are tempted to think that we cannot succeed, or have never succeeded in school, we should recall the accomplishments of our ancestors, over a hundred and fifty years ago. There is no such thing as "we can't." Our history proves that.

Our current schools manage to graduate some articulate, visionary leaders. But the percentage of successful alumni compared to our drop-out rate is discouraging. This book examines school problems and recommends new strategies. The authors insist that teachers need to be more intensely trained in cross-cultural communication in order to work effectively with students, parents and village elders, just as they would if they were Peace Corps volunteers destined for overseas assignments. Village educators also need to reconsider the curriculum as it is taught in middle and high school, incorporating relevant, meaningful courses that will interest and challenge all students, both the college bound and the majority who intend to remain permanently in their home villages. We will need to reexamine the way we teach reading and writing, to assure all elementary students can read to learn beginning in the fourth and fifth grades. School officials will need also to devise a way of documenting their successes, and sharing these with educators in other parts of their region and across the state.

My hopes are that, as stated in the book, Native corporations and Native organizations unite "and assist and insist in the creation of truly culturally responsive schools that are well-designed, positive places for Native children to learn" and this book is a catalyst to help make this happen. If we continue to rely on the Department of Education, the state university system, or school districts, at least based on observations and experiences of the last 30 years, very little is likely to change.

I highly commend this book to all who are interested and concerned about the future of schooling in rural Alaska, and hope that our corporation's support of this publication will result not only in a deeper appreciation of the task and obstacles we face, but a productive conversation about how we might collectively rethink and restructure the mission of our schools, to assure the success and well-being of future generations of Alaska Native children. This book is about education, but it's for the kids.

— Maver Carey
President/CEO, The Kuskokwim Corporation

Like many Alaska Native parents, I've been concerned about what schools do to our kids. We have too many drop-outs, and too many failures. As a school board member, I've been perplexed and frustrated by the educators, both administrators and classroom teachers who regularly circulate through our villages. We have too much instability and too little "institutional memory." I'm worried about an educational system that pays. so little attention to our cultures, our histories, our identities. I am upset about schools that seem to do more harm than good to too many wonderful kids.

Father Michael J. Oleksa and Clifton Bates have been concerned about the same issues, and have put their observations, criticisms, analysis and proposed reforms into this book. I am excited about its message, and the clear and informative way in which they present the complex problems we face in rural Alaskan schools.

I'm sure there will be some officials who will disagree and disapprove of some of the information in ***Conflicting Landscapes***, but I urge everyone interested in the education of Native children to read this book and consider its message. At least we have, at last, some of the most basic issues presented here for discussion and debate.

I am pleased that the Kuskokwim Corporation has decided to fund the publication of this book, which we hope will spark serious discussion of these critical and chronic problems, widespread and typical in our rural schools. We owe it to our kids to repair what is broken and improve what can be salvaged in our current system. Let's begin the conversation.

— Leo Morgan
Chairman of the Board
The Kuskokwim Corporation

PREFACE

This book has been written by two men who care deeply about children specifically Alaskan Native children and their communities. We realize that the health and well–being of villages are primarily village concerns and village responsibilities. No one can make a particular neighborhood, barrio, ghetto, ward or hamlet a healthier, happier place except the people who live there. Parents bear the greatest burden, together with Elders and tribal leaders. But the government has mandated that children attend school for most of their waking hours, five days a week for a minimum of ten years. Having assumed control and custody of the children, the school plays a central, critical role in their lives for a formative decade. How we treat those children entrusted to us, how we relate to them, guide and instruct them, have long-term effects on them, their families and communities. And having watched children enter school at ages five or six and leave between 16 and 18, our experience indicates we are doing serious harm to many if not most of Alaska's Native school children. While some certainly succeed and go on to perform well at the post-secondary level, many, too many, leave school damaged, hurt, wounded, depressed, angry and tragically suicidal. We believe Alaskans should reflect on what we have been doing for the last hundred years in the name of "education" and consider alternatives.

We do not mean to over generalize. Not all our experiences apply to all places or situations. We have punctuated our writing with real stories about real people, incidents we personally witnessed, educators, students and parents we have known while altering their names to protect their privacy and identity. Some of our anecdotes will resonate with teachers, administrators, parents and alumni. Others may not. We offer our experience for whatever it may be worth. But we are not writing fiction here. We are not making this up.

We do not intend only to rail against the establishment like two over-aged products of the 1960's. We do not want only to critique but to offer concrete suggestions, to propose genuine long-term reforms. We believe that what we have been doing and without significant change of attitude, direction or policy, continue to do is unnecessarily detrimental to children and communities about whom we care deeply, and we are indignant about this. Some of our anger erupts on these pages. But it is that frustration with the inertia, the lack of commitment and concern that inspires and motivates us to offer these pages.

The Alaska Association of School Boards has, for years, promoted the SEARCH Institute's ASSETS research. Hundreds of Alaskan rural communities have participated in the orientation to the 40 Developmental Assets as developed by Derek Peterson, using balloons to represent the kids, and yarn to symbolize the positive encouragement the Assets provide. The strands of yarn that form a network, a "dream catcher" of safety and support, are held by caring, loving adults, parents, Elders, and teachers. In Alaskan villages, teachers typically come and go more frequently than certified staff in other parts of the country. Even when teachers bond with particular students, or their families or communities, they are not permanent residents. They leave, cutting the threads of concern and affection they had provided. The next recruits arrive to teach at the school, not knowing which kids have become more vulnerable with the departure of the last ones.

But this institutional amnesia goes deeper. A teacher in one school discovers ways to interest, fascinate and inspire her class. For years that school does well. It may even be recognized as a model school for its amazing progress or accomplishments. Then that teacher moves on and the school returns to its former patterns. The new guys have no idea what the last ones did, why they did it, how it worked, and what they might do to perpetuate that success. The same occurs at the district level. One observant administrator offers a remedy for a particular problem, and it seems to work. For several years this idea is embraced by that district and the students' academic performance improves. But when the superintendent retires or possibly transfers to a larger district and a better paying or more comfortable position, the project collapses. We have no mechanism for documenting successful initiatives, and no institutional way of remembering and sharing them.

Teachers today are sent to rural Alaska as if they were going to suburban Massachusetts. Imported from elsewhere, 95% of Alaska's educators are non-Native and are given little or no relevant training in cross-cultural issues or Alaska Native history. We find this peculiar. The Peace Corps would not send volunteers abroad without significant training in the language, history and culture of the people to whom they are sent. When the methods and techniques they learned in college don't seem to produce the same results, teachers are forced to reconsider their approach. Is there something inapplicable here about the curriculum, the methods or the approach or is there something different about these children? If one assumes the theory and methods imported from elsewhere may not apply here, one adjusts the curriculum and approaches, but that is possible only if the teacher has interest, energy and opportunity for exploring alternatives. It is so much easier to conclude the kids are the problem, the parents are the problem, the village and culture and language and history are the problem. It is too easy to give up.

How many times have we heard professional educators complain about "these kids" or "this place" as if they could achieve higher success rates if they only had another group of children somewhere else? But they don't. They have these students in this village. And they are provided precious little guidance and support as they struggle to instruct and inspire their pupils. It seems that many have already given up and are content to collect their paychecks, build up their pensions, and survive another year, planning ultimately to escape elsewhere "outside," leaving the wreckage of cultures and lives behind them.

We understand how hard it is to teach in rural Alaska. The challenges can seem overwhelming. The temptation to give up looms large. But we think we can do better. We can prepare teachers better. We can develop more appropriate curricula and methods. We can develop closer ties with parents and community leaders. We can build ASSETS. We can help the school become a positive place where, together with churches, tribal cultural organizations, health care providers and state and federal agencies, we can build happier, healthier communities, where children grow up with a positive sense of their personal and cultural identities, and become productive citizens in the modern world.

So we ask the reader to consider the case we make, first in our critique of what has been and continues to be the destructive patterns embedded in the way we teach, the things we teach, the way we have historically operated for the last hundred years, just to make sense of the problems we face today, and second in our proposals for improving, learning from our mistakes and successes, and ending the ignorance or indifference to the cultural backgrounds of our children and their families, and our institutional amnesia which precludes reflection or reform. Read all that we have to say, both as critique and as suggestion. And then, let's talk. Let's stop denying we have a problem in Alaska Native education by pointing to the successes we have achieved or the progress we have made.

Of course we have some success stories. We do have Alaskan Native college graduates. We do have articulate, inspiring Native leaders, professional men and women in various professions around the state. But for every success we have twice as many tragic failures. For every graduate we have two or three drop outs. For every college alumnus we have five times more deaths, accidents, and suicides. For every star we have a dozen black holes. Our schools are failing too many of our children. We have seen this continue for over thirty years. We are weary, frustrated and upset by this, and we do not think we are alone. We are not ready to give up, however. And we hope the reader is not prepared to surrender either. We all have work to do.

We have divided our presentation into two parts, what has been and is, and what could be. The first section is necessary to detail what our story has been and how things got to be the way they are. Otherwise, people can jump to some strange and erroneous personal conclusions about the nature of the problem, so we think knowing the history is necessary and informative. But we don't want to stop with an indictment of past and present procedures and programs. We want to offer some concrete ways in which the situation might improve, today, right now, as well as over the next several years. We need to face, not deny the problems and understand them, and then proceed toward resolution. That is the structure of this book, and we hope that both parts will be informative and provocative. Our goal is not to impose our agenda. We hope to offer specific recommendations for serious consideration and debate to revitalize discussion about the chronic issues in Alaska Native education because we care deeply about these children, these communities. And we are certain we are not alone.

We offer this text as a companion to ***Another Culture/Another World***, previously published by the Alaska Association of School Boards. That book introduces the reader to five main Native Cultural groups in Alaska and recommends further discussion, investigation and study, with a selected bibliography. This volume, ***Conflicting Landscapes***, focuses intentionally on the history of the clash between cultures--the Global Literate Society (as Father Oleksa characterized it in the earlier book and on his four-part PBS television series, ***CommunicatingAcross Cultures***, produced at KTOO-TV in Juneau in 1994), and Traditional Local Societies--detailing the events that have shaped the direction of schooling in Alaska over the past two centuries. We have attempted to avoid duplicating material from ***AC/AW***, but urge readers of this presentation to consult its sibling for additional related information and insight into the issues discussed here.

How This Book Happened

Father Michael has been consulting on cross-cultural and Alaska Native history issues with school districts and health corporations for several decades. He met Clifton Bates in 1978, a teacher in rural Alaska at that time. Years later, as an assistant superintendent, Clif invited Father Michael to Kuspuk School District headquarters in Aniak, to speak to teachers, school board members and parents on several occasions. The two educators also met in airports and at conferences sporadically for several decades, until about 2002, when they discovered themselves both residing near Anchorage. They became the "we," the co-authors of this book.

Our discussions at periodic lunch meetings always ended with the same frustration and indignation until we decided to start recording our experiences and analyses and organizing them into themes, which after about six years became ***Conflicting Landscapes.*** We offer it as an invitation to all who share our concerns to join our continuing conversation on the direction, purpose and reform of Alaska Native Education.

SECTION I: AS IT IS AND HAS BEEN

PART ONE

A Personalized View of Native Schooling The Historical, Social and Cultural Context by Michael J. Oleksa

Introduction

I never planned to collaborate in writing a book on educational topics. My interests and focus have been in history, anthropology, linguistics and religion. My first childhood fascination was with American Indians. I wanted to be a Comanche or Apache when I grew up.

I don't recall why I identified so strongly with the First Americans. In the early years of television, westerns depicted them as savages, attacking and massacring innocent white folks for apparently no reason. But somehow I realized that the Indians were defending their homes and lands, and the Europeans were the invaders. I knew the Indians didn't have much chance against the more sophisticated weapons the cowboys and U.S. cavalry employed, but they were right and, from my perspective, the pioneers and soldiers were thieves, robbers and barbarians. I was in war paint and feathers regularly until I turned twelve.

My mother tried her best to convince me that this was impossible. A kid born to parents who were of Pennsylvania German and Lemko Ukrainian descent could not become a Native American warrior.

But they humored me. The 1955 family summer vacation took us to the Adirondack Mountains in northwestern New York State, where for me the main attraction was a tourist site named "Indian Village." There I met "Chief Smiling Bear" and his family, who were visiting from the Hopi Reservation in northern Arizona. Real Indians! I had my photo taken with the delegation and felt myself adopted into the tribe. "See! I can grow up to be an Indian, Mom!"

Years passed and my interests evolved. I was drawn, as a Yankee Pennsylvanian, to Gettysburg and a lifelong curiosity about the Civil War, the issues that fueled it, the passions it aroused, the leaders who were so totally committed to their Cause, especially Abraham Lincoln. I read the multivolume series produced by Carl Sandberg. I wrote essays and won contests with my knowledge of Old Abe, the most Christ-like figure in American history, complete with a hymn whose final verse explicitly linked Lincoln to Jesus. There was something noble, sacred about sacrificing oneself for others.

My study of language officially began in fifth grade, when my homeroom teacher offered fifteen minutes of conversational Spanish three times a week. He never translated what he was saying but through gesture and mime managed to convey his meaning, using games, charades and songs. I got all my practical language teaching methods from Mr. Moyer at Lincoln Elementary School.

But my interest in languages arose much earlier. My dad and his siblings normally conversed with my grandmother, whom we called "Baba," in the Lemko dialect of Ukrainian. I was never much of an ethnic nationalist, as many Ukrainian immigrants tended to be, since Baba told me that we had only identified as "Ukrainian" on this side of the Atlantic "What did we call ourselves in the Old Country, Baba?" "Rus!" she replied. But in America no one knew about these peasant farmers in the western Carpathian Mountains of what is today Poland, Slovakia, and Ukraine. Researching the ethno-history of this region many years later, I concluded my ancestors were a Slavic tribe, locally known as Lemko, who were exiled and persecuted for being different from their neighbors.

I spent my early childhood in a predominantly German-American neighborhood, whose central focus was St. Peter's Evangelical Lutheran Church. There was a bust of a famous man in the front yard, and I vowed that someday I'd learn to read well enough to decipher the inscription on its base. But passing by en route homeward in the third grade, I was frustrated in my attempt, since the monument was not only engraved in old gothic script, but in another language. I could recognize only the name "Martin Luther" in larger letters than the remaining German text. The nearby bulletin board announced meetings and services in both English and German and the pastor spoke with a pronounced accent. The congregation had brought Dr. Hagen Staak to serve its bilingual community and teach at nearby Muhlenberg College.

This was a bit more progressive than my father's Ukrainian parish, where the priest seemed to speak no English at all.

Up and down the streets were churches and clubs erected by their local constituencies, and labeled in various languages. There was a Polish-American and a Ukrainian-American Citizens Club a few blocks away. The Sokol Club, where my father regularly bowled, belonged to the Slovaks, who had their own parochial school as well. The Irish had a larger church, a school and even a convent. I was confused by the nuns' attire. They seemed like characters I'd encountered in a recent animated Disney film. I remember being hushed by my mother one afternoon when some sisters exited their residence and I exclaimed "Look, Mommy! The Queen of Hearts!"

The most exotic culture in our neighborhood was Syrian. I don't remember my first encounter with Arabic language, but I certainly remember being overwhelmed by Middle Eastern hospitality when, as a teen, I visited St. George's Antiochene Orthodox Church. And much to my amazement, worship there was conducted mostly in English. It was there that I heard the fourth-century Liturgy of St. John Chrysostom celebrated in my own language, and enjoyed my first taste of delicious Arabic cuisine.

Given this varied experience of different languages and customs, I developed an interest in international affairs and diplomatic history. I wanted to know where all these people came from and why they had left their homelands. The obvious answer was economic opportunity. Wars, class and social inequalities, revolutions and invasions had driven many from their ancestral lands to America's shores. Nearly all the Elders in my world had passed through Ellis Island and found jobs and a new life in the New World. Lee Iacocca, famous not only as CEO of Chrysler, but as the Chairperson spearheading the effort to restore the Statue of Liberty and the Ellis Island facilities, was my mother and uncle's classmate, a graduate of Allentown High School's class of 1940.

The only kid on my block, I could always find an elder to read stories to me, after which I entertained myself by pretending, acting the stories out, and performing them for my willing captive audience. I began reciting "pieces", memorized texts and poems at the age of three. I had the lead in many school productions, adding singing to my starring role in the Emperor's Nightingale. I sang in the youth choir, first at St. Peter's Lutheran and later in Slavonic at St. Mary's Orthodox church. And on Pentecost, my senior year in high school, I read the Epistle lesson for the first time—for myself and for the parish— in English. I was already a subversive revolutionary!

For some years music and art became my focus. I liked drawing and my high school instructors encouraged me to develop this talent, but I saw it more as a hobby than a calling. My mother and I enjoyed concerts, though we fought over my practice time on the accordion, where I gained some mastery of music theory and an appreciation for both folk and classical styles.

I was drawn to the study of theology during my three years catechetical study at the Lutheran church my mother attended. I became interested in historical and Biblical issues, but knew that entering the ministry would be problematic in my religiously divided household. It was more convenient and less controversial to pursue more secular studies. Lincoln's legal background drew me in that direction, but I had no real passion for criminal or civil law. Then John F. Kennedy was elected president.

I was only in eighth grade, but I was infatuated with JFK and inspired by his message. When an Irish Catholic was elected President of the USA, it said to our neighborhood that anything was possible. Even one of us could become the leader of the Free World. More than this, Kennedy's themes of self-sacrifice and seeking the betterment of others resonated with my earlier identification with the exploited and oppressed. "Ask not what your country can do for you, but what you can do for your country." Yes, that made sense to my generation. We had escaped the poverty of the Great Depression, though our parents recalled it well enough, and the turmoil and tragedy of the Second World War. We were living in the "Happy Days" of the century and we sensed that, and felt almost guilty about it. Our parents and grandparents had struggled and suffered. We had to do our part in our own way, somehow, somewhere.

And then came Viet Nam. Actually, after the assassination of JFK, nothing on the national political scene or our collective psyche was the same. Lee Harvey Oswald killed our innocence and optimism. Kennedy had challenged us to be of service, but he expected us to follow his lead and do so willingly, enthusiastically. LBJ had other ideas. With the draft in place, young men were going to serve whether they wanted to or not. And die in an effort to stem the tide of international communism, that it seemed threatened to engulf the world.

But as college students studying history and philosophy, we discovered that the war in Viet Nam had begun as a colonial war against French occupation and that the Vietnamese had won that struggle for national independence. However, the treaty ending that conflict artificially divided Viet Nam in half, awarding full independence to the north, and allowing several years for the southern half to decide, ultimately by a popular referendum, whether to join the north as one country or remain separate. The vote, however, was cancelled, because the US feared that South Viet Nam would choose to unite with a communist regime. So we set up a pro-American government and hoped that we could persuade the people of the south to remain a separate country. The duplicity here was clear. We were meddling in the internal affairs of Viet Nam, not for their benefit but for our own, in the global chess match known as the Cold War.

And the government, the State Department, the Secretary of Defense and the President himself had to regularly deceive the people by manipulating or distorting the facts to maintain support for their policies. As this became clear, my idealistic generation became increasingly disillusioned and ultimately angry. The anti-war movement not only opposed the policy of war, but the government that waged it. I was in the Georgetown University Edmund A. Walsh School of Foreign Service by then. I knew I would never take the State Department's entry exam. My service would have to be rendered elsewhere.

In the meantime, I lived within walking distance of St. Nicholas Orthodox Cathedral on Massachusetts Avenue, Embassy Row, and was overwhelmed with the simplicity and beauty of the choral music there. I bought serious theological texts at their basement bookstall, and increasingly was drawn to study Orthodox Christian history and doctrine. Having been baptized into the Orthodox Faith though exposed to it only at major holidays at Baba's house, I had chosen my spiritual home there at the age of 17, receiving the sacraments there for the first time on April 7, a day my family and I celebrate as a household feast each year. By the middle of my sophomore year, I was convinced that I would enter St. Vladimir's Seminary in suburban New York upon graduation. My parents were not especially pleased. Even Baba opposed the idea. But in the end, they relented and even embraced my vocation.

My college summers were filled with children, day campers at the Jewish Community Center's facility a few miles from our home in Biblically-named Emmaus, PA. I preferred teaching eight and nine year olds, who were aware and self-directed enough to express real preferences and interests, and not yet disenchanted with learning or suspicious of authority. I spoke to them periodically in Spanish, just to tantalize them, and without ever translating, introduced them to several hundred words during the camping season. Friday afternoons we observed Shabot, and I learned plenty of Hebrew. My Jewish roommate invited me home for Passover each spring, and I'd picked up quite a bit from that experience, but Day Camp introduced me to yet another world.

What a symbol of twentieth-century pluralism I had become: A guy with a Lemko last name, with a Lutheran mother of German descent, a Baba who spoke English with a Slavic accent, attending a Jesuit university, with a Jewish roommate, majoring in International Affairs with an emphasis in Arabic. Only in America!

It would seem any lingering interest in Native America had long faded, but in fact, on my first visit to the seminary campus, it was unexpectedly reawakened. A senior student had a map of Alaska prominently tacked to his dorm room wall, and when I inquired about it he explained that there were nearly 100 Orthodox communities in the 49th state. Didn't I recall that Alaska had once been part of the Russian Empire? I vaguely recalled a paragraph about that from my fifth grade history book. What! There are Native Americans who are also Orthodox Christians! My two lifelong fascinations united on American soil! This I gotta see someday! So I resolved that I would, somehow, sometime, travel north to visit this cultural phenomenon myself.

Unbeknownst to me, on Kodiak Island the destructive force of North America's most powerful earthquake had destroyed a tiny village on Good Friday 1964, and led to that community's rebirth. The tidal wave that had washed away nearly the entire town of Old

Harbor had left in its wake only two structures, the Bureau of Indian Affairs elementary school, torn from its foundations, and Three Saints Orthodox Church, the chapel where Alaska's oldest Christian congregation gathered for worship, as their ancestors had since 1784. The resurrected village, under the leadership of its young, energetic and visionary mayor Sven Haakanson, Sr., embarked on a plan to recruit a resident priest for the community.

Sven wrote to the bishop in Sitka requesting a pastor. The bishop replied that without a house for a rector, he could not assign one. The village remodeled a surviving structure and resubmitted their request. The bishop responded that without a salary on hand, he could not appoint a priest to this post. The town collected over $3000 as a down payment, and sent their appeal again to Sitka. The bishop then admitted that he had no one available at this time. With the money in the bank and the house vacant, Sven then decided to recruit a future priest, a seminarian, to work with the village children for at least three summer months. The letter requesting a volunteer to come to Alaska for the summer of 1970 arrived in Crestwood, New York in early May. A month later I was flying to Seattle and onward to Kodiak.

It was a love at first sight experience. The island reminded me of northern Greece, where I'd spent the tumultuous summer of 1968, in seclusion on Mount Athos, the "Holy Mountain" as the 250,000,000 Orthodox Christians of the world call it. An autonomous republic of twenty monastic communities, Athos has been a place of worship and prayer for over one thousand years. I wanted to visit its churches and pray at its shrines, and spent the summer following my junior year at Georgetown traveling across Europe, but spending nearly half my time at Simonas Petras, architecturally the highest and perhaps most amazing monastery on the peninsula.

Kodiak's dark blue sea, pale blue sky and the variety of a dozen shades of green on the land recalled the beauty of the Holy Mountain. Welcomed warmly by the local parish priest and his wife, born in Jerusalem and fluent in Arabic, I felt at home immediately. Traveling on an amazing Grumman "Goose" which waddled off the land and belly-flopped into the North Pacific in Kodiak harbor, then slid into the frigid waters again upon touchdown and waddled up onto the gravel beach at Old Harbor, I was enthralled. Most of the Alutiiq residents there were on hand to greet me as I disembarked. My first informal parish would be these patient, generous, hospitable, loving and loveable Aleuts.

My life, at this point, seemed to be coming together. So much of what I had experienced since childhood, converged and overlapped here. Languages, religion, music, art, history, Native Peoples, a desire to serve, a commitment to the underdog, a singing and speaking voice with some of my mother's dramatic, story-telling flare all would be useful and necessary in the coming four decades. My Alaskan adventure was just beginning.

CHAPTER 1

Saint Herman's People

I came to Alaska at the invitation of the Alutiiq village of Old Harbor, founded in the aftermath of the Battle of Refuge Rock in August 1784, when the Siberian entrepreneur and scoundrel, Gregory Shelikov, attacked and massacred hundreds of Alaskan Natives and forced them to accept his intrusion into their country. The terms of Shelikov's peace treaty were lenient, however. He had come to trade and establish a permanent base on Kodiak. For this he needed manpower. His two hundred promyshlenniki, Siberian frontiersmen, were bachelors. While his wife, Natalia, had accompanied him on this venture, the Shelikovs were returning to Russia to present their case for a commercial monopoly on all furs traded in North America to the Imperial government. If this colony were to grow, it needed women. So Gregory insisted that the Alutiiq establish a village on the north shore of Three Saints Bay. In 1791, the next Russian vessel to visit the island wintered at the outpost, and the chaplain aboard spent many afternoons celebrating the weddings and baptizing the children born from the couples who shared a love for each other and the place now called (since the founding of Kodiak in 1792) Sunalleq, the original or "old" harbor.

The children I encountered and then organized into church school classes by age, were the descendents of those early settlers and their Alaskan Native wives. Their surnames, Pestrikoff, Larionoff, Melovedoff, Ignatin, Malutin, Naumoff, were mixed with those of Alutiiq origin, Inga, Shugak, Chya, Ashouwak, (and a few Scandinavian fishermen who had jumped ship in order to remain in this gorgeous and growing community), Haakanson, Peterson and Christiansen. Allentown had had its diversity, but Old Harbor far surpassed even my hometown.

I settled into my cabin, which proved far more spacious and comfortable than my Athonite cell had been two summers earlier. I had a private room, a toilet, shower with hot and cold running water, and an expense account at the village store. The hiking trails beckoned. The salmon berries were already ripe. So was the "buchki" (wild celery), once the kids had shown me how to peal it and eat it properly, (without letting the stalk touch my lips). I learned new words like "cheetak" (a dessert made of mashed berries and evaporated milk), redefined old words like "jumper" and "kicker" (the former a leaping salmon, the latter an outboard motor) and discovered old ones (like banya, the Russian word for a sauna).

The village had neither radio nor television, which meant that visiting was the primary social activity of adults most evenings. And visits were filled with stories, old and new, ancient legends and folktales as well as family histories and autobiographical anecdotes.

And everyone had stories about the recent tsunami and its aftermath, and nearly everyone had a miracle to relate, attributed to Ap'a Herman, the heroic and saintly member of the missionary team recruited by Shelikov from Valaam Monastery, on Lake Ladoga, in Russian Finland, who was to be glorified (canonized) that summer in Kodiak.

I had my stories, of course, as Biblical incidents and parables, to share with my students, but the villagers seemed to have many more. The summer of 1970 was a story fest and I feasted on them all.

While some of my 200 students understood their ancestral language, few of them, except those being raised by or living with grandparents, spoke it. The Elders, on the other hand, and most of the parents, used Alutiiq as their normal language of communication, and the fishermen were adept at concealing their locations or their success from visiting boats by using Alutiiq exclusively on their CB radios. Although my task was not to investigate or to study this place or its culture, it would have been impossible to work effectively with either children or adults without becoming acquainted with my warm and hospitable neighbors.

Many of my students spoke on a beautiful musical score, using differing pitches and pauses in a way I had never encountered elsewhere. The village had its own "accent" and I deliberately tried to adopt it. Even my name was subject to musical re-interpretation. It was pronounced more like a question than a statement, with a slight glottal stop between the syllables. A favorite exclamation for surprise was Waaaaaah! and for pain, especially associated with heat "ahaah!" I didn't realize it then, but I was becoming "acculturated."

The stories Elders told from long ago described animals as intelligent and wise. Unlike European tales that begin by describing how a wicked witch or sorcerer had cursed a man, transforming him into a beast, Alutiiqs told stories like the "Mink Boy," in which the boy's ability to transform himself into a mink provided him with the necessary means of surviving dangerous situations, escaping from enemies, seeing the world from a new perspective. The "mink boy" even ends with the boy deciding to remain in animal form and live "happily ever after."

Alutiiqs, both young and old, were quiet, unhurried, respectful listeners and observers. They were sensitive to changes of wind direction and tide. They discussed hunting successes and hot fishing locations. They recounted voyages at sea and hikes over mountains, meeting bears, encountering whales, enjoying the soaring eagles and magpies overhead. These people were intimately connected to each other and their environment. They knew and loved their land, their families, their community, their culture and their Creator.

I don't mean to idealize the town. There were also problems. A perfect parish would not need a pastor. But all this was hidden from me during my first month or so in the village. I was drawn into its life and I loved it immediately. Only on Independence Day, July 4, did I discover that a significant number of my neighbors would periodically binge drink, mostly beer, and take several days to sober up. While this revelation was unhappy and unpleasant, especially as I welcomed refugee children into my house, I was not overly scandalized. Washington DC had had a lower drinking age for beer and wine while I attended Georgetown, so I had been accustomed to hundreds of carousing college students descending on our neighborhood every weekend for the past four years. *Alcoholism/Alcohol Abuse in the Diocese of Alaska* would become the topic of my master's thesis at St. Vladimir's.

I knew these people to be kind and generous, hospitable and incredibly forgiving. The kids behaved so well. The adults treated each other respectfully. The Elders, basking in the summer sun, huddled together at the store or post office and chatted quietly, remembering another time and another world when Old Harbor's entire population dwelt in semi-subterranean barabaras, the ruins one of which still anchored the village runway. Some still wove grass baskets in the style of their ancestors. For them, what the world called the "stone age" had been their childhood.

And yet these same unschooled grandparents came to the church and sang enthusiastically in both Alutiiq and Slavonic. I was amazed that they had committed so many texts, at such length, to memory. Certainly their pronunciation was distinctively Alutiiq, but my Baba could have understood everything they sang. We shared the same hymns, the same folk customs, the same faith, though mine had immigrated to the USA through Ellis Island, and theirs had crossed the Bering Sea.

Sitting for hours at kitchen tables, drinking gallons of hot tea in the old Russian style, I learned of their experience at school. These Elders had been forbidden to speak the only language they knew, and sat for hours trying to comprehend instruction in a language they did not. They had better things to do. Most left school before completing the elementary curriculum. Some did not return after the third or fourth grade. They considered themselves academic failures, "just dumb Aleuts" as one often said.

But these were resourceful and intelligent minds. They had survived seven thousand winters here and seldom knew severe hardship or starvation. They had designed, built and mastered the kayak and the throwing board. They had hunted whales and the largest terrestrial carnivore on earth, the Kodiak Brown Bear. They had harvested millions of salmon and preserved their catch as insurance against winter hunger. They had carved in bone, ivory and wood, sewn skins of otter, seal and mink, illumined their dwellings with stone bowl-shaped "lamps" and their spirits with myths, stories, art, music and ceremony. Their original name for themselves was Suget, or Sugpiaq, the Human Beings, or more accurately, the Real People. There was nothing "dumb" about them.

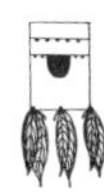

Human Beings/Real People

Tribes throughout the world have names for themselves. In Alaska, these generally translate as "the People." Tlingit means "the People," and Unangan, (the Aleut word for Aleut) means "We, the People." The various Athabaskan tribes of the interior call themselves "Dene" or Dineh (identical to the Navajo name for Navajo, in Arizona and New Mexico—linguistic proof that the Navajo had migrated from the subarctic to their current homes in the Southwest). The Eskimos add a suffix, "-pik" or "-piaq" to their name, a bit of one-upsmanship, for they call themselves the Real People, the Genuine Human Beings.

Regardless of what their name is, Human Beings believe that they originated in their land, and from the beginning of human occupation, they have adapted to their ecosystem appropriately, according to the way the universe was made. Their customs and traditions derive from the First People who were wise and were often divinely inspired to live in a certain way, to behave in a certain way. These attitudes and behaviors constitute the Way of the Human Being, and all must be taught, passed down by example and legend, reinforced in repetition and ritual, so that the next generation will learn how to live and behave as Human Beings should, as the People always have.

Of course this belief produces a rather conservative, unchanging view of life. Things have been done this way for ten thousand years and life has continued, under extraordinarily difficult circumstances. Don't mess with success! More importantly, however, life is viewed as meaningful. The patterns and customs passed down from the past infuse daily chores with meaningfulness that they would lack in another culture. When I do things the way my parents taught me, the way their ancestors taught them, I behave appropriately, I behave meaningfully, I behave humanly. If I accomplish the same task in some other way, even if it is more efficient, less time or energy consuming, I have violated the code, behaved in a way that has no meaning. I am no longer in solidarity with my parents and ancestors, but isolated, living in a meaningless and, therefore in-human way. Change is not only difficult in traditional societies. It can represent a kind of discontinuity and therefore rupture with the past and with the People. Change can be sacrilege. To be Real means to be in solidarity and live as Real People always have.

Almost every household had Ap'a Herman stories to tell, often biographical details about his holy life, on Elovoi or Spruce Island, just north of Kodiak, where Mayor Sven had been born. He recalled becoming deathly ill with what was probably pneumonia as a child, and elders from Ouzinkie, his village, brought soil from the gravesite of the venerable monk, who had died in December 1837. The Alutiiq had built a memorial chapel over his grave on the centennial of his arrival with the other nine missionaries in 1794, so that to reach the place now, one had to crawl under the chapel to pray and retrieve some of the soil. This earth was used, often mixed with holy water from the nearby spring, to create a mudpack, applied to the unconscious child's chest. His prayerful parents waited anxiously and expectantly, hoping their son would recover. Obviously he did. Ap'a Herman's closeness to God, his holiness, was communicable, healing the sick over 130 years after his passing.

Neighbors spoke of cures they had witnessed, attributed to the prayers of the holy "Grandfather" or to the earth or water brought from his shrine at Monk's Lagoon. Children had been weaned on stories of his prayerful life and his courageous defense of the Natives against the exploitation that followed Shelikov's conquest. The Alutiiq felt protected by his intercessions now much as their great-great grandparents had been defended by his eloquent pleas while he was still among them. And this August the whole world was going to learn of Ap'a Herman, as the Church in America was performing its first canonization, proclaiming to the world what the Alutiiq had known for generations, that the Monk Herman of Spruce Island was a holy man, who posthumously continued to guard and protect his people.

Here was someone with whom I could identify. A man of Slavic descent who spent his life serving and interceding on behalf of Native Americans for their civil rights and human dignity—my kind of hero! But it was not long before I realized that Father Herman's beloved flock was still being misunderstood, exploited and oppressed, now by people who had come here with the best of intentions.

CHAPTER 2

Monks and Monsters

The monk Herman was born near Moscow but fled to a monastery as a teen. Monastic life in the Eastern Church remains a lay movement. Few monks are ordained or receive seminary training. Monastics sell all that they have, give it away, and enter a community of prayer, fasting and almsgiving, renouncing earthly pleasures in order to enter into a more complete relationship with God. The vocation is to turn one's self- or ego-centric love into self-offering, self-sacrificial love for God, for each human person, and for the entire created universe. Overcoming the self as an idol requires real struggle, an inner spiritual warfare, which each monk undertakes under the direction of a spiritual master, the igumen or Elder whose community the novice freely chooses and enters.

Such was the life the Elder Herman had accepted in his teen years. He was the oldest of the volunteers whom Gregory Shelikov recruited for his Alaskan colony, promising that he would support them financially, claiming, in fact that he had already built a church and school for them. Arriving in Kodiak on September 24, 1794, however, the Valaam monks found no such structures. They were forced to reside in the common barracks with the frontiersmen and forage for their daily meals on the clam beaches and forests. Worse, they met the resistance and even persecution from the company manager, Alexander Baranov, who was exploiting Native labor and forcing Aleuts to resettle on distant shores as well as to hunt the local sea otter population to extinction.

The monks wrote letters of protest to the church and civil authorities in Russia, but the Company correspondence contradicted or mitigated their accusations. Several inspectors came to Kodiak to gather facts about the situation. Those from the church corroborated the monks' accounts, those sent by the Company administration backed Baranov. After three assassination attempts, Father Herman withdrew from St. Paul (Kodiak) harbor and relocated to Spruce Island, where he dug a cave, in the tradition of the desert fathers of fourth century Egypt, and later a hut, where he resided for the next three decades. Aleuts were amazed at his ascetic life, sleeping on a board with a rock for a pillow, going barefoot in a deer skin cassock year round, but constantly joyful, prayerful, kind and generous. They were aware that he stood by them, writing petitions to authorities in Russia for redress and relief.

When Baranov retired in 1818, his replacement hurried to Kodiak to interview Father Herman about the previous regime. The Elder reported that hundreds, perhaps thousands had perished, impressed at gunpoint into Company service and dispatched to outposts along the entire North Pacific rim, from the Kurile Islands, just north of Japan, to the Alaskan and Californian mainland as far south as Baja, Mexico. Most of those who had been exiled never returned. The plight of their surviving family and dependents on Kodiak had been desperate. Diseases brought by British and American vessels from the south had decimated the population as well. Father Herman, with the assistance of Sophia Vlasov and Gerassim Zyrianov, had taken many orphans into their custody, but the suffering of the Natives had been traumatic and overwhelming. Father Herman appealed to the new governor, Simeon Yanovskii, to "wipe away the tears of orphans," and to let the local people "know what comfort means."

It was his bold defense of the civil and moral rights of his Alutiiq neighbors and friends that provided the basis for a relationship of trust and ultimately of love and devotion between himself and the Native people of the Kodiak region. They never forgot him. On the 100th anniversary of his arrival, they dedicated a church over his gravesite, the cave he had dug and in which he had lived, as a sacred shrine, to which they regularly resorted in time of calamity or need.

Hearing these stories from the locals, I too was inspired by this forgotten old monk, whose life and teachings had had such a tremendous impact on them and their culture. While the Siberian frontiersmen had been harsh and the company policies illegal and immoral, the example of this one pious monastic had confirmed them in the faith and inspired them for over a century and a half. There were no atheists among these people, not even skeptics. Their experience of the sacred, in nature, as in pre-contact times, and in God and His saints, was firm and unquestioned. They observed the customs and rules of their new faith with devotion and sincerity. No one ate a mouthful of food or took a sip of water without invoking God, making the sign of the cross. No one entered a house without invoking God, praying as they entered, bowing toward the icon corner in each parlor. No one neglected to visit the graves of their relatives in the cemetery overlooking the village, and kiss the cross that marked each burial site, remembering their ancestors with reverence and respect. People prayed, worshipped, cooperated, supported and loved each other. There were, of course, misunderstandings and even some longstanding feuds, but essentially these were kind, hospitable, open, honest and generous people, eagerly forgiving each other and reconciling. In a town of 300 no one can afford to bear a grudge for very long.

Reverence for Life

Subsistence resources were shared. Boys caught fish, sometimes with the simplest tools, a tin can and a fish line and hook, and eagerly offered them to neighbors and friends. Fresh sea mammal meat, from seals, seal lions and more rarely whale, was still a staple in the local diet, along with various shell fish, clams, sea urchins, and mussels. The salmon runs were amazing. The creeks and streams of Kodiak are clogged with fish for weeks each summer. It is no wonder that brown bears prospered here so well that they evolved into a super species named for the island, the Kodiak. Amid this beauty and bounty, the Alutiiq had become sincere Christians and it was this commitment that had brought me to their island paradise.

Gradually I came to understand their view of the world as essentially spiritual. Life was itself a sacred mystery. It had to be approached respectfully, carefully, with humility and gratitude. There were dozens of ways in which this attitude was conveyed. Food was treated with respect. Everything humans ate came from the earth and had been alive. Whether it was dried fish or a cracker, its composition had been a living thing, plant or animal, and had to be appreciated as such. In order to feed us, to keep us alive, this living reality had to die. The wheat had to be harvested, ground into flour and mixed with other ingredients to create the bread. If even a crumb fell to the floor, children raced to retrieve it, blow on it and make the sign of the cross before consuming it. No doubt the breath of exhaled air was supposed to clean it but the sign of the cross consecrated it, restored it to sacredness. These simple rituals were a constant reminder that life itself was sacred and had to be respected, treated with reverence.

Gift of Beaver

We were traveling down river one summer afternoon when a beaver plunked himself loudly into the slough, thirty yards in front of us. I thought this peculiar, since our 50 horsepower outboard motor certainly was making plenty of noise, enough to alert any wildlife of our position and trajectory.

The Yup'ik man who was steering the boat slowed and picked up his .22 rifle, watching the waters toward the bow. The beaver reemerged and he shot it, accelerated the engine and pulled the beaver on board. We had not been on a hunting expedition. We had only planned to go to the local hub and purchase some groceries. But here was more food than we had expected.

I'd been looking for a way to express, in English, and to convey to my colleagues at the village school, this new way of seeing I was encountering the longer I spent time with The Real People. This situation presented me with an opportunity to try my latest theory.

"How nice of him to give himself to us!" I exclaimed to the captain/hunter.

At first he looked a little surprised, even a bit puzzled. And then he confirmed my perception by replying, "That's what we always say."

As the years passed and I lived in other parts of the State, I realized that all Native Peoples shared this reverence for life, and for food that came from the lives of other creatures. Eating was a sacred act by virtue of the fact that living things had given themselves to sustain us. This was never to be taken lightly.

And when the meat had been taken from an animal the providers of the family had personally taken, the reverence was even greater. The tradition throughout Alaska was that when a boy caught his first of any specific species, his family shared it with others, giving it away. The boy himself ate none of it. The animal, no matter how small or large, whether duck or seal or moose, had offered itself to the community, and the hunter was the "conduit" through which the animal's self-sacrifice sustained the village. The pattern of offering one's self for others was repeated in nature. Life was a pattern of self-giving in relation to others and for the sake of others.

Other Ways of Seeing

This way of seeing, I appreciated, was ancient and older, Neolithic. Anthropologists and ethnographers had documented the hunting and gathering rites and beliefs of "primitive" peoples across the globe and concluded that their worldviews were essentially spiritual in ways that far surpass the most "religious" people in today's secular society. For these people, religion was not a matter of certain worship practices or moral teachings, nor the observance of particular holidays or fasts. Life was spiritual. There was no distinction between the secular and the sacred. Everything was viewed in what we can only call "religious" terms.

The monks, as they crossed Siberia, encountered many tribes, visited many monastic communities that had, each in its turn been founded beyond the frontiers of the Empire. The founding fathers had studied the languages and customs of the local people, and often invented alphabets for their language, ultimately translating passages of Scripture and the liturgical services of the Orthodox Church into the local vernacular. Schools for the training of local leaders, not only for service in the church, but for secular positions evolved from this monastic core, so that within a generation or two, the traditional tribal leadership were literate and usually bilingual, speaking Russian as well as their ancestral tongue.

In order to bridge the gap between the ancient and new religious faiths, the monks undertook studies of the Native languages and collected their myths and legends. Without exception, they discovered that tribal peoples had deduced, as a matter of spiritual perception and common sense, most of the moral rules contained in the Biblical Ten Commandments. People cannot live together harmoniously for very long if they rob, kill, kidnap, plunder or deceive each other. Adultery, theft and murder can break up a village pretty quickly. Most traditional hunter/gatherer communities told stories of the origins of the world, of the various animal species, of the human race, and of the structures of the universe. They told stories, too, about the respectful way people should interact with each other and their environment, and celebrated these primordial events in song, dance and ceremony. In many annual feasts recalled and enacted those determinative and foundational acts according to a sacred calendar. On Kodiak, the Kashaq was specially trained to calculate the times for these celebrations and directed the sequence of the rituals.

In addition to the public structure of religious life, where the Sacred Stories of "those days" were told and recounted in music and art, with dancing and feasting, there were the angalkut, the shamans. These were the clairvoyants, those who had fallen into deep near-death sleep, or through some catastrophic accident had been temporarily dead, who had had what we might consider today to be have been an "out of the body" experience. They had journeyed to the spirit world beyond this one, and encountered spirits, souls, angels or demons, and returned to their bodies, now intensely aware and personally familiar with this other Reality. Their unique experience empowered them to prophesy the future and to heal the sick, or do harm to others, depending on the nature of their helping spirits. Shamans corroborated by direct experience the Reality about which the myths spoke, the ceremonies celebrated. They were the "proof" that the old stories were true.

The Valaam monks understood this by the time they arrived on Kodiak. They spent the winter of 1794-5 collecting the myths and legends of the Kodiak Alutiiq, expressing no surprise that they had in their repertoire tales of a Supreme God, Creator of the world, and of the first people from whom all humans are descended. They reported a flood story similar to the Noah account in Genesis, and concluded that the Spirit of God had been here long before their mission arrived. They had more stories to share, and would present their faith as the completion, the fulfillment of what the People had known long before.

Father Herman did this and more. By working miracles of healing and predicting the future, he became the Alutiiq Christian "shaman," whose wisdom and miraculous deeds corroborated the new faith, just as the angalkut had done in times past. The Monk Herman became for the Kodiak people the proof that their new faith, in continuity with their ancient beliefs, put them in touch and harmony with the Spiritual Reality that governs the world. The transition from Shamanism to Christianity was amazingly swift and complete.

What I was about to witness, however, was the forced secularization of Alaskan Native society. At first I understood this only as a local tension between the purveyors of secular modernism and the local traditional people. But gradually I came to see this struggle as global, a planetary process in which the ancient, spiritual worldview would be suppressed and overwhelmed by a global, literate and highly sophisticated technological society. The instrument by which the latter imposed itself on the former would be the public school. The destruction of the old by the new would be done in the name of "Education."

CHAPTER 3

Winning the West

The history of official American Indian policy is not particularly happy. Anyone familiar with the Plymouth Colony's treatment of their indigenous neighbors knows that within a half century of their arrival in 1620, the Mayflower men had massacred the Massachusetts and taken possession of their lands. The pattern was repeated from so-called "King Philip's War" across the continent for the next three centuries. A growing number of European colonists grew eager to expand their domain inland, and met Indian resistance. The pioneers pushed, the Indians were provoked, and the full military might of the newcomers was brought to bear on the Natives. The settlers moved into the now vacant territory and the pattern repeated. Today, happily, we treat endangered species of birds and beasts with more respect and sensitivity.

This policy came under scrutiny and re-evaluation during the presidency of Thomas Jefferson, who had, after all, read Rousseau and Locke, and had penned the immortal words about all men being created equal and endowed by their Creator with certain inalienable rights. Now, whether all "men" included Native Americans might still be open to debate, Jefferson clearly had qualms about the extermination policy that the country had embraced for the last two centuries. Having purchased the Louisiana Territory from Napoleon, Jefferson also realized the newly expanded nation now included hundreds more Indians, whom were already being labeled "the Vanishing American." It would not be long by all estimates that the Indian "race" would perish. George Catlin picked up brushes and paint and headed for the wilderness, hoping, before they disappeared, to capture the life and images of the original Americans. Extinction seemed imminent.

Jefferson's cabinet shared his anxiety about the surviving tribes, and decided to adopt a new approach. Instead of killing them off, Indians should be relocated to areas in which the Europeans had little or no interest. They could resume their lifeways on lands set aside for their exclusive use, far removed from the alien and corrupting influences of "civilization," provided, of course, they would kindly vacate the lands new settlers coveted. Please go west, young men, far west. We have reserved vast areas of Oklahoma and South Dakota for you. And the Reservation System was born.

Tribes East of the Mississippi were relocated westward, the most famous of which were the Cherokee whose "Trail of Tears" marks one of the new republic's most tragic and disgraceful chapters. Long before the term was coined, the USA was ethnically cleansing its Eastern quadrant of any indigenous peoples who had survived. Tribes that resisted relocation were attacked as "outlaw" and 'renegade," as if being born in one's ancestral homeland was itself a crime. This policy remained in place for most of the 19th century.

The basic European assumption at this time was that people who were racially or culturally or linguistically distinct could not live in harmony. One needed to kill off the other, or they needed to separate. The modern concept of mutual respect and toleration, under the banner of "Diversity," had not been conceived yet. People who are different, it was presumed, could not get along, apparently overlooking every married couple on earth.

The Great Watershed of American History was and remains the Civil War. The conflict engaged hundreds of thousands of young, able-bodied men, hundreds of thousands of which ended the war as casualties, dead or no longer able-bodied. This left the Republic with a tremendous labor shortage, just when it was time to return to more productive enterprises, laying railroad track, digging mines, constructing canals and roads, smelting ore, running mills and sweat shops. With an entire generation of American manhood deceased or disabled, where was the country going to get the necessary manpower to harness and conquer the continent?

In 1876, the USA celebrated a century of Independence, and received a birthday gift from the people of France, the Statue of Liberty Enlightening the World. School children on this side of the Atlantic raised the funds for the pedestal, and the copper covered image was erected in New York harbor, appropriately inscribed with the famous poem, "Give me your tired, your poor, your huddled masses yearning to breath free..." And in the next half-century, nearly 20 million huddled masses accepted Miss Liberty's gracious invitation.

The problem with the new immigrants was that they were not like the original Mayflower variety. Few of them spoke English. They came mostly from Eastern and Southern Europe. Few of them were Protestant Christians. They were Catholic and Orthodox Christians, Jews from many various sects, Moslems and even atheists. Most were illiterate peasants. They settled in the tenement houses and slums of the larger cities and entered the workplace, breeding more offspring than the average Anglo-Saxon household, and causing widespread alarm among the "Native" Americans who calculated that within decades, these newcomers would soon outnumber them.

The country developed a long, painful migraine headache. For several decades the solution to the self-created immigrant problem eluded solution. These alien people could not be expelled. The US had just invited them here. They could not be enslaved. Slavery had been the issue in the recent "troubles" and had been abolished constitutionally. Extermination was not an option. The country needed these workers to do the work many of the established families shunned. The solution to one problem had led to the rise of a yet greater and more complex one.

The Last 500 Years: Your Choice

If we consider the history of the United States, focusing on inter-racial/intercultural relations and the official policies of the government, it's easy to see we're making progress:

1500-1800 ***Official Policies: Extermination and Enslavement (The only "Good" Indian is a ....)***

1800-1875 ***Official Policy: Removal (to Africa for liberated slaves, to reservations for Native Americans)***

1875-1975 ***Assimilation: the "melting pot." (All Real" Americans came on the Mayflower)***

1975 Pluralism, Multiculturalism Our National Motto?
E Pluribus Unum (From Many, ONE)

How do you get your Unum with so much Pluribus?
Here are the choices we've considered and tried:

—Kill those who are different (the Nazi Approach)
—Kick out those who are different? (Ethnic Cleansing)
—Force everyone to act, believe and behave the same? (back in the USSR)
—Respect and learn from each other? (Each person affirmed and valued)

The quickest and fastest way to Unum is murder, but only a few skin heads and neo-Nazis would embrace that approach today. That's Progress!

Separation, segregation, apartheid has been tried and rejected as well.

Assimilation, squeezing everyone into the same mold and suppressing differences is still popular, but obviously tyrannical and often counter-productive.

Appreciating the perspectives and contributions people of other cultural backgrounds offer us is the only approach consistent with the human values we have enshrined in our Constitution and Bill of Rights.

What holds us together, then? What makes us ONE? Our common commitment to what we teach the kids to recite every morning as they repeat the pledge. We promise ourselves a country where there will be, (as we have been moving toward the goal) "with Liberty and Justice for All."

We all must choose our own "policy" toward Americans who are racially and culturally different.

These are the choices. You pick.

Searching the world for a strategy, American philosophers stumbled upon a possible solution. The Kingdom of Prussia had recently instituted a program of compulsory public education. Children there were required by law to attend school for a decade. They wore uniforms and were treated like soldiers, who reported promptly for duty, spic and span. Their officers inspected them as a sergeant might review his troops, and admitted them to the day's training exercises. They were regularly tested. They were disciplined harshly for any misconduct. And illiterate German peasants were being prepared appropriately for new lives in factories and mines. All this was imposed and accepted in the name of patriotism, for the children were all taught to be grateful to their government for the benefits of this compulsory educational system. Perfect! State by state in the USA, local governments outlawed child labor and passed compulsory school attendance laws. For the first time in history, young people may not work but they must attend school at public expense.

The motivation in America arose from the need to assimilate the children of the new immigrants, to assure that they would assume their proper roles as working English-speaking, preferable Protestant-believing citizens as true Americans, in the image of the Pilgrim Fathers.

Melting Pot Meltdown

For about a century after the Civil War, the USA pursued a policy of assimilating immigrants and indigenous people into what was called the "Melting Pot." The Pot itself was made in England. It came on the Mayflower. Real Americans came from Britain, spoke English, were Protestant Christians who washed their hands and kept appointments punctually. Those who were male could vote, and all were Caucasian. So the very definition of "American" boiled down to WASP males.

Immigrant kids would go to school and learn all about this group. The curriculum was designed to foster admiration

and respect for these heroes who crossed the Atlantic, revolted against British tyranny (taxes and protection of Indian land rights) drafted the Declaration of Independence, the Constitution and the Bill of Rights, fought in the Civil War and had conquered North America, freeing it from savages and settling it with slaves, then freeing them and erecting the Statue of Liberty to invite others to join their noble experiment in representative democracy.

New Stories entered the history books, showing this group to have been super-human demigods. Washington was incapable of lying. Abe was so incredibly honest. Franklin was a real sage. Both Lee and Grant were extraordinary generals. And remember the Alamo! Thanksgiving, a national holiday declared to offer thanks for the Union victory at Antietem, was transformed into a remembrance of the Pilgrims at Plymouth, who sat down with their Indian friends and shared an inter-racial feast, the very image of the kind of America we were building: the tribes sat down with the English and prayed to the Christian God who had saved and blessed them all. We still dress up the first graders, half as pilgrims and half as Indians in November to teach this important inter-cultural lesson.

All this made sense for a hundred years, but by the late 20th century, too many Americans could not melt into this pot. There were the Catholics, who were suspect in their American identity for not being Protestant, like all good Mayflower passengers were and all Real Americans should be. And the Jews. And the Buddhists from Viet Nam and Cambodia, and the Moslems from the Middle East, and all those folks who had come to the USA across the wrong Ocean: from Japan, China, Korea, India, Polynesia. Too many weren't fitting in, the way the curriculum had been planned and implemented.

It took a Chinese couple living in the Bay Area, near San Francisco to challenge the Melting Pot concept at its roots.

Why is one culture the standard against which all others are judged? If we've lived here for a hundred years and have never been accepted as "real Americans" when will that ever happen? We are not White, not Anglo-Saxon, not Protestant. We are Chinese, we speak Mandarin, we are Buddhists and Taoist and will never be Mayflower types. When do we get included?

And the Supreme Court ruled "Now!"

The Melting Pot Cracked. It's time to throw it away.

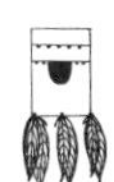

Immigrants and Indians

The school day began with inspections, just as in Germany. Children had to be in their seats, or standing by them, neat, clean, and punctual. Being "on time" was essential, for graduates would be expected to appear for work with equal precision in adult life. Peasant children had to be taught how to dress properly, clean and preen themselves appropriately, and make a good impression socially. And of paramount importance was an ability to speak English properly and to appreciate all that the Anglo-Saxon founders of the Republic had done to assure them the blessings of life, liberty and the pursuit of happiness.

For the Ellis Island immigrants, the offer of free education seemed only a blessing. They had come from impoverished rural societies where formal school was the unique privilege of the rich. Teachers charged fees, schools charged tuition, and books and supplies were the student's responsibility. But here in America, children had to go to school, but education was free of charge. What a country!

Immigrants accepted and embraced public schools because they had decided to come to America to begin a new life, and they welcomed any outreach designed to help them adapt the cultural ways and norms of this Anglo society. You want to teach my children English? Wonderful! You are going to add math, science and history to the curriculum? Terrific! My kids will soon be able to fit in, so that within a generation we will no longer be outsiders or aliens, but full citizens?

Thank you very much! Having decided to leave their homelands to seek a better life in the New World, the newly arrived rejoiced at being so warmly welcomed, so carefully and practically informed on how best to adapt and being adopted by their new country.

Their ancestral culture was not jeopardized by this. There were millions of their relatives and friends back in the homeland, preserving the traditional language and culture of their ancestors. Immigrants were free to assimilate without recrimination or guilt.

However, when Alaska was transferred to US rule in 1867, the cultural assimilationist policies that had gained such widespread acceptance in the lower 48, would soon be applied to Native Americans, first on reservations there, and imported and imposed on villages here, with disastrous consequences.

CHAPTER 4

"Sages" and "Savages"

Soon after the Russian government offered its American colonies to the USA and negotiated the sale of that sovereignty to Washington for less than eight million dollars, the US federal government began wrestling with the "Indian Problem." The West was rapidly filling with farmers and ranchers, and it seemed that the land reserved for the use of the Indians was more valuable than originally thought. How could pioneers gain access to the silver in the Black Hills or the oil on Indian land in Oklahoma? Weren't we doing the Native Americans a disservice by not providing education to their children, as we were to the children of the new immigrants? Why should Cherokee or Lakota be deprived of the obvious benefits of our civilization? Wasn't it our moral duty to elevate them from "savagery," to civilize them? Of course! And in the age of labor shortage, wouldn' t it be best if we gave the First Americans the rudimentary outline of a basic English Education, so that they too could join the workforce of miners, teamsters, mill workers and rail road laborers, and enjoy some of the same benefits of a cash economy?

What was good for the immigrant should be good for the Indian!

But there were serious differences between them. First, the Native Americans had not chosen to leave their homeland and journey to another, there to be assimilated into an alien culture and worldview. They had been minding their own business in their traditional homes, when these strange, alien people had intruded. They, unlike the immigrant, had not left home and had not opted to become something they were not. More importantly, assimilation for the Natives meant the demise of their culture and language. To the extent that they adapted to the new, they had to abandon the old. Those who adopted the new ways could be viewed with suspicion, as "Uncle Toms," or what Indian people often call "Apples," (red on the outside, white on the inside). Those who rejected the new could be seen as backward, ignorant, rejectionist, stubborn or stupidly conservative in the face of all the advantages and comforts the modern world offered.

American society invited both the immigrants and the Indians to assimilate by accepting the Pilgrim Story as their own. Immigrants from Europe could readily accept, but who among the Indians could realistically pretend that they too had come on the Mayflower? Absurd as this may seem, federal policy precisely extended this same offer (with which it had enticed the children of immigrants) to the Native Americans, expecting them, rather unrealistically, to accept it with the same enthusiasm as the immigrants had. In the eyes of the national political establishment both groups were aliens, both needed schooling and both should eagerly adopt. But their stories were radically different. Assimilation worked well for the immigrants. It was a catastrophe for the Natives.

Various missions had competed across the US for the opportunity to convert tribes to their particular denomination, often entering into direct conflict with rival church groups. The Federal government had little money to spare after the Civil War for Indian Education, and before the civil service reforms later in that century most Indian Agents were political appointees, men who had supported the latest victor in a presidential election. Pay was poor and conditions primitive, corruption rampant. Treaty obligations to provide schools and clinics went unfulfilled. President Grant was especially plagued with scandals involving his old army buddies, illegally or unethically profiting at the expense of the tribes whose welfare had been entrusted to them.

The Society of Friends, the "Quaker" Church, stepped forward with a proposal. What if the reservations were divided equally among the competing denominations, and the churches contributed to the support of Indian schools? The government would pay a portion of their salaries and mission societies would contribute another percentage. This would assure dedicated, honest, high-quality teachers at a reduced cost. Scandals would end. Indians would be taught and assimilated, as well as "saved." It looked like a win-win proposition and the Quakers were allowed to inaugurate the experiment on certain reservations in Minnesota. Everyone seems to have been pleased with the results.

In later years, all the reservations in the lower 48 were divvied up among various American Protestant groups, and the federal government oversaw the administration of the nation-wide system.

When Congress passed the Alaska Organic Act, this pre-existing style of schooling was imported and imposed by the first Commissioner of Education, Dr. Sheldon Jackson, who was also simultaneously the head of the Presbyterian Church in the USA, and received salaries from both the federal government and his denomination. Today this would be viewed as both a conflict of interest and a violation of the basic constitutional principle of separation of Church and State. But in the late 19th century, no one in power seemed to be bothered by these details. Alaska Natives now would also have the chance to re-write their story, and like the immigrants and Indians in the rest of the country, pretend that they too, had arrived on the Mayflower.

The Aleut Alterative

Of course, no one in Alaska had any inkling of this new policy. Alaskans were only vaguely aware that they had passed under American rule. The US Government established a naval presence at Sitka, and periodically the revenue cutter, The Bear, visited Bering Sea ports more or less regularly. Otherwise, the territory may have just as well remained under Russian rule.

The clergy who served in Russian America during the last forty years of Imperial rule had studied the languages and devised alphabets for Alutiiq, Unangan Aleut, Yup'ik Eskimo and Tlingit, published books and primers, and opened bilingual schools for Native and Creole (mixed-race) children. The prodigy of Russian fathers and Native mothers, the Creoles emerged as an important class, able to work effectively in two or more cultures. They served not only as translators and traders, but were trained to assume middle and upper management positions in the colony where there were never more than 800 ethnic Russians at any one time. Alaska was overwhelmingly Native, and Natives were educated to become priests and school teachers, ship builders and accountants, musicians, artists, cartographers and navigators. Several graduated from the Russian Naval Academy at Kronstadt and sailed around the world. When the US government decided to establish schools in the territory, Sheldon Jackson wrote a polite letter to the Orthodox Bishop Nicholai, asking where his schools already existed, noting that there was no point in overlapping the two educational efforts. Bishop Nicholai complied, but Sheldon established schools in each of the villages listed, and entered into direct competition and conflict with the "Aleut" Schools.

The architect of the bilingual, Native-operated schools, Father John, later (Bishop Innocent) Veniaminov, had spent a decade in the Aleutian Islands and several more years in Sitka. He spoke both Aleut and Tlingit and devised alphabets for both. Later elected to head the entire Russian Orthodox Church as Metropolitan (Archbishop) of Moscow, he founded a mission society for the continued support of schools and churches in Alaska, so that, in these early years, more support was being sent from Russia to fund the Aleut Schools than the US government was appropriating in Washington.

American Missions

Sheldon Jackson and the officials back East viewed these Native run schools, using Native languages as an affront to American culture. Even when English was added to their curriculum, the Federal government did all that it could to suppress and close them. The Orthodox press throughout the final decades of the 19th century and indeed into the first decades of the twentieth reported monthly incidents of discrimination and abuse at the hands of federal officials, particularly in Sitka, Kodiak and Unalaska. The Bolshevik seizure of power in Russia ended this uneven duel, since the Communists ended all financial support for the struggling multi-lingual Native schools.

Their very existence continues to be questioned by American historians who would prefer to deny that by 1845, the Russian school system was producing Alaska Native graduates. On the other hand, everyone familiar with the history of the Alaska State Museum and the Alaska State Historical Library knows that these were founded by an Aleut who could read and write four languages fluently: Russian, Aleut, English, and Tlingit. The so-called "Russian Bishop's House," restored by the National Park Service in downtown Sitka was more than a residence for a church leader. It functioned as the All Colonial School, where generations of Native leaders attended a six-year course, preparing them for leadership positions in their communities long after the Transfer to US rule in 1867.

Alien Invasion

In any case, the Federal decision to establish Bureau of Indian Affairs elementary "Day Schools" in Alaska produced a decade of confusion and frustration in most Native villages. No one expected a barge-load of lumber to arrive from Seattle, yet suddenly, there it was. On the treeless tundra in Southwest Alaska or the Aleutian Archipelago, this in itself was an amazing event. People there had never seen so much long, straight boards.

Within weeks, a crew of carpenters came to erect the new schoolhouse and teacher's cottage. These looked totally out of place on the flat, open terrain of the Yukon-Kuskokwim Delta, and proved highly impractical on the windswept shores of the Bering Sea. Among the domed roofs of the traditional Native sod homes, the pointy, angular style of the European structure might as well have been a space ship from an alien planet. The villagers were curious about the purpose for these incongruous buildings, but the construction crew could not explain to them what a "school" was.

A month or so later, the first teachers, usually volunteer missionaries hired by their home denomination and subsidized with a federal pay check as well, appeared, equally unexpectedly, disembarking from yet another mysterious barge. In the style of the day, they wore the most impractical clothing.

Imagine in 1880's or 90's attire, a middle aged man in a three piece business suit, a derby hat and spats strutting ashore, sporting a handsome, handle-bar moustache. Since buttons had once been valued as much as coins, this guy had to appear quite wealthy to the villagers, covered as he was in buttons— on his shirt, vest, jacket, sleeves and even up his shoes! He was pale by local standards, and resembled by some accounts a walrus. But his lovely wife was even more novel, holding a fashionable parasol that quickly blew inside out with the first good gust of Aleutian wind. Her hairdo was spectacular, piled high on her now exposed head, complete with pins, combs and perhaps an ostrich plume or two. And her dress! There was something unusual about her posterior, since it stuck noticeably out. The villagers wanted to inquire if that was really her rear end, but no one dared ask or experiment.

A few days later, Mrs. Fanny began making some disturbing early morning noise in front of the angular and pointed "skuuluuq" as the Yup' iks called it. What was all that racket about? And the clanging continued for several minutes before the village returned to its usual quiet. The teachers expected their pupils to scurry schoolward, but not a soul showed. Day after day, they had no scholars, until they decided to take matters into their own hands. They would capture unsuspecting students and shanghai them up to the school if they had to. This classroom would be filled with volunteers or prisoners!

Eventually the weary instructors managed to fill their school with captives, whom they arranged in rows, seated behind long tables on benches that stretched the width of the room. Once quieted in their seats, the school rules were announced---in perfectly clear English! First, everyone should come to school as soon as the bell rang. Charades conveyed this concept adequately. When we ring the bell (thusly demonstrated) you all come here, Okay! Got it!

Englishhh Only!

And secondly, you must not speak your language on school property or during school hours. This is a federal regulation and we will strictly enforce it. If anyone is caught speaking their Native language they will be punished with spanking, soap or iodine on the tongue, or worse! This rule was also promulgated in English, but no one understood its meaning, until two squirming six year olds in the front row began fidgeting and whispering in the only language they knew. They were immediately reprimanded, slapped across their faces. The entire room got silent—for the next seven years!

Some students decided they never wanted to attend school again from that first experience. Others returned out of curiosity. Few learned very much. As this history was told again and again, at kitchen table after kitchen table around my village, I got a clear sense of what school had meant to the Elders and even some of the parents in Old Harbor. This was the place they were attacked and humiliated for being who they are, for speaking the only language that they knew. I later asked my Yup'ik wife when she remembers learning anything at school, and she replied that by fourth grade she had begun to understand enough English to actually benefit instructionally. But for the first three years, she was just struggling to make sense of what these strange people were trying to say.

On the other hand, it seems widespread that children wanted to learn English, wanted to know what these aliens were trying to convey. They even played school at recess, (thankfully, not by slapping each other!) by sitting on the ground outside in neat rows (somehow this formation seemed essential) and pretending to speak English. The play teacher would imitate the sounds of English by using the unfamiliar consonants SH and R in rapid succession. In Southeast Alaska, students pretended to speak English, an elder later told me, by imitating the alien sound "L" saying "La LA La La La LA!" This was "school" for several generations of Native Alaskans.

Educational Exile

After twenty or even thirty years, some perseverant scholars managed to complete the eighth grade, the highest level available at the local Day Schools. The most promising were encouraged to apply for entrance into something called high school, always some distance from home. The system of boarding schools was inaugurated originally at the old Spanish fort in St. Augustine Florida, where Apache and some Navajo boys were incarcerated literally in the dungeon, removed as far from family, friends and familiar culture as the government could ship them. The great hope was that they would forget their people and, having mastered English and gained some job skills, assimilate into the American workforce, as millions of immigrants had done. Refugees have always sought acceptance into the proverbial "melting pot." Indigenous people have historical struggled to define and protect their distinctive identities. Most of the boys at the "school" in Florida died. But this did not discourage the BIA.

A new, more suitable but equally foreign site was chosen for Native American teens at Carlile, Pennsylvania. Here the boarding school paradigm was developed and exported. For decades Native American teens where shipped off to exotic distant locations like Chemawa, Oregon, Chilocco, Oklahoma and Haskell, Kansas, and later Mount Edgecumbe, Alaska. Trade schools operated for a time at Eklutna, near Anchorage, as well as Seward and Wrangell.

The community and region-wide impact on thousands of Native Americans is difficult to assess. From my many interviews with Native survivors of this system and their parents, however, a clear pattern emerges. Parents felt helpless and depressed, having their adolescent children removed from their homes and communities. Certainly this occurs, tragically, when family problems or crises make such removal necessary for the safety and wellbeing of the children. But these were loving homes with healthy family and community networks of loving support. The only "problem" was that these were Native children being raised as Natives by Native families, friends and neighbors. Left to these care providers, these kids would grow up to be another generation of ...Natives! In the heyday of assimilation, authorities believed, that was unacceptable. So in the name of Education, and in the "best interests of the children" they were exiled to distant dormitories where their daily existence was monitored more closely than convicted felons are today within the state correctional system. Parents were deprived of their children and teens were virtually incarcerated for the crime of being Native American.

Many, if not most of that first wave of school refugees returned home after a year or perhaps two, and refused to resume their studies. Of course, they often felt as if it was they who had failed, they who could not endure, they who could not succeed. Somehow they were not smart enough to graduate from high school, let alone to attend college. Within a generation the prevailing attitude was that secondary education and university level success was natural, even easy for non-Natives, but too difficult for indigenous people. A community of dropouts viewed themselves as failures.

How many times an articulate, tri-lingual Aleut Elder has said to me privately, "Don't expect too much from us, Father Michael! We're just dumb Aleuts in this town!" Who had branded them so unfairly? Where had they gained this self-concept of being "just dumb" Natives? Who had taught them that? The answer, upon further inquiry: at school, from the teachers. There have been times when I was tempted to conclude that our people may have been better off if the federal government had neglected them for a couple more centuries.

By the late 1960's, another generation of village students was, however belatedly, completing high school successfully. They had grown up hearing the horror and later the comic stories of the arrival of the first teachers, the construction of the first school. They had been intrigued by tales told by older siblings of their travels outside Alaska to exotic destinations in Oregon, Kansas and Oklahoma. And they had resolved that they would venture there and persevere. They would travel to high school and graduate. And many did.

Native people are adaptive. Their cultures require members to be creative, tenacious, flexible. We can do whatever we need to succeed and survive. So with determination, after years of painful and confusing alienation and tears, students began coming home with diplomas. This was a new situation for both Elders and graduates. Imbued with a spirit of western individualism and personal success, many of the newly educated youth viewed their grandparents as illiterate, stone-age barbarians. While they still loved them as family, they were also ashamed of their social ignorance and backwardness. Of course they could not voice these criticisms, but they found reintegration into village life difficult. They longed to fit back into the roles they had enjoyed before their sojourn "abroad," and many quickly did. Others found the readjustment painful. And the tension was mutual. The new alumni thought they understood the world and its problems in ways superior to their chiefs and elders. The Elders viewed the returnees as contaminated with new ideas and attitudes alien and even hostile to the traditions of the People. Unable to accept some of the practices and beliefs of previous times, the graduates felt a sense of loss and separation from their own families and their culture. Sensing this alienation, one elder commented, "These kids come back from school, and they are strangers to us. But worse than that, they are strangers to themselves."

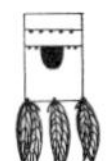

Family Values

What makes something a precious heirloom? I suppose most parents have saved, through the years, all sorts of mysterious handicrafts their offspring produced. There are barely recognizable valentines and mother's day cards, birthday gifts that only vaguely resembled their archetype. Most folks would consider these poorly executed examples of children's cutting, pasting, coloring or painting simply junk. Why are these stored carefully in closets and cedar chests all over the earth?

Value can be derived from the material from which an object is made. Gold, silver, diamonds and sapphires have an inherent value because these are rare and beautiful commodities. But other items retain their value despite their almost insignificant composition. Their value derives from their origins, the process by which they were created, their story. The old afghan that great-grandma painstakingly crocheted is far more valuable than those of higher quality and superior craftsmanship woven by machine. The time, energy and commitment that the elder "put into" the blanket confer on it an almost priceless and irreplaceable meaning.

So it is in rural communities, where men hunt and fish, devoting their time, talent and physical strength to providing the food, the women their talents to sewing, weaving, knitting and cooking, to provide clothing and meals to their family, friends, neighbors and strangers. The berries from the store freezer may be tasty, but they lack the value of the ones our daughters labored all day to pick, on the tundra, near the summer fish camp. There is no story in that frozen fruit, no value beyond the price tag. What we bring home from the land is always a gift, a gift from nature, a gift from the hunter or gatherer, a gift from God. They are sacred, and we receive them with gratitude and respect.

We don't want food stamps. We just want to be able to survive on our land, as we always have and hope always will.

A Destructive Dilemma

Here is the dilemma for all Native Americans. Insofar as a person adapts to modern western ways of thinking and behaving, he or she will be viewed by the dominant culture as progressive, intelligent, wise, but also as turncoat, one who sold out his cultural identity for the goods and services of the modern world, and therefore no longer a "real" Indian. To the extent that one holds onto the traditional ways, speaks the language, observes the traditions of the tribe, that person will be seen as a genuine Native, but backward, stupid and ignorant. Each Native Alaskan has to find a spot on the continuum represented by these two extremes. Entire villages have sought to resolve the dilemma by asserting either its total commitment to traditional ways, or by renouncing them. Neither has proven particularly healthy or practical.

Many graduates have found it impossible to articulate, let alone choose a comfortable place between being a traditionalist or an assimilationist. For some, the emotional and psychological strain of being permanently placed in this irresolveable problem gives way to anger, depression, guilt and/or grief. The anger arises from having been deceived. All were encouraged to leave for school in the hopes of a brighter future, a higher standard of living, of jobs and money and comforts available to those with "an education." But having struggled through the program and graduated, the returning alumnus finds no such future awaiting back home. The jobs are elsewhere, and one must choose to remain close to family and friends or strike out on one's own. Yet the skills and basic information for making this transition, to ultimately assimilate into the dominant society, were never provided. Urban survival was not part of the boarding school curriculum.

So even those who might have opted for this lifestyle have no practical way of pursuing it. They are trapped, and angry.

Depression arises from either this sense of entrapment or for the sense of loss and separation. Graduates did not gain the same competence in the spoken language or in traditional skills or practices that those who never left home have mastered. So much of what was central to the high school experience seems meaningless and unimportant back in the village. School imparted western values of self-sufficiency and independence, while the village operates along different lines, where mutual support, sharing and interdependence are paramount. Where do I fit? Which way is "right"? Who am I? What does it mean to be Native today? The personal and collective issues, questions without any apparent or acceptable answers loom large, forever.

Loss

Every time an Elder dies, we lose a living connection to our continuing story. Imagine what it was like to be born in 1915, just a few years after the BIA built a school in the winter village. Fall, spring and summer months, hardly anyone stayed there. It was the place we gathered in the cold and darkness of winter to remember the departed family and tribal members and thank the animals for giving themselves to us as food and clothing, to tell the stories, observe the ceremonies, sing, dance, feast and enjoy as well as support each other. The rest of the year, we were nomads.

But the teachers began insisting that we stay in the village in spring, so the kids could attend school. We didn't see the point. Spring camp was always a wonderful time of renewal and rebirth. After eating mostly last summer's smoked salmon for weeks, we were eager to return to the wilderness and get some fresh meat. They made such a fuss about it, though, that we left the younger kids with older relatives and went to spring camp without them. When that proved too stressful, we gave up spring camp back about 1955. Nowadays no one ever goes, and the younger generation never heard about it, except when the elders reminisced about their own youth.

No one in town had electricity, except the school and the teachers' houses in the BIA compound. No one else had indoor plumbing either. Everyone had temporary cabins they used when in the village, and lived in tents the rest of the year. A century ago, these were made of caribou hide, but eventually folks switched to store bought canvas tents. Folks traveled by dog sled in winter and home made boats and even kayaks the rest of the year, but gradually they saved the money to buy aluminum skiffs and outboard motors. The first we saw was just four horsepower, but we thought it moved so fast! Snow machines gradually replaced the dog teams, fueled by dogs that ate the fish we stored in summer. Now we needed gasoline (at $6 a gallon) to go anywhere during the winter. Things got easier, moved faster.

The Federal Government decided our cabins were too poor and primitive, so they sent in pre-fabricated houses with oil furnaces. No one had to chop wood anymore, but we had to find a way to pay for heating oil now. And the new houses came with electricity and high utility bills too. The tough times were ending.

Radio, television and eventually telephones came in the next decade. When I think of it, Grandpa, as he grew up, between 1915 and 1975, witnessed all that the outside world had invented in the last 6000 years: writing, books, schools, electricity, fossil fueled engines and generators, telephones, radios, televisions, airplanes, and space craft sailing to the moon and back. He was born in a stone age and died in a space age culture. He wore the clothes made from animal skins his mother sewed as a boy, and was in Eddie Bauer down jackets and REI socks 60 years later. He hunted and fished and gathered as a teen, but in retirement rushed home in his 50 horse power boat to throw his lunch into a microwave to watch his favorite satellite TV show each afternoon.

Value is accrued not only by the money spent for but the personal time and energy devoted to producing a product. This is the inherent value in subsistence fish or meat. The equivalent can be bought at the store today, for two or three times the Seattle market price (which no one could afford) or it can be harvested, using the snow machine or boat, the precious gasoline, the rifle and ammo, plus hours, even weeks work, time, energy and commitment, to bring the food home to feed others.

As an Elder said in the early 1970's, "When I was young, things were difficult but also satisfying. Now they're not so hard. But they're also not so satisfying."

I guess we're losing our ability to understand what this lady meant, every time another Elder passes away.

Grief and Guilt

There is often a sense of grief for the undeniable loss of cultural information and wisdom that each generation fails to learn and therefore cannot transmit to its own offspring. Customs once cherished and enjoyed fall into disuse. Rites and traditions that formed the core of family and community life go unobserved, and will in another generation be forgotten entirely. As each generation ages it becomes painfully aware of this steady but apparently irreversible erosion of traditional life. Something we love is slowly dying. A sense of loss and grief pervades the community.

This is coupled with guilt. Somehow we are ourselves responsible for this decline and feel helpless to reverse it. The whole world seems to militate against our survival, the continuation of our way of life, and while we cannot surrender, we cannot resist appropriately. We lack the strength and the creative power to turn things around. We cannot teach what we do not know, and we know so much less than our parents and grandparents. We are to blame for the demise of our own culture. An entire generation, and sometimes two suffer on the cross of guilt, grief, depression and anger. But they keep it hidden. Seldom do members of this tragic generation speak about their feelings, their silent suffering, their alienation, or their pain. Only after a couple of beers, in my Kodiak experience, did any adults speak of their trauma and tragedy. But gradually a great distortion of the story began to permeate it. Native Alaskans assumed a negative self-identity. Many started to blame themselves as victims often do. It is our own fault. We don't measure up. Those old teachers were right. We really are "dumb." We just can't succeed in the modern world. That's it. We CAN'T. White folks can, but Natives cannot. Secretly this lie begins to take root in the collective psyche. The history of schooling in the last decades of the Russian period reveals this to be untrue, but not knowing their own history, (and the story denied or ignored by Alaskan historians) perpetuates the lie. We CAN'T. So why bother?

During the next decade, usually with the importation of alcohol or drugs, the next generation implodes. Under the influence of controlled substances of one sort or another, the community erupts in an epidemic of anti-social and self-destructive behaviors. Domestic violence, child neglect and abuse, Fetal Alcohol Syndrome, rape and murder result in high levels of incarceration. The modern world addresses crime by arresting and imprisoning the offenders, removing children from their abusive or neglectful homes, and burying the victims. Some are obvious, some not. Suicide can be direct and violent, with guns and nooses, or slow and painful, with alcohol or drugs, or invisible, as in the case of "accidents." Alaska is, of course, a dangerous place and people have always perished by drowning, falling, crashing, or just getting lost. But today the number of accidents surpasses all previous levels. Young people take unnecessary risks. They venture onto thin ice, into storms and blizzards that, had they heeded their experienced Elders, they would have never traveled. But there is an increasing sense of meaninglessness, of nihilism in today's generation. Warned that conditions might be dangerous, they leave anyway. They seem to believe it doesn't matter whether they live or die. Nothing matters. I don't matter. You don't matter. Everything is pointless. Who cares anyway?

After a century of this downward spiral, the modern world re-intervenes with emergency "help." Often this help arrives in the form of a mental health 'SWAT' team that comes into a village after an incident (plane crash, suicide, etc.) and stays a day or two and leaves. One of the first responders is usually the school counselor. Non-reciprocal assistance arrives in the form of programs, staffed by experts imported from elsewhere. We have drug and alcohol counseling centers, suicide prevention hot lines, shelters, social workers, financial aid, grief experts, nutrition experts, exercise experts, birthing, child rearing, and how to die experts. All have advanced degrees. All have a sincere desire and commitment to help. All come from somewhere else, and all will leave in a year or two or three. Their collective importance, their clear message to the Native population is "You're right. You CAN'T. But don't worry. We're here to HELP." And we are being helped to death.

For indeed, we have come full circle, back to the missionary lady in her bustle, who has come to save us from ourselves, confident that she is doing good, even God's work, by transforming us into her own image. The clear message indigenous people receive from the dominant culture reinforces all the confusion and frustration of that first generation a century or more ago. It takes a hundred years to mess things up this badly, but we have worked hard at it and can now claim success. The Native people, their languages and cultures are dying. They could and or would not assimilate and now they're doomed.

PLY's

The staff at the hospital in Juneau introduced me to this concept, PLY's, Potential Life Years. It helps to quantify the kind of grief, loss, anger and despair that invisibly envelopes and swallows entire communities.

Let's suppose the life expectancy in a region is 80 years and an 85 year old grandmother dies there of natural causes. No PLYs are lost. Grandma had had more than her share of birthdays, holidays and anniversaries. The number of PLYs lost to the family and community is zero.

Then suppose a 55 year old man suddenly collapses and dies of heart failure. He should have been here for another 25 years, a full quarter century more of holidays and celebrations. He should have been here 25 more years to guide and inspire his siblings and grandchildren. He should have been here with his parents as they aged and needed him, depended on him more. So the loss is quantified as 25 PLYs.

In a town of 500, the community can reasonably expect a loss of 25 PLYs in a year. The loss and grief then remains at acceptable, predictable levels.

But what happens when a child or teen drowns, gets sick and dies, commits suicide. The level of PLYs is much increased. The community must deal with three or four times the normal level of PLYs. It will soon be drowning in grief, but since this is invisible, no newly arrived outsider will likely become aware of this in the first year or two of residence.

Rural Alaska is drowning in invisible grief, and we continue to work there as if conditions were normal and the PLYs had never been calculated.

Well, the "Vanishing American" has been disappearing for two hundred or more years already, and there are more Native People today in North American than any time since 1492. There is hope. But given the decline of cultures and languages, what will be the point, the purpose, the meaning of being Native in the centuries ahead? That is a question for the indigenous peoples themselves.

But I have witnessed this cycle take its toll on families and friends. I have buried too many victims of both suicide and accidents. I have shared the grief and the trauma, the anger and the sadness of elders and parents who have watched as their children drift off into lives of addiction, crime, sickness, suffering and death. And I am convinced that the seedbed out of which these destructive behaviors emerge is the school. Our schools are killing our kids.

CHAPTER 5

Bootleggers, Binges and Booze

I don't recall now how I gradually came to the realization that the effort to retain some vestige of their traditional lifestyle and world view that has characterized the Native American response to European colonization, and conquest across the Americas had become a global phenomenon. I remember agonizing for months, perhaps years, over the fate of my community. As the village pastor, I was having daily services. We had renovated the historic church and enlarged the rectory. I met with people daily to discuss spiritual matters and their own issues. I visited the homes, encouraged the Elders, guided the parents, instructed the children. And all this was not enough. My flock was in a permanent state of depression. During the economic depression of the 1930's, alcohol abuse and suicides skyrocketed in the majority culture, but that traumatic era lasted less than a decade. My parish had been depressed for half a century! People didn't like to talk about it. It was too painful. They felt humiliated, hurt, and angry. But these feelings were just below the surface. It only took a couple of beers to bring them boiling out.

Repeatedly I witnessed calm and quiet men become easily enraged, violent and abusive. I saw parents deal with their inner doubts and demons with the bootlegged anesthesia in a bottle. These people were in deep pain and had no apparent or healthy way to deal with it. There were two patterns, in my experience. There were, as there nearly always had been, the town "drunks," the guys who used alcohol to drop out of life, and drank to excess whenever they could. But these were the quiet ones, whose inebriation attracted little or no attention and seldom created any serious disruption. They smiled a lot, staggered a little and went home to sleep it off, until tomorrow. These were the textbook alcoholics made famous and funny in literature and comic skits.

But there were also many binge drinkers in the community. This was not the norm anywhere else I had been. There were certain times of the year when many if not most of the village would get premeditatedly drunk, continue to drink for a certain number of days, and then stop, sober up, and go back to work. My first experience with this was the Fourth of July. Parents deliberately drank to the point of intoxication, became rowdy and unpleasant, forcing their children to seek sanctuary in more sober neighboring households. After a few days, the storm passed, people cleaned up themselves and their homes and life returned to normal. The End of the Salmon Season marked another such binge, as well as New Year and sometime after Lent ended. The village gave itself permission to "let off steam" according to this informal calendar, so that the kids dreaded the approach of certain holidays, hoping the damage would not be too severe. This was conscious, planned, scheduled alcohol abuse.

There are theories that posit a genetic trait, a propensity toward alcoholism and abuse in Native Americans. Research indicates that populations with long historic experience with and exposure to alcohol have developed some resistance to addictive behaviors. Certain sects of Jews have the widest use of alcohol and the least incidence of problems with it. The substance is not itself chemically addictive. Otherwise everyone who drinks would eventually become alcoholic. But this is not the case with 90% of drinkers. They can drink, drink responsibly and never crave alcohol the way alcoholics do. But for 10%, alcohol becomes emotionally and psychologically addictive, and whether there is a genetic cause or whether the reason is more sociological or psychological remains a matter of debate. No one would deny, however, that booze, as the cheapest semi-legal drug, is the scourge of rural Alaska.

Shaking the Bottle

Some years ago, a drug and alcohol counselor approached me for advice. He said the elders in his village believed that alcohol was itself the problem, and if importation of it could be effective banned, the problem would be solved. His own analysis was that the problem went deeper. How could he demonstrate this to the community's leaders?

Overnight I pondered this question and proposed this demonstration. Bring to the meeting, I suggested, two bottles of carbonated beverages, two liters of soda pop. Explain that for most people drinking was not a problem. Drinking did not affect their ability to function as parent, spouse or employee. Drinking did not lead to anti-social or self-destructive behaviors. They could drink responsibly and self-regulate the quantity they drank. Using the pop bottles, declare that alcohol is a bottle opener, and open the first bottle. Nothing happens. Now violently shake the second bottle and open it. The agitated soda inside foams and explodes as the cap is removed. Did removing the cap, the alcohol cause this eruption? No, the agitation did. What is inside the bottle will determine whether the application of alcohol produces silence or an explosion. But the bottle opener was only the release of the energy within. People manage to keep their pain, their rage, their grief, their guilt under control, hidden from view, but once alcohol is introduced, the eruption is inevitable.

Like lava from a volcano, these eruptions can themselves do serious harm, inflicting further pain, guilt, rage and grief. Most domestic violence occurs when one or more parties are drinking. Many if not most fatal accidents are alcohol related. Nearly all crime is committed under the influence. I have been visiting Alaskan prisons for nearly thirty years and have never met an inmate who was sober at the time of his offense. People are in pain. They seek relief. They drink to numb themselves and forget. In the process they hurt others, who in their pain seek relief. They drink for the same reasons. The condition is communicated to another generation.

Descent into Drink

When I first came to Alaska forty years ago, the town drunks were an embarrassment, teased and joked about. The community wide binges were an anomaly, a behavior for which people sought reconciliation and forgiveness, acknowledging that their behavior had been irresponsible and ungodly. They recognized that this was unhealthy and improper and repented tearfully and sincerely, but like most addictions they found it impossible to break the cycle by will power alone. This increased the grief and guilt and led to another round. They knew it was wrong but continued to resort to binge drinking because, it seemed to me, this was their only release.

Knowing what is right and doing it are very different things. There is a passage in Scripture where the Apostle Paul writes, "The good things I know and seek to do, I don't do. The evil that I know and even hate, I find myself doing." That's the human predicament. Knowledge and will power are not sufficiently strong to propel us toward the Good. There are psychic realities that hold us back, and even prompt us to behave in ways that logic and reason disapprove. I could understand and forgive my flock. But how could I help them?

It was then that I began researching their history. Discovering that three generations earlier, Kodiak Alutiiq had assumed leadership positions in the Russian American Company, that they had produced college graduates who had completed post-secondary degrees in Siberia and Europe, that they had a record of amazing accomplishments stretching back more than a century provided me with tools to begin rebuilding the wounded souls of my friends and neighbors. "Dumb Aleut!" There is no such thing!

And I could point, at least at that time, to elders who could read, write and speak three languages, Russian, Aleut and English. There were educated, genteel ladies and gentlemen in nearly every village. They conversed in Russian and drank their tea from samovar and imported china. They addressed each other with formal respect, and wrote letters with impeccable penmanship. They also harvested fish and sea mammals, enjoying traditional Alutiiq cuisine, maintaining a subsistence lifestyle much as their ancestors had for millennia. Their homes were decorated with photos of their children and grandchildren, precious ancient icons with vigil lamps aglow, lace curtains, and heirlooms. They considered all these cultures their own. Having intermarried with Siberian frontiersmen, Scandinavian fishermen and neighboring tribes for two hundred years, the Kodiak Aleuts were a cosmopolitan and sophisticated elite. They had explored and mapped Alaska's shores, built and operated churches, schools, stores, trading posts and ships, recorded their legends and histories, studied in foreign universities and sailed around the world. "Dumb Aleuts!" What a lie that was!

My interest in Native cultures, both anthropological and historical research, arose from my pastoral concern for my friends and neighbors, for the children in my classroom at both the church and public schools. At least part of the response to the tragic situation I had encountered lay in rebuilding their dignity and self-respect, which the forced assimilationist policies had robbed them. I also pioneered the first attempt to teach Alutiiq in the public schools in Akhiok and

Old Harbor, receiving a state-planning grant to fund the development of materials and compensation for the teachers. Affirming the value and importance of the language, within the walls of the school that had worked so hard to suppress it, was a complete reversal of the old pattern. But this was not enough.

Telling the Story

Getting the Aleut story told would not be easy. There was nothing available in English, no academic research to prove that Native Alaskans had made significant contributions to the development of their society. These accomplishments had to be accepted and acknowledged, and the path to this was solid scholarly research and publication. That would be one aspect of the struggle. But in the meantime, the same attitudes and policies remained. The curriculum was still filled with assimilationist material, every page declaring the "normalcy" of the White Anglo-Saxon Protestant and mostly Male heritage, as the standard against which all other races, languages and cultures would be judged. Real Americans came on the Mayflower. People of other ethnic backgrounds, cultural and religious traditions or even genders cannot expect equality despite legal and constitutional guarantees. "Liberty and Justice for all," the final words in the Pledge of Allegiance, most students recite daily at school, remain an unfulfilled promise rather than a reality for millions of minority children and their parents.

Most teachers recruited to teach on Kodiak had no idea that all this had happened in the centuries before their arrival. They were coming to a magnificently beautiful place, inhabited by incredibly kind, generous and hospitable people, who were drowning in grief, guilt, sadness and indignation, and had found no appropriate means by which to heal. In their ignorance, the new wave of professionals would only aggravate rather than ameliorate this pain, and unknowingly perpetuate it unless they learned more about these people, this place. Would they? If they wanted to, how could they? Where would one begin to tell the story?

I discovered that meeting the newly arrived and introducing myself to them as their neighbor and the village pastor, sitting and discussing this story with them and offering my support and experience did not suffice. I was, after all, just the village priest from down the road. My responsibility was the church. Theirs was the school. They had been trained in teaching methods and classroom management and they were confident they were up to the task. If I did my job and they did theirs, everyone would be happy, and we could all get along harmoniously.

I did plenty of substituting at the school, however, and as the academic year progressed, I heard with increasing frequency, complaints about "these people," and "this place." Intercultural communications were predictably breaking down. And when miscommunication occurs, whoever has less power suffers the consequences. That's the rule. Miscommunicate with your boss, and you pay. With your doctor, you pay, with the traffic cop, you pay, with your teacher, you pay, with your parents, you pay. With your spouse, it depends. But whoever has less power in the relationship will be unable to repair the damage. Only the person in the superior position can fix it, if they recognize there is a problem at all.

Most miscommunication is also missed. Or rather, it is defined as rudeness, dishonesty, deceit or stupidity. And this is how my students were being treated by imported, well-educated certified staff who had no idea that they were misassessing the behavior and the competence of their students because of the cultural gap they failed to recognize existed between them. I visited classrooms where I was told over 90% of the students were "learning disabled." I have encountered small schools where 28 out of 32 students have been classified as "special ed." The mislabeling and misunderstanding of children at the very start of their academic careers practically assures their eventual failure. We consistently take bright, beautiful, energetic and enthusiastic five year olds and, in ten short years, transform them into depressed, angry, suicidal fifteen year olds. Isn't it time to stop this? Why can't schools stop killing our kids, if not physically, then emotionally, psychologically, spiritually?

This is not a uniquely Alaskan situation. Wherever the global society, with its economic, social, political and military power has imposed itself on a local, traditional, tribal culture, the same forces have been brought to bear with the same results. The population we have been sent to "help" is placed in a position of inferiority and dependence, leading to years of confusion, frustration and anxiety, followed by decades of accumulated anger, depression, grief and guilt.

The population becomes clinically depressed and demoralized and seeks relief from the pressures, stress, the chronic psychic pain, and finds release in addictive behaviors, principally alcohol. This leads to another level of problems, a destructive cycle of violence and suffering after which the dominant culture intervenes with more professional, non-reciprocal (and therefore addictive) "help." And the cycle self-perpetuates and strengthens like a tropic depression gaining hurricane force. The sun might be shining, but this town is in the midst of an invisible, destructive and deadly storm.

And this is any town, anywhere, not just rural Alaska.

CHAPTER 6

Unintentional Harm

The bad news is that well educated and enlightened professionals are doing serious though unintentional harm to Native Alaskan children. The norm is that when miscommunication occurs, whoever has less power in the relationship suffers the consequences for that undetected miscommunication. And when this happens often enough, students are dismissed as disrespectful, deceitful, dishonest, unreceptive, inattentive, uncooperative, passively aggressive or learning disabled. The tendency then is to survive. Teachers adopt a mindset that enables them to "get through" the day, without further qualms about the academic achievement of their students. We can teach for the standardized test, the results of which will determine whether they have made "adequate progress" which alone will assure job security and stability in the era of No Child Left Behind.

The national standard by which all students are to be assessed, however, fails to take their cultural background and inherent strengths into account. School requires initial competence in oral language, that is school assumes fluency in speaking and understanding standard American English. One cannot assume that rural Alaskan students have the same grasp of this dialect that most urban Anglo children have, but the norms for the tests use this latter group as the standard against which all others will be judged. We are, in an odd sense, back to the Mayflower once again.

Learning styles differ cross-culturally. For ten thousand years, Native Alaskan kids have learned by watching, observing, listening, imitating and repeating. Most Yup'ik parents, for example, will only silently point to indicate that a child should watch a particular activity closely. There is not much emphasis on wordy explanations or preparations. Observation and imitation are key. Silence is appreciated, often even preferred. This has produced generations of thoughtful, reflective, resourceful and creative people who have survived in some of the world's most difficult and dangerous ecosystems.

Quiet People

You are invited with a nod to help yourself to the soup and ladle your portion into a bowl from the adjourning cabinet. Sitting down you pray quickly and silently and join those already seated. No one says anything. You ask for someone to pass you the salt, and silently they do. You say "Thank you," but no one responds. You request the bread and thank the person who hands you the plate. He says quietly "Not yet!" You try to spark some conversation, but everyone stares down at their bowls, continuing to eat their lunch. Tea is served. You ask for sugar and it arrives. You again, according to your usual protocol, say "Thanks," and again hear in mutter tones, "Not yet!" Around homemade jam and freshly baked bread, someone begins a short anecdote about an incident that occurred this morning at the post office. Everyone listens attentively and laughs at the punch line. The meal ends with everyone standing, making the sign of the cross and turning to you saying in unison "Now!" The chorus now emphatically expresses thanks and leaves.

Silence in this culture is golden. It is better to be quiet than to talk. Conversation comes only after the food has been carefully and reverently consumed, not during the meal. Even the expression of thanks is postponed until most of the food has been eaten. Only over the sipping of tea do stories erupt, and one "Quyana" at the end suffices to thank verbally, God, the hunter, the cook, and all those who assisted in any way at the meal.
These are quiet people.

In the pre-technology days, before television or even radio, evenings were filled with stories, often told in the dark as everyone lay in their early wintertime beds. Grandparents recounted the old myths and legends, filled with wisdom and truth, informing the next generation of the adventures ahead, the struggle to grow up, to become an adult, a provider, a member of the community, a Real Person. There was time and place for long orations, during which the young could imagine the sights and sounds of a long ago place, when heroes and monsters and ghosts and spirits, demons and angels, visited the Human Beings and taught them all that they needed to know about their place in the world, and the appropriate and respectful ways they should live. In the age of 400 television channels, a thousand DVDs and ten thousand compact discs, much of this tradition and heritage has been neglected. The Elders told the old stories with talent and eloquence, but they have been lost in translation, the older generation capable of telling the tales in their original language, but the younger generation incapable of understanding them. There is, among the Elders, a sense of loss, guilt and grief attending to what is now unspoken, untold, lost.

Visiting

This is perhaps even more true in the dominant culture. During my childhood relatives and friends visited. They sat around in the living room and talked, shared stories, caught up on news and gossip, and reminisced. They shared stories, connected, talked. When guests arrived, the television was turned off, refreshments served. Family histories were recounted, origins revealed. Children eavesdropped until the adults realized that some stories were not appropriate for young ears, and they were sent out to play. Nevertheless, the next generation discovered their roots at such family gatherings, when by oral tradition the deeds of the ancestors were recounted, the heroic deeds of the Elders revealed.

Villagers visit daily. It is still a major village activity, perhaps its core. My wife and I made it our custom to walk on Sunday afternoon to the far end of our village and begin visiting, stopping for a few minutes in some homes, for an hour or more in others. We' d take the whole day just to visit, to connect, to catch up, to communicate. Other residents visited certain neighbors or family daily at about the same time. The routine of village life is established by regular visits. Those who have never lived in a village have little or no concept how just visiting cements relationships, provides the fuel for friendships that last a lifetime.

Teachers, it seems, never visit. They somehow do not realize that they are welcome. The villagers often sense that they do not want to connect, do not want to be involved in the life of the town. They have their own concerns, interests, and agenda. But they remain separate and alien just like Mrs. Bigbutt a hundred years ago. I recall being criticized at the school for not only writing a revisionist history of the island, but for trying to revive an extinct language. The teachers, it seems never heard Alutiiq spoken. That was predictable, since teachers had as a profession and a matter of policy suppressed the language for many decades. So when a teacher, even a new recruit who knew nothing of this sad legacy, approached, villagers switched to English. I heard Alutiiq all the time, every day. They never did. Even linguists sent to study the language around Kodiak met with resistance. One scholar told me that she spent weeks trying to get locals to speak to her in Alutiiq and they insisted they had forgotten it. "We speak only Russian here!" they proclaimed— until she caught them speaking to each other in Aleut at the local post office. I am often amazed at how different the teachers perceive the community from the way people who have lived there all their lives do. There can be a complete disconnect.

Breakdown

And here, the breakdown is predictable, given that the teachers have never been prepared for life in a rural Native Alaskan community. Nothing in their personal experience has enabled them to bridge this gap, and nothing in their educational background or orientation has prepared them for the experience. We would not send Peace Corps volunteers to India without some intensive classes in Hindu religion, history, languages, culture, politics and cuisine. We would teach them Hindi, coach them on forms of etiquette and politeness styles, provide them with essential information about customs, beliefs, traditions, holidays and religious rites. We would hardly expect them to succeed in establishing appropriate, harmonious relationships without this essential background information.

But we do nothing comparable to prepare teachers for success in rural Alaska. There may be several explanations for this, but none of them justify this neglect. Certainly there are other ethnic minorities in the state. But they all immigrated here willingly. Only Natives have been overrun in their own homeland and subjected to policies of extermination, relocation and assimilation for the last five hundred years. Only Natives were sent to boarding schools, alienated from their own cultures and communities and returned home without much hope of readjusting to either the world of their ancestors or assimilating into the modern global society. Unlike the others, Native Peoples are our responsibility because we have spent too much time and energy, allocated so many resources to destroying them.

Bridging the Gap

As a minimum, people planning to teach or administrate in rural Alaska should be required two full semesters of substantial courses in anthropology and history specifically designed to prepare them to appreciate and embrace Alaska's indigenous cultural heritage (this would also be a part of the training center curricula outlined in Section II). They should have some knowledge of the structure of the local language and the role it continues to play in the social, economic and political life of the region. The way Yup' ik continues to dominate the worldview and identity of people in Southwest Alaska is radically different from the way Tlingit language permeates the culture in Southeast. But teachers should not go to either area ignorant of this! The moiety and clan structure of Northwest Coast Indian tribes, their complex system of respect and honor, their use of poetry and metaphor, their rich oratorical style contrasts with the egalitarian society of the Inuit and Yup'ik whose dancing traditions and celebrations offer a unique insight into their worldview. All have "potlatches" but each has its own structure and meaning. There are many worlds in rural Alaska, and new comers should be prepared to understand and explore them with appropriate background information and continuing support.

Unless and until we provide this sort of informed, scholarly background and continued personal contact and support, we preclude, for the majority of professionals working in "the bush" any full appreciation of the joys and satisfaction that Native people derive from their identity and home. I am amazed how disconnected most teachers and social workers feel from the most interconnected people in the world. We miss each other completely, living in separate worlds, side by side.

Curriculum reform and teacher education are two necessary areas to reconsider. If we teach Alaska history, neglecting or ignoring completely the contributions and accomplishments of Alaskan Natives, we perpetuate negative stereotypes, and allow the Great Lie to stand, unchallenged. This is a fatal sin of omission. I believe it would be better not to teach "Alaska History" at all rather than use a required course to perpetuate the Lie. And if we fail to provide new and continuing professionals with the information they need to enhance their appreciation of Native languages and cultures, and to interact and communicate appropriately and effectively with Native children and their parents, we allow the wound, the gap between school and community, to continue untreated, to fester, to infect and poison the lives of both teacher and student The situation is far from hopeless, but we need to recognize the problem before we can address it, propose remedies. Left to their own isolated devices, too many professionals have fallen into cynicism or depression. They can give up and move away. But the harm this does to children, the damage this does to communities already suffering and wounded, is unconscionable. I feel a sense of both outrage and urgency.

One Life in Two Worlds

It is time to rethink our direction, reform our curriculum and our training programs, our continuing education and our support systems to allow teachers to teach meaningfully, effectively and enthusiastically, and for students to delight in their schools, to celebrate their academic successes, and to live healthy, productive lives, accepting and embracing their cultural heritage and identity and enjoying all the benefits of full citizenship in the modern world. Our children need both to affirm their identity with pride and confidence, and to become contributing members of the wider society.

All our children, all human beings, are seeking to restore this balance between their personal ethnic and spiritual heritage on one hand and their role as autonomous, productive citizens in a global society on the other. In Alaska we have the perfect laboratory for working out this balance, a small, scattered highly diverse population with plenty of talent and resources for the effort. What we need is vision and commitment to proceed. And if we find a way of bringing together all that is best in our ancient cultural traditions into harmony with the modern global economic and political systems which have engulfed us, the rest of the country and indeed the world are eager to hear of our success. This is not the backwaters, the boondocks, but the front line, the cutting edge. It is here that we will work out ways of bringing the conflict between the local and traditional with the global and modern together harmoniously. And for us it is not an academic exercise. The survival of our people depends on it.

Sitka Sense: Leader T

I lived for nearly two years in Sitka, in the Tlingit heartland and then was invited north to Southwest Alaska, the Yup'ik Eskimo region of the state. While I had been interested in Tlingit language and culture, I had enjoyed little success in studying or learning much about them during my residence among them in 1971-2. Returning to Sitka a decade later, I was invited by a very respected Tlingit aristocrat to have dinner at his home in "the Village," where he began to tell me a series of legends. I was honored to be invited and highly flattered that such a high-ranking Elder would share this traditional wisdom with me.

The orator told me one story. I wished I could have recorded it, but thanked him sincerely for sharing it with me. He rejected my expression of appreciation and continued immediately with a second story, more fascinating than the first. It was, as if in retrospect, he was drawing an arc in the air with the first story, and continuing the curve with the second. I was beginning to discern his agenda, but his point was not quite clear. When I attempted to thank him for his second story, he again insisted that I listen to yet a third before replying. And with the third legend, the masterful orator closed his circle, or I might say verbal "trap." He had spoken for over an hour, weaving three traditional Tlingit legends into a carefully constructed circle around his clear but never explicitly stated central point. And then class was dismissed.

I stumbled toward the door dumbfounded. How had he done that? I couldn't do that! He delivered his message clearly and firmly by constructing his argument in curved lines and joining them especially and uniquely for me, and he could see plainly from my reaction that I had understood, I had gotten his point, which was "Since we Tlingit are so fascinating, why are you bothering with those Eskimos?"

A History of Traditional Education

Schooling and Education should never be confused. Education is much older. It refers to anything learned or taught that is useful, meaningful or relevant to the lives of others. Parents have been passing on useful, meaningful and relevant ideas, attitudes, behaviors, techniques and tools for millennia. Schooling is what you do in school. And to be honest, much as I love schools, we should readily admit that not all that we do in them is ultimately useful, meaningful or relevant. In fact, we know, having been to college, that we have taken classes, and paid good tuition, for courses that proved to be useless, meaningless and irrelevant.

Traditional, non-literate cultures, nevertheless, have curricula, methods, goals, objectives, and even graduations, none of these committed to writing, accessible in libraries or the World Wide Web. Most tribal peoples identify themselves as "the People." Tlingit means "the People" or "The Human Beings." Unangax, (the name the traditional indigenous people of the Aleutian Islands have for themselves) means, "We the People." Alaska and Canada's Athabaskan Indians call themselves "Dene" or "Dineh" as do the Navajo and Apache in modern Arizona—the linguistic evidence that these are former Alaskans who moved to the Sunbelt some centuries ago. The Eskimo tribes of the western and northern coastal plains and tundra play a bit of one-upsmanship with their neighbors, for the Yup'ik and Inupiaq identify as "The Real People." But the goal of all education among Alaska's indigenous population has been to educate the next generation to know what it means to be a human being, to accept the human place in the cosmic scheme of things, and to think, speak and act as "real people" should.

The Way of the Human Being was not, however, humanly devised, discovered or invented. The Creator, in the Beginning, taught the First People the way they should speak, and even gave them their language, their homeland, their identity, and the appropriate ways in which they should relate to the natural and spiritual as well as social environments. There has always been "the Way we do." Knowing "the way we do" is the curriculum.

Patterns and Paradigms

The primary method for raising human children to human adulthood is by example. It is essential for the elders and parents to embody, to live by the ancient code that the First People learned and exemplified. Animals follow the same pattern, the parents teaching their offspring by demonstration and repetition. Eagle parents teach their chicks to fly. Wolf parents teach their cubs to speak, act, hunt and eat as wolves do. Whales show their calves how to swim, breath, navigate, migrate, feed, fish, breach, play, and mate. But while these creatures seem always to succeed, human beings have uniquely failed in producing children who follow the examples and teachings of their Elders. Human children just don't listen!

Hundreds of legends recount the misbehaviors and rebellions of human teens, usually with happy endings brought about by the intervention of an older, wiser Elder. The clear lesson derived from this genre of oral transmission is that children should watch closely, imitate faithfully and respect attentively the example and teachings of their parents, grandparents, extended family members, older siblings and in general, their entire community.

The oldest stories, the "Myths" about the origins and beginnings of things, constitute the basic context in which this curriculum is conveyed. The wonderful story of *K͟aax͟'aach goox,* a Tlingit hunter washed far eastward until he was marooned on a distant island where the trees seemed like huge blades of grass (probably bamboo) demonstrates how knowledge of the eternal structures of the world can be used to great profit. The hero of the *Kaagwaantann* clan navigated successfully home to Sitka across the open sea because he knew the structure of the world, and was able to locate his home on the distant horizon after the summer solstice. Knowing how the world works, what its fixed structures are and creatively applying this data to one's situation can provide the basis for survival and success.

First People

Legends enhance, support and give further evidence of the applicability of the old stories to current situations. Ostensibly stories like Kaxaach.goox's that happened long after the First People, they emphasize the need to refer constantly to the wisdom contained in the Origin Stories. Human beings, for example, appeared in this world unexpected and unprepared. The Creator met the First People on the beach and was not impressed favorably by their physical attributes. "Not enough hair and no feathers!" were the initial assessment. "Pitiful! You've got no future here!"

But the Creator felt sorry for these new arrivees and called a conclave of all the Arctic animals. They concurred with the initial prognosis. The first heavy frost and these new humans would be extinct. But the animals had a solution to propose. "What if we give them our flesh for food and our hides for clothing? Couldn't they survive then?" Yes, the Creator agreed, that would work. But what would the animals want in return for their meat and skins? "Gratitude and respect" the animals replied. And that is how human beings relate to the animals in their ecosystem, with gratitude, humility and respect. For the animals will give themselves, sacrifice themselves to keep the otherwise hopeless and pitiful humans alive, as long as they follow the protocols, established in the beginning, to express that respect and maintain the relationship of gratitude.

This includes the way the hunter's weapons and tools are treated, cleaned, handled, the way he hunts and kills his prey, the way it is skinned, shared, used, eaten and the unuseable leftovers disposed of. Traditional art, music, song and dance as well as annual ceremonies all focused on this central theme of traditional tribal life. Real People know how to be respectful, humble, and grateful. They know who they are, they know where they fit in the cosmic scheme of things, and they know how to relate with respect to each other, to their natural environment, to the plants and animals, and to the spirits.

Elders

When I first visited rural Alaska in the early 1970's I was introduced to Elders. These were older people, but not every old person is an Elder. Surviving to old age used to be a guarantee that the person had lived well, lived appropriately, lived as the First People had taught. Today this is not necessarily true. Modern medicine has prolonged the lives of many who were not necessarily observant of the old standards and ideals. But most villages still treasure Real People who embody the cultural ideals of kindness, humility, generosity and patience and who love to tell the old stories, whose standards, beliefs, and behaviors they have come to embody,

I was drawn to and have remained most of my life in Alaska not because of the natural beauty, though the place is extraordinarily and spectacularly beautiful. The long, cold dark winters were not all that attractive. What kept me here was the encounter with the Real Elders, the people who are qualitatively superior, kinder, gentler, more generous, more patient, more forgiving, more loving, than any I have met anywhere on earth. Their way of life, their way of seeing and living, relating and making sense of their world, of life, should not be maligned, attacked, suppressed or ignored. The Way of the Human Being is as meaningful and relevant today as ever. But the Elders are often invisible to outsiders.

They are in nearly every village the least acculturated residents of the community, often unable to communicate effectively with the newcomers, the least likely to drop by the school for a visit, except perhaps to see their grandchildren in a play, an athletic tournament, at a concert. Most teachers never see them at all. The certified staff at school is responsible for schooling. The Elders are responsible for education.

But the twentieth century was not kind to the Elders. There was, of course, the Great Death, the 1918-19 influenza epidemic that killed thousands, in some cases entire villages, but nearly everywhere the oldest citizens. Before they had time to impart their wisdom to the next generation or two, they were suddenly, often overnight, gone. Survivors were taken to children's home and orphanages, accelerating the federal policy of forced assimilation. At mid-century, rural Alaska was plagued with tuberculosis, and another generation of Elders either died or was sent to distant sanitoria, from which only a minority returned after years of exile. Family life has been disrupted in rural Alaska for nearly 100 years. The boarding schools often exacerbated the breakdown of whatever was left of "normal family life" in many communities by the 1960's and 1970's.

Old Wisdom/New Knowledge

The desire to maintain and even resurrect old cultural norms and values, however, remains strong. While it is not and cannot be the primary mission of the public school to promote or enhance the indigenous local culture, the schools' policies, curricula methods, discipline, focus and personnel must be supportive of the basic right of its constituency to affirm their identity, to teach and maintain their sense of Who they are, Where they fit in the world and make sense of it, and How they have always and continue to live respectfully with each other and meaningfully within their ecosystem. The old wisdom is still valued, even as the new knowledge is accepted and appreciated.

These are not uniquely Alaskan concerns. Everyone on the planet, in the face of the overwhelming influence and power of the Global Society, must come to grips with the same issues, defining their humanity in the face of the homogeneous but unyielding and overpowering dehumanizing presence of a worldview that has imposed itself on nearly every community and person on earth. How any of us maintain our human sense of who we are, where we fit and how to relate appropriately to our world constitute critical spiritual, moral and ethical questions for us all.

The School is by definition an institution and instrument of the Global Society. Can it be humanized to serve higher purposes than economic progress, social status or military power, or will the Global Society and its values ultimately overwhelm not only Native Americans but all humankind? The global forces of homogeneity and therefore the pressure to abandon the higher moral and spiritual standards (promulgated by all the world's religious traditions and the essentially spiritual cultures of indigenous peoples everywhere) are combatants in a war that a century ago moved from the battlefields of Little Big Horn and Wounded Knee into the school and classroom. Paradoxically, the only way for the Local Traditional Cultures to survive requires them to embrace this very institution, for the School is the only place for Real People to gain the knowledge they need to survive, economically, socially, politically, intellectually, in the modern world, we hope without losing their souls. That this is a real danger cannot be denied. The crushing of an entire People's positive self-identity, the eradication of their languages and cultural traditions, the suppression of their stories and customs, the death and exile of their teachers, tradition bearers and Elders, the removal of their children, have all taken and continues to take their toll. That has all happened. It is past. The question remains, what now? Must we continue to perpetrate such senseless injustice on another generation of innocent children, or can we stop, reflect, and imagine a better way to both school and to educate Real People?

Schooling

We are told that writing was invented about five different times, by five very different civilizations. Babylon, Egypt, India, Guatemala and China all had very different writing systems, but each attempted to inventory and preserve great data banks of knowledge. Writing is in a way almost magical. It allows the thoughts, ideas, observations and discoveries of one generation to be passed down to the next. Literacy informs generations yet unborn of the heroic struggles and insights of their ancestors. Getting published confers a kind of intellectual immortality on authors. Your name will be forever listed in the Library of Congress' catalog system.

But there is so much written, no one could possibly absorb all knowledge in one lifetime. Students are introduced to a smorgasbord of information in high school and the first year or two of college, but must necessarily chose a focus for their continued study, a "major" with perhaps a "minor" in another related or subordinate field. Unable to learn everything about everything, a scholar must concentrate on one small "sliver" of reality, necessarily neglecting, for lack of time or interest, most of what the human family has learned in the past 5000 years since writing first appeared.

Children are taught to read in order that they may read to learn. Those with advanced degrees in any particular field know a lot about their field of interest, but relatively very little about ideas, discoveries or even basic principles outside it. We have necessarily become increasingly and more narrowly specialized as the centuries have passed. It was possible, five hundred years ago, for some learned men to have read most of the library, knowing all there was to know about astronomy, mathematics, chemistry, physics and even anatomy. A scientist knew all the sciences, primarily because there were only five or six books published in each field. Today, these fields are further subdivided. There are few "general practitioners." Nearly everyone today has been forced by the shear volume of information to choose a more specialized sub-set. Doctors must pick an organ, heart, liver, bladder, nerves, skin, eye, brain, and the yellow pages of every telephone directory list them according to their specialty. Literacy allows knowledge to be stored and retrieved, schools offer courses in various disciplines, and graduates know a lot about their specialty and often little or nothing about unrelated fields.

This narrowing of focus relates directly to the way society utilizes its experts. Those who have studied and earned degrees in one area are licensed to practice in that field: law, education, economics, psychology, engineering, architecture, chemistry, botany, music, meteorology, medicine or monkeys. They are hired and paid according to the competence and experience their degrees imply. They are now ready to play the game of life in the modern, global economic, social, political society whose foundations lay in literacy in one of the planet's seven great Literary Traditions, English, French, Spanish, Russian, German, Arabic or Mandarin Chinese. The entire corpus of human knowledge is available in any of these, and most school children are invited to become functionally literate in one of these global/international languages, which afford them entrance into the World's Data Bank at the post-secondary level.

Becoming an "expert" however means that those at the highest, doctoral level, where research, the discovery of new ideas, events or realities, contributing to the data bank one's self, requires an increasingly narrow focus. Those we call experts in this society necessarily know more and more about less and less. The boundaries between disciplines also means, that we cannot always see or navigate the connections across them.

I had a student nearly 30 years ago who was interested in many fields. She decided, in the early days of computer technology, to major in both mathematics and music, and requested this at the university registrar's office. Her petition was denied and she sought my support. When I asked why her petition had been rejected, the Registrar scoffed, replying as if this were self-evident, that on our campus, no one could major in these two very different fields. "Where would she sit at graduation!" was her dismissive response.

Here we have a classic example of academic boundaries and reality in conflict. The University awards two sorts of bachelor degrees, Arts and Science, BA and BS. Music falls into the arts category, math into science. One cannot earn two bachelor degrees in two such opposite disciplines at the same commencement!

The data enshrined in the non-fiction sections of our libraries is recorded in linear, concise, precise, and often more sophisticated dialects of each of the major languages. Most writers, sharing the same information with a colleague over cocktails, would not employ the same structure, style or vocabulary. Doing so might come across as pretentious or arrogant. But the same idea on paper is expressed differently, since it is now a truth, disconnected from the person writing, and available to anyone, regardless of his personality, location or status. Non-fiction writing must be "true" anywhere, anytime, and therefore necessarily de-contextualized and impersonal.

Students worldwide read the same texts to garner the same information to pass the same tests to earn identical degrees and compete for identical jobs, to move into similar neighborhoods, with similar amenities and mortgages, to raise another generation of children who will go to school, learn to read, develop interests, major in other fields, develop marketable skills to qualify for their own home and car loans and raise, in turn, their children.

The quality of life is conceived, here, as a factor of job satisfaction as much as income. Just making lots of money is not necessarily a sign of success. What matters most is how one can balance one's work and free time. A person who earns a substantial salary at a job he/she finds satisfying and rewarding, who uses that income to enjoy quality leisure time as well, is "winning" the game of life in this culture. None of this is possible without literacy. Those unable to read are disqualified from playing the game at all. They lack fundamental, basic skills to even try out for the team.

We have students in our classrooms today who do not know this game exists, and we have others who have opted not to play. We do them both a disservice by not explaining the ball game rules, its benefits and shortcomings, and encouraging them to play, if only to defend themselves from social, political, military and economic power of the Global Society. For whether or not they want to play this game, its influence will impact them and their family and community for the foreseeable future, at least as long as fossil fuels are available to keep its cars moving, planes flying and generators running. And increasingly, every village will need well-schooled, literate people to lead and guide them into the future, or they will be overwhelmed by social, political, economic and military powers beyond their comprehension, influence or control.

Survivors

I feel passionately about education in rural Alaska because I love the people, especially the children there. I am indignant that after witnessing the destructive impact of public schooling for nearly four decades, and researching its tragic history, our post-secondary educational system can continue to ignore the damage that has been done and continues to be done to children in the sacred Name of Education. We have many talented alumni, of course, those whose innate abilities and personal interests as well as family backgrounds and communities have promoted their success. They are the heroes, the survivors. But for every one of them there are those who have perished. Their graves silently indict us. I take pride in the students I once taught who have become prominent leaders in their communities. But they themselves can recall the names of their classmates, members of their graduating classes, who have died. Of my Wrangell Institute class of 1972, few have survived. They did not live to their 40th birthday. And there were more than 80 Native students in that class.

Consider that in the late nineteenth century, about the time schools were introduced among the Yup'ik, observers explicitly noted that, despite the difficult, challenging and often depressing circumstances of their lives--the struggle to survive in a beautiful but dangerous and unforgiving natural environment--suicide was unknown. After a century of contact and schooling, suicide rates among young Native Alaskans have tragically reached alarming and devastating levels.

I have intuited that school is the seedbed from which widespread depression, anger, misdirected or unarticulated bitterness and anger arise, and produces the anti-social and self-destructive behaviors we see rampant in rural Alaska. Since the kids enter kindergarten happy, healthy, and even enthusiastic and so many leave or drop out frustrated, embittered or depressed, we should conclude that we are doing something highly detrimental to their mental and spiritual welfare while they are under our watchful control during those years. So why don't we figure out what it is we have been doing and stop doing it? When do we start doing more of what could be, should be encouraging, ennobling, life affirming, and uplifting?

V. Rev. Michael J. Oleksa

SECTION I:
AS IT IS AND HAS BEEN

PART TWO

A Description of the Seedbed Conflicting Landscapes by Clifton Bates

Introduction

Thinking About Kim-boy

After rising, I close the door behind me and climb into a watercolor painting of this Sunday tundra town. The snow-covered, iced earth rises up to meet the low, reddish-brown scrub bushes and light, straw-colored grasses, to various shack-type dwellings and on up to the band of lavender sky. Fish camps are eerie with apparitions as they are seemingly deserted and things flap in the wind and tap a haunted sound.

For a while I could hear the bell from the church, but I've walked too far now. It is just the dog and me and we are far enough away to share the sense that is present in the quiet white. The tundra is full of reflections from the ice and sun. The land and the sky in the dead of winter become shades of blurred white on cloudy days. Only when the sky is clear are other sections of the spectrum dispersed. Then, lavenders, oranges, pinks, and gold flush the cold.

An oval pond reflects the sky changes. Look into the pond for the weather: a pewter sky is a pewter pond. It was a windy day when the pond froze for good. Waves, caught in the act, leave a surface in turmoil. And, as if angry over its fate, the pond's protest is captured like the expression on a vindictive corpse.

It took me longer than I thought to get to this pond I know so well. I scar its features that have been softened by snows. I sit comfortably on a familiar knoll of tundra blown bare by the wind. The dog circles and sniffs at fox tracks that are about in nonsensical patterns. He turns, comes to me, pushes his head at my hands then resumes his canvassing, and I lift my face to the sun and feel its distant warmth. I nestle into my Thinking Place. My thoughts bounce around, touching on various subjects before settling on thinking about Kim-boy last Friday.

He was really down. He is thirteen and has lived with his old grandma for the last twelve years. She speaks Yup'ik and maybe a few words of English. They live in a one-room, uninsulated little house on the riverbank. Kim-boy sleeps in one corner on the floor. He has a blanket and some towels where he gets cozy at night.

He doesn't know how his mother died. His father drowned one spring when he fell from the riverbank into some overflow after drinking too much. He had a brother a few years older than him who recently quit high school and committed suicide.

Kim-boy is really into wrestling now. And he has discovered he is very good at it. He has a heck of a time reading and writing though. This is his first year of junior high and he can now turn out for the wrestling team, and he has been practicing after school for about a month. He has been so excited about the meet next week with some nearby village schools.

I've always marveled at how he gets himself up, dresses and gets to school day after day, year after year. Friday he was really down. I tried talking with him when I had the chance to see him alone, but he surely didn't want to talk.

That afternoon I learned that Kim-boy was failing in history, health and science, and he was not eligible to wrestle. I looked at his eligibility slip and read the comments by teachers:

"doesn't turn in his homework", "fails his tests", "no answers turned in to the questions on chapters one through five". So, no wrestling for Kim-boy.

I pondered the logic, the rationale, and the irony, related to Kim-boy's situation and thought of similar tragedies in the making before I finally stood and began trudging back to the frozen settlement. The wind driven ice snow blew into my face. I stared at the earth, huddled as I marched with the dog in my shadow. I left the expanse behind me and let poetry do polkas and minuets and death and life celebrations with the foxes and wolves that change form when darkness comes. All I saw were white changing ice shapes, conflicting landscapes, and rolling snow in shadows in twilight. The cold was far away and the white before my eyes became regular and distant.

This took place three decades ago. It was when I began wondering about the various ways schools could change so the Kim-boys of Alaska could experience success, develop healthy spirits, have choices and do what they can do in today's world as Alaska Native people.

"Everyone sees a tear in the seam, but talks about the weather."
— Lindsey Buckingham

Make the Child Fit the Desk?

The K-12 Western education system, a model devised in Prussia in the mid-1800's, has been superimposed over Alaska's indigenous people with few, if any, adaptations to meet the particular characteristics and needs of this very different student population. Various current educational and social statistics pertaining to Alaska Natives provide adequate cause for concern as to how the global society is interacting with Alaskan traditional cultures. The education system is at the heart of the matter.

The notion of creating culturally responsive schools has been bantered around for many years as, at least, a partial solution to the alienation and difficulties many Native students experience that result in social and academic problems.

"Culturally Responsive Schools" commonly refers to a smattering of attempts to ensure local activities and interests are a visible part of the education efforts. Examples are such measures as incorporating the local environment in science instruction; including local history in the social studies; encouraging Elders to visit classrooms to tell stories, share arts and crafts; using Native American literature as a language arts resource; and inviting adult males from the village to teach net repair, sled building and trapping as a part of the vocational education program. For the most part, but for some isolated incidences, this is the extent to which I have seen the Alaska Native Network's Alaska Standards for Culturally Responsive Schools be manifested in the schools and classrooms.

These are readily observable cultural activities. Many educators and concerned folk are quick to conclude that with these kinds of things going on, the problem is being addressed enabling the schools to get back to the task at hand: preparing the students for the state tests so that the demands for adequate yearly progress can be met.

But there is a very different and essential set of criteria for making our schools truly culturally responsive that would allow Native students better access to academic success, increased opportunities for developing positive, healthy attitudes and would enable successful interaction with the global society without them having to sacrifice their cultural self. By the beginning of the twenty first century, one would think the dominant society, the world's foremost superpower, would know how to positively interact with its own indigenous people. Creating truly culturally responsive schools requires more than mentioning it in a university, school district or state department mission statement or checking off that certain things are being done no matter how superficially.

Judging from how well the western education system has adapted to meet the needs of Alaska Native students in rural Alaskan villages, I can only surmise that if we were to superimpose this same system on a population whose five year olds were over six feet tall, we would unquestionably continue to equip the classrooms with the regular kindergarten desks we find in schools all over America. The students would be forced to squeeze into these seats and the schools would march on oblivious to this mismatch. Undoubtedly consultants would be hired to fly in from California to provide staff training on a special program designed to ease the unusual amount of fidgeting of these students when they are seated.

Ample evidence exists that gives cause for concern about how our schools are educating Alaska Native students. There is a leak in the main gas line, so to speak, and generally educators and agencies put forth efforts in designing gas masks and other peripherals instead of concentrating on the actual leak. This leak relates to the school system not taking into account the particular characteristics and needs of Alaska Native students; the lack of mandatory research-based, appropriate structures that are not personnel dependent in our rural schools; and inadequate educator training. This writing offers specific recommendations that deal directly with this leak in the main gas line.

This writing does not intend to be critical of the child or the culture. It is critical of an imposed system that has not adapted to meet the needs of Alaska's indigenous population. It is a system largely manned by individuals who have received no specific training regarding Alaska Native education, the land, the history, the people, traditions, or cross-cultural issues. Some very effective, creative educators and programs have and do exist for Alaska Native students. If it seems that this writing deals with too much negativism and ineptness, it is because these two factors are too often the case.

How can schools be truly culturally responsive when the vast majority of the teachers and administrators running the show are unaware of and not trained in the history, cultural traits, cross-cultural issues, language considerations, or appropriate interactions and teaching methodologies for the Native students they are there to serve? Educators come and go on a regular basis and have limited vested interest in where they are temporarily living and working. Because of this there are no sustained efforts, there is no continuity nor long-term assessment information available to determine what specifically is and isn't working. Efforts depend upon the views, concerns, whims, and interests of whatever individual happens to be in a particular position, whether as a teacher, principal, superintendent, school board member, commissioner of education or governor.

This situation of stops and starts, tangents and uncoordinated, chaotic efforts by educators not prepared and unfamiliar with the circumstances they find themselves in has resulted in educational and societal difficulties and continued alarming statistics concerning Alaska's Native people. The educators and the imposed system must make the adaptations to achieve success instead of the indigenous people continuing to be subjected to a form of cultural imperialism.

"The effects of such instruction are highly visible in withered Native souls: the nation's lowest life expectancy; the lowest annual income; and the highest rates of suicide, alcoholism, infant mortality, unemployment, and tuberculosis (Spindler, 1987). In spite of their increasing numbers, Native Americans are still underrepresented in government, institutions of higher education, professional positions, and.... the statistical evidence demonstrates the need for both Native and non-Native educators to reexamine their mainstream teaching methods, materials, and attitudes in order that they may offer more suitable programs for America's Native youth." Grant & Gillispie, 1993

CHAPTER 7

A Parade of Educators

You're hired!

The young couple looked like they just climbed down off a wedding cake. Fresh, pink, twenty-some year old faces, eager and excited, holding hands and with 'intent-to-hire' teaching contracts in their pockets. They just landed their first job teaching in Alaska. Up from Lansing to the Anchorage April Job Fair and now moving to a sub-Arctic village come fall.

They were beaming when they bumped into the middle-age lady from Oklahoma they had met earlier in the registration line. They explained to her that they both were offered jobs teaching in a four-teacher school in the Bush. They looked at their papers in order to tell her where they were going. They tried but stumbled to pronounce the name of the village, so they just showed it to her on the paper.

"Oh wonderful, where is it?" she asked sharing in their excitement.
"It's that way," Debbie, the wife, pointed toward the hotel's restaurant.
"It's west on a big river," the husband, Dave, stepped in and clarified.

They told her that there was no use in them spending any more time and money at the Job Fair since they were all set. They were changing their tickets and flying back home. They didn't have to be at their new job until mid-August. There was plenty of time to buy winter clothes, pack and get ready to move. They were full of smiles and nervous energy as they shook hands and wished the Oklahoma lady good luck in getting the position she wanted.

Ready? Set? Teach?

There are young couples like Dave and Debbie. There are couples in their fifties who have been waiting for their kids to be off on their own so they could do what they have always wanted and experience Alaska. He's dreamed of the fishing and hunting in the northland, and she's with him. There are single older women, widows and divorcees, from Texas, Oklahoma, and Arkansas wanting to teach in Alaskan villages. There are single men and women in their twenties and early thirties, REI equipped, used to camping, hiking, biking, kayaking and skiing, seeking an Alaskan teaching adventure. They can be seen camped out on the upper decks of the Alaskan ferries traveling up from the Washington terminal to find their way to the summer Job Fairs in Fairbanks. There are these stereotypes as well as individuals with a wide array of reasons for seeking a job as an educator in Alaskan villages. Some educators from in and outside Alaska are still being hired after a telephone conversation and a review of their resume.

One attribute they all have in common is that, prior to moving to their new position, they receive no training or instruction as to how they can effectively teach Alaska Native students or how they can live and positively interact in a village community. They receive no instruction regarding the history of the area where they will live and work, the people or the culture. It is likely they have also never attended an education system that did not reinforce their own cultural identity and value system.

The federal government spends a great deal of money to train Peace Corps volunteers to be successful in some village in Bolivia, Thailand, or other places around the world, but educators are hired and move to remote Alaska Native villages in our own country with virtually no preparation. It is a sink or swim situation. Their ability to adapt and succeed is left to happenchance.

Peace Corps volunteers'service is generally for two years. It is a given that they are not planning on settling in their host country. They are trained and acclimated to be most effective during that short time they are there. They are somewhat prepared to "hit the ground running". The goal is for them to be trained and prepared so that their stay is most effective. Some volunteers with unsuitable characteristics are weeded out during the training. At the least this allows for the possibility of diminishing the number of volunteers whom, like many educators who move to a village, land, take a look around and decide to take the next plane out.

Minimal efforts are done to screen applicants or truly equip educators to be effective and successful when moving to and then teaching in a remote, environmentally and culturally very different place that is the home of an Alaskan aboriginal people. Often those involved in teacher training, even within Alaska, have little or no experience in rural schools. And if they do, it doesn't necessarily mean it was a successful experience. There is a good chance they are not knowledgeable themselves as to how to provide appropriate schooling in village schools. The training they do offer is usually not specific to Alaska Native students, and if it is, it is still within the framework of the standard western school system model.

Upon beginning a career in Alaska there are four main categories of educators: there are those new to the profession and new to Alaska, experienced educators new to Alaska, there are some non-Natives who were born and raised in Alaska, and there is a small percentage of educators who are indigenous Alaskans. Alaska Natives compose 34% of the total student population while less than 5% of the educators are Native. The majority of educators fit in the first two categories, thus, 95% of the educators staffing the schools in the state are non-Native.

There is a variety of very different teaching situations found in Alaska. There are large urban and suburban schools with few Alaska Native students to very remote one and two teacher schools with all indigenous students. And there is about everything in between these two extremes.

As an administrator I interviewed hundreds of applicants over the years for education positions in Alaska. At some point in the interview the individual is given the opportunity to ask any questions he or she might have. The majority of inquiries from newcomers related to the weather, hunting, fishing, salary, what to bring, what the housing is like, and other such items. It is difficult for newcomers to fathom the size of Alaska and just how different areas of the state really are. What might be true in some village on the Bering Sea would likely be quite different in some place in the southwest, the southeast, or in some village on the North Slope. It is not easy to generalize.

Another common question relates to what do the Natives think about this or that. Their assumption being that there is one collective set of beliefs for all of the five major Alaskan Native groups (twenty-one indigenous cultures) in the state. Some Native groups are more vocal than others, some more "aggressive" while others are perceived as more Asian-like in their stoicism and patience. There are groups that have been more isolated than others: thus, outside influence has been more recent. They may or may not be more traditional than those whom have been exposed to westernization for a longer time period.

"Just as physical appearances of Native people differ, so do their philosophies about life. Despite acculturation, Native languages, spirituality, traditions, values, and ways of life survive..." Grant & Gillispie, 1993

The situation new educators enter into is so unlike anything they are familiar with that they understandably don't know what questions to ask. Unbeknownst to them, they are really not "ready" to teach.

Are You Prepared for Living Remotely?

One question I asked potential teachers in an interview, to try and determine if living in a remote village was something they were prepared to do was, "What life experiences have you had that enable you to believe that you would be able and comfortable living in a small, isolated place with limited amenities?"

One man in his late twenties looked puzzled when I asked him this. He asked me to clarify what I meant. So I said, "what have you done in life that makes you think you are OK with living in a far away place where there is not much of the usual type of things available for you to do. There are no restaurants, no theatres, and sometimes the weather is so poor that you can't even go outside".

He thought for a minute and then answered hesitantly, "Well, I was in the navy, and I was on a submarine. Sometimes we would go underwater and not surface for up to eighty-eight days at a time. You mean something like that?"

"Yeah, something like that."

A Possible Scenario

It is a formidable task new teachers must face when they move to a village school to live and work. The reality of the situation is often something they are not prepared for in the least. If Dave and Debbie are not provided accurate information and at least a glimpse of the reality of what they will be facing, and if the only preparation they do is read *Tisha* or some Jack London they are likely to be in for a very rude awakening. They may envision a little log cabin in a glen of trees as their home with a path winding down to a schoolhouse with smoke curling from its chimney filled with eager, excited Native children hanging onto their every word.

To be fair to Dave and Debbie, the students, and the people in the village as authentic a depiction as possible needs to be presented to new educators beforehand. When there is a shortage of educators, school districts trying to recruit for their position vacancies sometimes purposely do not paint an accurate picture. Appropriate preparation is critical and educators new to this situation need to be equipped with the skills and information that will help them succeed as new members of this unfamiliar community and as teachers of indigenous children in the classroom.

Teachers like Dave and Debbie might find themselves entering a school district that is in the midst of changing to a Quality Schools Initiative Model, a district in the mid-stages of doing so, or a district in which the QSI Model was recently abandoned. This is a model that is an entirely different concept that could further compound all the unfamiliarity and strangeness they are experiencing in this new culture and new environment. It is a model that in a decade, though some remnants may survive, will likely become another passing fancy in the dim memory.

Dave and Debbie might receive some paperwork in the mail over the summer regarding their upcoming employment. Some districts do have brochures and printed information concerning basic living needs and possible contacts to help them establish housing.

Some teachers might fly to their village first and then return to the school district headquarters for an initial in-service prior to school starting. The two or three days of training and acclimating are usually jam packed with activities. School district personnel are introduced; retirement, insurance and a variety of other forms are filled out; district procedures are provided and there are usually some training sessions available concerning whatever district curriculum and instruction efforts are currently underway. There is so much information provided during this short time that newcomers often have difficulty sorting things out, and it becomes a blur of activity.

There are new faces and others whom have been around for varied lengths of time. A person's longevity with the school district and length of time in Alaska are usually clarified quickly when people meet. There is often a feeling of one-upmanship when Susan meets Joe and she learns that she has been in the state three years longer than he has.

Some districts assist new teachers in finding housing or they provide places to rent. In some districts, you are on your own. The quality of housing varies tremendously but has generally improved over the years. It ranges from well-equipped, modern trailer homes or houses to very rustic, substandard living quarters. Often it is at the school where the teachers shower and do laundry.

At the in-service Dave and Debbie met the other two teachers they will be working with at the school. One is an elderly lady from Arkansas, the other a young, fresh-out-of-college woman from Oregon. Dave has been asked, and he agrees to take on the responsibilities of principal/teacher. He has nine students from ages twelve to eighteen, and he teaches language arts, social studies, and health. Debbie also has nine children, ages five to seven. This is her first year teaching.

The first year of teaching is stressful no matter the location. But Debbie finds herself living in a small Yup'ik village accessible only by small plane. There is a village store on the porch of someone's home that has a limited array of expensive canned goods and some odds and ends. It is a flat, windy land on a large slow moving river that is unlike any place she has ever been. Everything is new. She soon discovers she must be the school cook on Mondays and Fridays because there is no one available to work those days.

Dave has taught two years in Michigan but it was the usual graded classroom in a suburban school. He is just beginning to realize that he will be teaching these nine students with a wide range of ages and abilities these different subject areas. And he has no idea how to handle this situation. It has not ever been mentioned as an issue with which he would be contending. His principal/teacher duties grow quickly and he finds himself spending a huge amount of time dealing with the few classified staff, some disgruntled parents, filling out forms for the district office and in keeping the gym open and chaperoning each evening and on Saturdays and Sundays. And the ice, wind and snow and extreme temperatures have not even arrived yet.

He changed the tire on the van on the way to picking up students who live across the slough and need a ride to and from school each day. Last week he found himself repairing a fitting on some copper tubing that was leaking oil for the school furnace. Debbie and Dave are swamped.

The expectations and demands on teachers in the small schools are tremendous. For those new to the profession as well as being new to the environment and culture, it is overwhelming. There are housing issues; groceries need to be obtained; access to medical help is very limited; there are village politics that Dave and Debbie are clueless about; there are perplexing politics within the small number of Native personnel at the school as well as within the whole school district; the manner in which students and adults are related is confusing; nasty weather and darkness arrive; there is a school to run, classes to teach, a gym to keep open, holiday events and extracurricular activities to manage and what seems a steady stream of school district people, specialists, health corporation personnel and other visitors that need to be picked up from and returned to the airport after disrupting the daily schedule. They are baffled.

And they are both beginning to realize their students are having huge problems with reading and writing. Dave is finding his texts are just not appropriate and the explanations he gives his students get him nowhere. He can't get his students to discuss anything. Debbie is equally as frustrated with her kids.

Two of Dave's students have been tentatively diagnosed as having Fetal Alcohol Syndrome. Two of his youngest are very proficient readers and high achievers. His eighteen year old is a special education student. The seventeen-year old reads on about the level of an eight year old. He is not sure about the other three students. The only information he has is state test results he ran across when he cleaned out the school office. They do not appear to him to be very motivated, interested or curious about what he is trying to teach.

Debbie has discovered that many of her students have great difficulty in following directions, paying attention, listening and remaining in a chair. Fortunately the previous teacher had the where-with-all to administer, on her own accord, some individual, diagnostic assessments. These test results show that five of her kids do not possess the most basic concepts about print, there are obvious letter/sound identification needs, and all her students are dramatically low in oral language proficiency. She also has a couple FAE/FAS students it appears and, at least, one special education child. They are all very pleasant to work with and quite charming. Several of them seem exceptionally bright, alert and clever in ways she doesn't understand. Her frustrations reduced her to tears several evenings a week the first couple of months.

It seems there is simply no time, no opportunity to inform Dave and Debbie about appropriate instruction and cross-cultural issues affecting their classrooms. They vaguely recall a session at the district in-service at the beginning of the year that had something to do with Alaska Native education. But if it was of import or relevance, the content was lost amongst the deluge of information they received at that time. It is painfully evident that the stress and difficulties that they face, as will the next two teachers who take their place when Dave and Debbie move on, could be alleviated by making it a definite priority to provide them with at least some of the needed knowledge and appropriate skills prior to them entering this situation.

We've Got A Problem

An astronaut was recently a guest on a radio talk show. He explained how frustrated he and his fellow crewmembers were in the earlier days of space travel due to difficulties in responding to some of the communications from ground control. Ground control consisted of individuals who never had been in outer space. They provided the astronauts with instructions and directions and made comments that simply did not make any sense to the astronauts in the space capsule. There was a definite disconnect between the communication from the ground and the actual situation in which the astronauts found themselves.

This is analogous to much of the instruction rural Alaskan educators receive in teacher preparation and training programs. Whether it is instruction received while the educator is employed in a village school or if it is provided prior to moving to the situation, the educator discovers this same disconnect the space travelers experienced. Much of the information and instruction supplied by university professors, consultants, and teacher trainers simply does not jibe with the actual situation in which they find themselves.

Useful, appropriate, relevant training curricula are a rare commodity. To illustrate this disconnect a proposal was recently offered by a university instructor that was deemed important and appropriate enough to be included in the content of a brief university summer training session a group of teachers received before heading out to teach in an Alaskan village school for the first time.

This instructor wanted to include the philosophical foundation of Aristotle, Plato, St. Thomas, Descartes, Rousseau, Kant, Nietzsche, Locke, John Stuart Mill and Dewey. A ten-hour time allotment was suggested for these topics. It was recommended that the other two hours be filled with lecture or student reports on the different schools of educational philosophy such as Essentialism, Romanticism, Progressivism, Idealism, Realism, Pragmatism, Constructivism, Existentialism, Post Modern, Native American, and Eastern Philosophy. The instructor added that some legal stories involving in loco parentis might also fit well before the novice teachers began their year teaching in village schools.

Making this content enough of a priority to include in the very limited training time that was available is another questionable decision made by 'Ground Control University'. It is dubious, at best, how this would be of any value in helping Dave and Debbie successfully deal with the situation in which they find themselves.

Two Ears, Two Eyes, One Mouth

Prior to taking up residence in a village new educators need to be made aware that there are obscure political influences operating within the district, school, and community. To assist in their success as educators and as new residents, they best be cautioned to hold off making judgments and decisions too quickly. There are friendships, kinships, grudges, jealousies and other intangibles that affect opinions that are expressed, decisions that are made, and behaviors that occur. Reliable information regarding the politics of the village, the school, and the district cannot be obtained through the view of any one individual. That would be like the story of the blind men describing an elephant and relying on what the one holding the tail had to say.

Newcomers need to listen and watch and not come to conclusions prematurely. Over time they can begin understanding, at least to some degree, the covert and subtle forces operating in this small, but complex, society.

School personnel with quite different viewpoints and opinions will present to the newcomers their own explanation as to "the way things are and why." Long time teacher, Al, will tell you how it is, with hopes you will see it his way and join the faction he represents. Linda has been there a while, and she will tell you exactly why "these kids" are like they are and just how to deal with them and their parents. Mark explains that everything would be fine if there just was a better administration. Judy's stance is that State and Federal requirements prevent educators from doing their job. Carol's solution is more instructional resources. Principal J's answer is simply more money. But many tacitly agree that, for the most part, the kids just aren't up to it academically.

Ms. Texas

Ms. Texas was hired at the last minute to teach in a small village elementary school. She arrived Friday afternoon, stayed at the school over the weekend and resigned Monday morning and flew back to San Antonio. In an attempt to learn what caused her to make this decision, she was asked via e-mail. She responded the same way:

"I was sleeping on the floor in this portable classroom and my luggage was there with me. I heard there was a place available that I could rent, but the principal teacher visited me on Saturday. She told me that the kids were all dirty, everyone in the village were drunks and no one cared. Then Sunday evening some kids knocked on the door and wouldn't go away. I was scared and all alone."

It was the elementary principal teacher who provided to her this distorted view of the students and the people in the village. This woman and her husband were a teaching couple who had lived there about ten years. Ms. Texas figured they must have known what they were talking about, and she didn't want anything to do with a place like what was described to her.

A Litany of Reasons

Usually new teachers are excited about their adventure and are very anxious to do well. The opinions freely provided to them by long time teachers are often quite biased, not encouraging or are downright negative. They paint a picture that is the world according to Mark, Judy, Linda, or Al. New educators must listen and observe and not fall into the trap of blindly adopting what these people espouse.

There is a litany of reasons provided by these naysayers as to why students are not learning like they should be: it is because of the uncaring, out-of-touch administrators; it is because necessary and appropriate classroom resources are not available; it is because of the substance abuse in the village; it is because the parents are apathetic; it is because the kids are lazy and just don't care; it's due to State regulations and inadequate funding. The commonality being that blame is placed not on one's self or the education system.

If teachers are hired with no prior exposure or knowledge of Native learning styles, the history of the village and the people, appropriate methodologies and cultural variances, and they find that no matter what they do in the classroom, the students generally do not perform as expected, they are likely to become frustrated and discouraged. The negativity supplied to them with authority by the experienced naysayers begins to seemingly make sense, and they can easily develop a similar attitude.

They may take on the job as a very positive, enthusiastic and open-minded person but their style and methods of teaching that fit in suburbia and urban schools can fail drastically when applied to the rural Alaskan Native. Witnessing this repeated failure, they may soon become discouraged and point their finger at the child. Some conclude that there must be something wrong with theses students, not their teaching practices or the manner in which school is held.

"But cultural discontinuity is not the only dilemma facing Native students. The lack of respect for Native culture and the misinterpretation of Native student resistance to school culture has led to widespread, often institutionalized, racism and prejudice." Grant & Gillispie, 1993

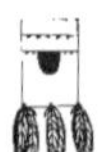

One "Solution"

It was a K-5 village school. Pretty much Alaska Native students. There were a few teachers' kids; a couple of students had parents who managed the store.

The teachers were frustrated, not happy. Seems it just wasn't working. They griped in the teachers' lounge day after day, month after month. They fussed and blamed and continued on. It reached a point, though, where a discussion occurred that seemed to make sense to them. They informally tossed the idea around, and it wasn't long before it began to gel. At a staff meeting the idea emerged and a direction was unanimously agreed upon. A unified front was established.

The answer was two fold: one relied on retaining students who couldn't read at grade two. "Keep them there until they can read!" (There was no mention, though, of investigating and altering the manner in which reading was taught). The second solution required the grade three through grade five kids to be divided into three groups: the high group, the middle group and the low group.

But! To quote the lead teacher explaining this proposal in all her wisdom, "the teachers will be rotated so no one will be stuck with the dumb group".

The Quandary

Needless to say, there are other more positive and legitimate solutions to the quandary teachers find themselves in village schools than the one decided upon in the true example above. The attitude leading to this strategy is frightening enough, but without being provided guidance, information, and training in effective schooling practices for this situation, this is an example of how frustrated teachers on their own might proceed. It may be convenient for these teachers, but it is certainly not in the best interests of the children. And there really is nothing in place to prevent something like this from occurring.

Task and Student Proficiency

Mr. Science, an ex-state biologist, now teacher (graduate of an Alaskan university, school of education), was having trouble teaching his students because they didn't understand his explanations or the reading material he assigned. He said, "If they are in my 10th grade biology class they should be able to do the 10th grade work and use the assigned biology text and deal with the work I provide."

"But they can't read and comprehend this level of material that is being presented," was the reply that was supplied.

"Then they shouldn't be in my class," he answered with certainty.

"But they are in your class and don't you think it is your responsibility to do what you can to teach the students who are in your class no matter who they are and what their ability is? This might require learning a variety of techniques that would assist your students in comprehending the science content but does not rely on them to independently glean information from your lectures and texts that is beyond their ability to access," was (in so many words) the gist of the response.

"I am not about to dumb down what I do. I have high expectations and a 10th grade science student in my class does 10th grade work," he replied with an end-of-discussion tone of voice.

This is not an uncommonly held attitude.
Ms. Florida was having the same problem in her fifth grade class of Native students. She had taught for years near Tallahassee and was very confident in her skill as a teacher. She was new to the village and was frustrated by her students' inability to read and understand her explanations. She had, though, completed her required three credits in multicultural education.

"I want to have my students read the same novel and work with them on it as a class. I used to do it all the time, but I can't do it with these kids."

She was somewhat receptive, but very skeptical about a plan. Each student was tested with two different, reliable, one-on-one diagnostic reading instruments and an estimated level was established for each child. The students were ten to twelve years old. The reading levels ranged from 7.5 years to 12 years of age. A high interest novel determined to be written on about the second and third grade level (seven to eight years of age) was selected and a classroom set was provided. There were a few students that might need some specific individual attention. Ms. Florida had a week and a half of activities and lessons planned related to this book. One of the culminating exercises was a teacher-made test of about five comprehension problems requiring written responses.

"See? It didn't work she seemed almost proud to report at the end of the unit. The students did horribly on the final short essay test. They showed almost no comprehension."

The questions on her self-made test were entered into three different reading level evaluation programs. Results? The students' questions were written on or above grade level 9 (age fourteen). The students likely had access to the novel, but the test questions were definitely beyond their frustration level. The concept of ensuring the level of the reading material is matched with the students' reading proficiency was the issue once again.

Father Herman: Line drawing or icon of St. Herman
(Image courtesy of Alaska State Library)

St. Herman entered monastic life as a teenager in Russia, was recruited to join the Alaskan Mission in 1793, walked across Siberia and sailed to Kodiak in September 1794. Finding the Shelikov trading company exploiting and oppressing the Alutiiq people there, he began a forty year writing campaign to civil and church authorities in Russia seeking to alleviate this suffering, winning the love of the Alaska Natives and the violent opposition of Alexander Baranov, who had him and the other monks placed under house arrest. Retiring to nearby Spruce Island, Father Herman welcomed the refugees, orphans and destitute to his settlement, where he built a school and continued his resistance to the Company policies. The Aleuts considered him a saint, and visited his grave regularly after his death in 1837, where hundreds of miracles convinced Church authorities of his sanctity. He was the first saint canonized in the New World, at ceremonies in Kodiak where his beautifully carved reliquary adorns Holy Resurrection Cathedral. Despite his significance to thousands of Native Alaskans, he is almost never mentioned in any histories of Alaska. For more information on the significance of St. Herman, see Father Michael Oleksa's ***Orthodox Alaska.***

Three Saints Bay, Kodiak Island: Sketch by Luka Voronin, 1791
(Image courtesy of Alaska State Library)

The site of the first Siberian settlement in Alaska, Three Saints Bay was Alaska's Plymouth Rock, where, after the battle and massacre at Refuge Rock in 1784, Gregory Shelikov required the defeated Alutiiqs to establish a village on the shore opposite his. In 1791, the Billings Expedition, sailing around the world, wintered there, and the chaplain aboard that ship registered dozens of weddings and births. The intermarriage that had characterized contact in the Aleutian Islands over the previous 50 years continued on Kodiak, producing a mixed population of Russian-speaking Alaska Natives, who became the mainstay of the Russian colony for the next 50 years and served as a Native "intelligentsia" after the transfer of Alaska to US rule in 1867. Census data seems to indicate that the Aleut population continued to decline in these years, without noting the corresponding increase of hundreds, eventually thousands of "Creoles," of mixed ancestry, nor the transfer of Aleuts, (often forcibly under Baranov 1791-1818), to settlements outside their homeland, as far west as Hokaido, as far east and south as Baja California. In 1867, Sitka, the Capital was 60% Creole or Native, Kodiak and Unalaska were 90%. For more information on the contributions of Creoles, see Barbara S. Smith's ***Russian Orthodoxy in Alaska***, and ***Russian America: the Forgotten Frontier***, and Oleksa's essay in ***The Legacy of St. Vladimir***.

Arriving at Unalaska in 1824, Father Ioan (John) devised an alphabet and published the first books in Unangan Aleut, founding a bilingual school, where students became literate in their own language as well as Russian. Transferred to Sitka, he learned Tlingit and founded the "All-Colonial School" there, and repeated this pattern once more, after 1858, among the Sakha people in Yakutia as well. Some of his students were recruited by the Russian Naval Academy and became seamen and officers, sailing around the world, while others entered the clergy, becoming priests, musicians, translators, writers and school teachers. Elected Metropolitan (Archbishop) of Moscow in 1868, Veniaminov founded a Mission Society which continued to fund bilingual schools in Alaska until the Bolshevik Revolution in 1917, ended nearly a century of Russian support. He was canonized in Russia as "St. Innocent, Apostle to the Aleuts," in 1979 at the request of the Orthodox Diocese of Alaska, an overwhelmingly Alaska Native faith community with nearly 100 parishes across the southern half of the state. For more information on Veniaminov see Paul Garrett's ***St. Innocent, Apostle to America***.

Father Ioan Veniaminov/Metropolitan Innocent: Portrait
(Photo courtesy of Alaska State Library)

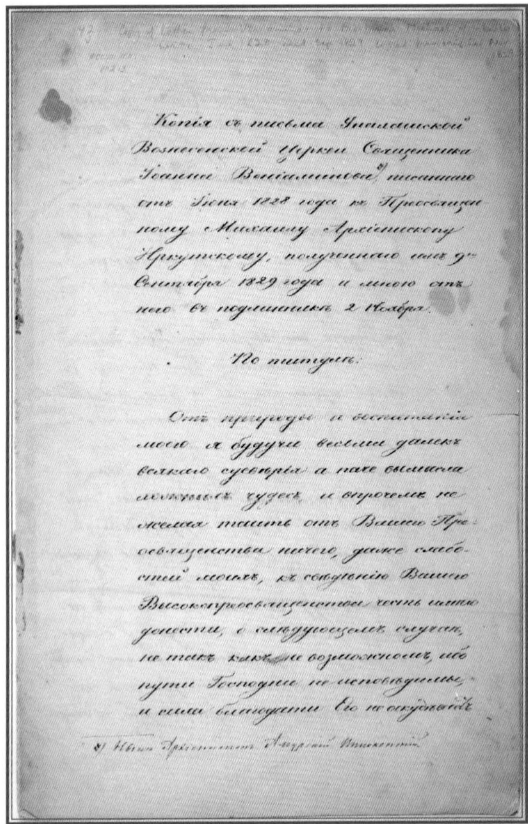

Veniminov's Letter: Photograph of first page
(Photo courtesy of Alaska State Library)

In 1828, Father Ioan Veniaminov encountered a shaman who had accurately predicted his arrival, healed injured and dying villagers, and reported meeting daily with his helping spirits, who provided him with his knowledge and powers. Father Ioan became convinced the man was not a charlatan but an authentic healer, whose spirits were indeed angels, and asked to meet them. When the shaman, Ivan Smerennikov, replied that they had agreed to appear to the priest, Father Ioan became apprehensive, wondering whether it was appropriate for him to meet with "angels," and filed this report with his bishop in Irkutsk, near Lake Baikal. The incident reveals the Siberian priest's openness to the possibility that Alaska Natives were already in touch with genuine holiness prior to the arrival of the Christian missionaries, and his willingness to build on, rather than eradicate this heritage. For more information on Russian Orthodoxy and Shamanism see Soterios Mousalimas' ***The Transition from Shamanism.***

Pictured here is St. Innocent already elderly with his son and grandson. Orthodox parish clergy are generally married men who seek ordination after being wed. The Russian Orthodox church became a major cultural, spiritual and educational institution in Alaska primarily because it welcomed Native men into the clergy during the first decades of Russian contact. The first Aleut priest, Father Iakov (Jacob) Netsvetov, married a Russian wife during his seminary training in Irkutsk, served for twenty years as parish priest, missionary and bilingual teacher at Atka in the Aleutians, and another eighteen years at Ikogmiut, today's "Russian Mission" on the Yukon, where he mastered Yup'ik Eskimo and devised an alphabet for it. Netsvetov not only translated texts into Aleut and Yup'ik but introduced icon painting in both these regions, and was active in inoculating his flock against the outbreak of smallpox. He retired to Sitka where he died and was buried in 1862, and was canonized as the first Native Alaskan saint as "Enlightener of the Native Alaskan Peoples" at ceremonies in Anchorage, in 1991. For more information on Netsvetov see his ***Journals,*** translated by Dr. Lydia T. Black.

Veniaminov Generations: Photograph (Photo courtesy of Alaska State Library)

Tlingit Brotherhoods at Sitka: Photograph, clergy in vestments, banners, flags, 1917 (Photo courtesy of Alaska State Library)

Recognizing that the Tlingit Nation was divided into to moieties (confederations of matrilinear clans) the Orthodox parish founded two complimentary Brotherhoods, the St. Michael and the St. Gabriel, to promote sobriety and conduct charitable activities in their communities. Following traditional Tlingit protocol, each Brotherhood had its own insignia, hymns, and regalia, providing the context out of which the later Alaska Native Brotherhood arose, devoting itself to obtaining full citizenship and civil rights for Native Alaskans. Pictured here, about 1914, in Byzantine-style mitres in the front row are the future bishop of Alaska, Father Amfilokhy, who served for many years in the Yukon Delta and became conversant in Yup'ik Eskimo (using Father Netsvetov's published translations) Biship Philip (Stavitskii) later imprisoned by the Communists upon his return to Russia, and Father Andrew Kashevarov, founder of the Alaska Territorial Museum and Historical Library. For more information on Tlingits and Russian Orthodoxy, see Sergei Kan's ***Memory Eternal.***

The large, bright yellow two-story residence on Sitka's Lincoln Street, completed in 1844, served as residence for Orthodox bishops and also the dormitory and classrooms for the "All Colonial School," a six-year program of advanced education, roughly equivalent to today's high school and junior college level. Since Sitka, as the capital, was a predominantly Alaska Native city, the student body there came from Alutiiq, Unangan and Tlingit backgrounds, and were required to study their own languages as well as Russian and English. The school produced multilingual, multi-literate graduates who served as accountants, merchants, artists, musicians, missionaries, teachers and seamen. One illustrious graduate, Major General Alexander Kashevarov, sailed around the world several times, and upon retirement, settled in St. Petersburg, a citizen of the Russian Empire. The Russian American Company depended almost totally on Native Alaskan leadership, since there were never more than 800 ethnic Russians in the Alaskan colony, and the fur trading operations depended on the Alaskans, whom the Russians called "the Americans" to retain their traditional subsistence hunting skills, while becoming familiar with European technology. For more information on Natives in the service of the Russian-American Company, see Lydia Black's ***Russians in Alaska***.

Adults Gathering outside the "Russian Bishop's House" Men in Brother sashes, women in modern clothing, 1910 (Photo courtesy of Alaska State Library)

Students at the "Russian" School or "Orphanage": Photograph with teachers, 1889 (Photo courtesy of Alaska State Library)

After the worldwide influenza epidemic in 1919, many schools became in fact orphanages, assuming responsibility for raising children whose families had perished, often in a matter of days. The disruption this caused traditional cultures can hardly be calculated. The US government attempted to address the need, and many American denominations established orphanages in the larger settlements, sometimes combining these with previously established boarding schools. The removal of Native American children from their home communities and families became federal policy soon after the Civil War and continued in Alaska for a century, further disrupting traditional life. The outbreak of tuberculosis in the 1940's and 50's meant that yet another generation would be deprived of the wisdom of its elders. "Normal family life" has not been known in most rural Alaskan communities for more than a hundred years. For more information on the impact of the 1919 "Great Death" in rural Alaska, see Harold Napolean's ***Yuuyaraq: The Way of the Human Being.***

The site of Veniaminov's Unanagan parish and school, Unalaska became the economic and cultural "capital" of the Aleutian Islands. The residents were often multilingual, taking pride in their cultural heritages as Native Alaskan, Siberian/Russian and American. Aleuts kept diaries, wrote letters and even attempted to publish a monthly magazine, *Orthodox Alaska*, in three hand-written, mimeographed languages. Aleuts brought petitions and filed suit in federal court at Unalaska, Kodiak and Sitka, demanding that their citizenship rights, under the 1867 Treaty, be honored, but usually without success. They also engaged in correspondence and debate with local American missionary teachers, challenging them to respect the rights of Native Alaskans to operate their own schools and churches, as the Aleuts had been doing for generations. For further information on this struggle, and also the petitions these articulate Native leaders addressed to the McKinley White House, seeking redress, see ***Alaskan Missionary Spirituality***, edited by Fr. Michael Oleksa.

Unalaska: Photograph of town from hill (Photo courtesy of University of Alaska, Fairbanks)

Holy Ascension Orthodox Cathedral (Photo courtesy of Anchorage Museum at Rasmuson Center)

Built by Aleuts on the site of Veniaminov's original chapel, this church dominates downtown Unalaska. Aleut carvers devoted their ancient talents to the carving of many of the furnishings inside, and painted many of the icons as well. When they were forcibly evacuated after the Japanese bombardment of the town in 1942, Anfesia Shapsnikof supervised the burial of the cathedral's treasures, probably saving them from the looting that occurred in many other evacuated Aleutian towns. The wartime internment of the Unangan Aleut people, and the permanent relocation of the residents of several smaller villages after the war, represented a further disruption, even persecution of their traditional culture. This church, however, was restored, in part, with reparations the US Government paid to the Aleut People nearly fifty years after their removal to deplorable internment camps during the Second World War. Nevertheless, as late as 1968, the US Fish and Wildlife Service, despite the unanimous opposition of the Aleut residents, invited American Protestant missionaries to establish a rival church on St. Paul Island, for "the religious diversification of the Aleuts." For more information, see Dorothy Knee Jones' ***A Century of Servitude***.

When Dr. Sheldon Jackson became Commissioner of Education for the Alaska Territory, he reportedly met with the leaders of various Protestant Christian denominations in Philadelphia to divide the region into spheres of influence. His own Presbyterian church accepted responsibility for the Southeast Panhandle area and the Arctic coastline. The Baptists were given Kodiak Island and the adjoining Alaska Peninsula. The Lutherans were assigned the Seward Peninsula, around Nome. The Friends (Quakers) got Kotzebue and its hinterland. The Episcopal church assumed responsibility for the interior, where they were already active, having entered Alaska from Canada. The Moravian Brethern accepted Bristol Bay but soon moved into the Kuskokwim Delta. The Swedish Covenant church took Nunivak Island, and the Methodists the Aleutian Chain. Their twin goals were to make the traditional tribal peoples of Alaska English-speaking, literate and Christian. Conflicts soon arose when the missionary/teachers encountered multi-lingual multi-literate Alaska Natives. The federally supported missions had not expected to find Natives running their own schools and churches—but they quickly decided these were the wrong kind of schools, teaching in the wrong languages and the wrong kind of church. For more on the conflict between mission philosophies see Richard Dauenhauer's ***Conflicting Visions in Alaskan Education.***

Children at the Jesse Lee Home: Photo of group (Photo courtesy of Anchorage Museum at Rasmuson Center)

The Bear: Photo of the vessel without sails, smoke stack active
(Photo courtesy of University of Alaska, Fairbanks)

For decades after the transfer of Alaska to US rule, the federal government paid little attention to the newly acquired territory. The US Revenue Cutter "the Bear" remained the only sign of American interest in the region, the only safety or law enforcement presence in Alaska. The Bear brought supplies and personnel, including the first missionary teachers from the "lower 48," arrested criminals, smugglers and bootleggers, and imported reindeer from Chukotka, a project engineered by Dr. Sheldon Jackson who frequently traveled with Captain Mike Healy, the son of an Irish immigrant and his slave mistress from rural Georgia, who successfully kept his racial identity secret throughout his extraordinary Alaskan career. For more information about Captain Healy, see the PBS video production: *Captain Mike Healy*.

Villages along Alaska's major rivers, the Nushagak, Kuskokwim, Yukon, Tanana, Koyukuk and Kobuk continue to receive most of their annual supply shipments from the outside world by river barge, vessels that sail from Seattle, Portland or San Francisco to deliver lumber, oil, groceries and building supplies. Since only the Southeast quadrant of the state is connected by railroads or highways, most of the state is still supplied by water or by air. The arrival of the summer barge has been a major event in village life for over a century now, dating back to the coming of the first unexpected shipment of lumber for the village school and teachers' residence. Thoughtful teachers even today do well to order as much of their annual supply of groceries and household goods by barge each year, rather than depend on the much more costly inventory at the village store.

The Barge: Photo from Allakaket *(Photo courtesy of Anchorage Museum at Rasmuson Center)*

The School: Photo of exterior of building, Friends School, Point Blossom, with bell tower
(Photo courtesy of University of Alaska, Fairbanks)

Federal school buildings and their adjoining teacher housing were often the first expression of government presence and authority in a rural Alaskan community. They were and are often the largest structures in the village, as well as the largest single employer in the town. In some communities, where teachers have devoted time and effort to developing respectful, harmonious relationships with the elders, parents and students, the school has become the focus of community social life as well, hosting carnivals, tournaments, memorial feasts, and traditional dancing, as well as offering culturally relevant instruction. In others, the school is viewed as an alien institution whose mission is directed toward the destruction of the local culture and community. Teachers need to ask themselves when they consider themselves successful, when their students remain in the village or leave it. Their response will determine whether their efforts will be appreciated or rejected. For further information see KYUK-TV video production *Uksum Cauyai, the Drums of Winter.*

In the early days of schooling, students were usually provided seating on long, wooden benches and arranged by size, with the youngest and smallest in the front rows, and the older, taller students in the back. No doubt everything about the school environment seemed alien, strange, and probably irrelevant to the real life of the community the central subsistence hunting, fishing, gathering and sharing concerns of the village. The first generation of children seldom advanced beyond the third or fourth grade, since their parents saw little value in sending them to sit on the benches all day, when they frankly had better, more important things to do. Since the students seldom or never understood any English, instructional time was mostly wasted effort, frustrating for the teachers and often humiliating to the children.

The Classroom: Photo from Point Hope, students on benches, teacher with flag
(Photo courtesy of University of Alaska, Fairbanks)

The Bath: Photo of seven boys in wash tubs at Allakaket

Boarding school administrators often erroneously believed that Native Alaskan children were dirty and orchestrated campaigns to clean up the kids. In the Wrangell Institute dormitory, the sign at the entrance to the showers read "Cleanliness Is Godliness." Since most villages did not have indoor plumbing or running water in any form until late in the 20th century, and the teachers usually had the only well in town, children would visit the teachers' house to examine the sinks and toilets more closely, asking to use the facilities when the opportunity arose, whether

(Photo courtesy of University of Alaska, Fairbanks)

or not they actually needed to. They would stand in the bathroom and flush the toilet just to admire the swirl of the rushing water. The same was true for the carpet. Visitors would remove their shoes, as they had been told was appropriate, and stand silently along the wall, letting the fibers of the rug tickle their toes. Teachers often wondered why they were visiting or what was so funny, mistakenly believing that they were the focus of the visit. For more information see Kwethluk teacher and author Pauline Evon Morris' *cultural autobiography* (manuscript).

The Kayak: Photo of three-person Kayak at Afognak (Photo courtesy of Alaska State Library)

Teachers, like tourists everywhere, enjoyed sending pictures home to show what a beautiful or exotic place they had found. While Native Alaskans paddled kayaks or drove dog teams from one village to the next as their only means of transport well into the 1950's, the ancient has given way to the modern by now in every community. Local languages also tended to survive well into the twentieth century, with a decline noted after teachers began physically abusing students caught speaking their home language. Today, sled dog races are a major tourist attraction and raising sled dogs is a popular hobby, but nowhere does anyone rely on these traditional modes. The rising cost of gasoline, however, could reverse this trend, as the rise in the price of stove oil has promoted a return to wood stoves. The revival of declining languages will require much more time, effort, commitment and encouragement. For more information see Michael Krauss: ***Alaska Native Languages, Past, Present and Future.***

During the decades of federal schooling run by the Bureau of Indian Affairs, attempts were often made to make the curriculum more relevant to local students who had no ambition or desire to leave their hometowns. While the curriculum today is geared primarily for those who might want to attend college elsewhere, to prepare for a professional position elsewhere, most students and their parents seek ways to support themselves and live more traditionally, and embrace schooling that will prepare them to survive and succeed in their community. For more information on curriculum reform see *Appendices*.

Building a Kayak in School: Photo from Hooper Bay (Photo courtesy of Alaska State Library)

Photo: A Classroom with lesson on the Blackboard *(Photo courtesy of University of Alaska, Fairbanks)*

This photo, taken in the 1950's, documents how alien the imported curriculum could be. The teacher has written a reading lesson on the blackboard, informing the Inuit students that animals have houses. This would have been a rather perplexing revelation to Arctic Alaskans, a reality far removed from their experience. That this house is called a "barn" and that they like their house, would seem unlikely, preposterous, incredible, to these children or anyone else in their village. The instructor seems not to have noticed the obvious incongruity, as if she were not teaching in Alaska at all. Unfortunately, such incongruities continue to this day, as teachers prepare their students to score well on standardized tests designed for middle-class Anglo-Americans who live in another world. For more information on culture and communication specific to Alaska Native children, see Oleksa's ***Another Culture/Another World***, and Ron and Suzie Scallon's ***Interethnic Communication.***

Alien as the building and the curriculum must have appeared to students, nothing compares to the absurdity of 19th century western-style clothing in the Arctic. This photo could be the "icon" the very image of what "school" meant to the first generation of students who were herded into an alien structure, taught in an alien language and confronted by people so strange they might as well have been from another planet. For more on the history of the US assimilationist philosophy see ***Hall Young of Alaska, an Autobiography.***

Derbies and Bustles: Photo from Wales (Photo courtesy of Alaska State Library)

Eklutna Vocational School: Photo with student body at RR Station (Photo courtesy of Anchorage Museum at Rasmuson Center)

Many federal boarding schools were considered "vocational" since their focus was to produce skilled and semi-skilled workers for offices and factories. The Eklutna school offered courses in mechanics and assembly-line skills, none of which served any purpose in villages. The assumption was that graduates would leave the state to find employment "outside," which seldom happened. Even when alumni might have been interested in making such a transition, the urban survival information and skills needed to succeed were never provided. While some heroic and talented individuals did assimilate into the dominant society, many more where emotionally and psychologically harmed by their experience in boarding schools, directly contributing to high rates of drug and alcohol abuse, domestic violence, child neglect and sexual abuse and suicide. For information on social problems in rural Alaska see First Alaskans Institute *Report*.

The Alaska Native Brotherhood was founded to lobby for US Citizenship for Alaska Natives. Founding members promised to renounce their former tribal customs, traditions and language and accept the norms of "civilization," in order to "uplift" their people and encourage them to achieve full citizenship by assimilating into the American "melting pot." For the Tlingit, who had been overwhelmed by thousands of prospectors during the 1895 Gold Rush, the most promising avenue for gaining respect and regaining control of their lives seemed to lie in this strategy. Within a generation, William L. Paul, a Tlingit, had graduated from law school and been elected to the Territorial Legislature. For more on Tlingit cultural and political leaders see Richard and Nora Dauenhauer's ***Haa Kusteeyi.***

The ANB: Photo of Convention in Sitka, 1914 *(Photo courtesy of Alaska State Library)*

William L. Paul: Photo, portrait (Photo courtesy of Alaska State Library)

Lawyer, Territorial Legislator, Native activist and civic leader, William Paul represented all that was best in the assimilationist philosophy, an Alaskan Native who by his success in the "White Man's World," proved to all Natives that they too could achieve great things if they renounced their traditional ways and adopted those of "civilization." Entire villages attempted to follow this pattern, only to discover that their social problems became more pronounced and violent. One village even voted at one point to destroy their traditional art and forbid the speaking of their ancestral language in an attempt to conform to these alien standards. Within fifty years, that town had the highest teen suicide rate in the United States. It seems that while some can disconnect from their cultural heritage, and many immigrant families have done so within a generation or two, the attempt to renounce one's own background in one's own homeland has been socially, emotionally, and spiritually disastrous for many more. See: State of Alaska, Department of Health and Social Services, *Alaska Suicide Prevention Plan*.

A graduate of the Orthodox schools on Kodiak and at Sitka, Father Andrew represented all that was best in the multi-cultural philosophy introduced in the Russian period. Fluent in Aleut, Russian, English and later Tlingit, Father Kashevarov founded the Territorial (today the State) Historical Museum and the Territorial (today the State) Historical Archives. An historian and author, he researched the first biography of Ioan Veniaminov, and published it in *Alaska* magazine. He served together with William Paul in the Territorial Legislature and won wide acclaim for his civic and pastoral work. Well into the 20th century, the leadership of most Aleut villages was composed of multi-lingual elders who could read, write and speak several languages. Sergei Sheratin at Afognak, for example, could converse and write in Aleut, Russian and English with equal competence, and when asked where he learned all this, he replied, that his uncle, Tikhon Sheratin, had attended the "Russian" School in San Francisco and brought this knowledge back to his village where he instructed another generation of multi-lingual, multi-literate Alaska Natives. Only when the last of these teachers were passing from the scene did Kodiak Aleuts begin searching for someone from "outside" to continue "Aleut School." For more information on "Aleut Schools" see Oleksa, ***Orthodox Alaska***. For reprints of Alaska Native language texts see www.asna.ca *Alaska Native Texts*.

Rev. Andrew Kashevarov: Photo, portrait
(Photo courtesy of Alaska State Library)

The Alaska Territorial House of Representatives, 1925 (Photo courtesy of Alaska State Library)

Although Alaska Natives were the majority of the population in the Territory, they were not recognized as citizens, and thus disenfranchised, until 1924. Unaware of their voting rights, most did not participate in the political process in the early years of home rule. However two Native men were elected to the Territorial legislature in 1925, William Paul and Rev. Andrew Kashevaroff. Funding for education remains a deeply political issue in Alaska, allocations usually made for one year at a time. This tends to politicize decisions of the state university and the public schools, since current enrollment and "success" will determine the next year's appropriations. A program or department that suffers a drop in participation will predictably receive less money the following year, forcing faculty to focus on "retention" and "recruitment," often to the detriment of standards and long range planning. Not knowing what the legislature will or will not continue to fund also pits one program against another, regardless of their long term potential contribution to the students. The Legislature and Governor determine the direction of education and no significant reforms can be initiated without their vision, commitment and support. Educational reform in Alaska will require political will and political action.

February 18 is a neglected state holiday in most of Alaska, but in the Southeast Panhandle, everyone knows it is Elizabeth Peratrovich Day. As president of the Alaska Native Sisterhood, she, (together with her husband Roy, of Serbian and Tlingit descent, as president of the ANB), continued the struggle toward full civil liberties and rights for all Natives. Well educated, totally "civilized" in the Anglo-American sense, the Peratrovich's were scandalized that despite their complete assimilation into the "melting pot" they could not buy a home, enter a theater or eat at certain restaurants when they returned to Juneau. Some establishments displayed signs reading "No Natives" or even "NO Natives, NO Dogs." The ANB and ANS joined forces to pressure the government to outlaw such flagrant discrimination. The bill passed the Territorial Legislature and was signed into law Gruening on February 18, 1945. Mrs. Peratrovich's experience, therefore, constitutes a victory for the assimilationist approach but also reveals the limits that racism places on it. An Alaska Native leader and legislature once remarked without bitterness, "I have given up expecting to be treated as an equal by The White Man." The Peratrovich legacy, like that of Dr. Martin Luther King, reminds us that there is still work to be done to combat racism, bigotry and discrimination. It should be noted, however, that the ANB/ANS won their victory over blatant public discrimination nearly thirty years before Civil Rights Laws banning such policies were enacted at the federal level. For more information on Elizabeth Peratrovich, see Oleksa's *Alaska Native Women Leaders, Pre-Statehood***.**

Elizabeth Peratrovich: Photo of Gov. Ernest Gruening signing of the1945 Anti-Discrimination Act *(Photo courtesy of Alaska State Library)*

Boarding School Students leaving Shungnak *(Photo courtesy of University of Alaska, Fairbanks)*

For over a century, federal social and educational policy favored removing Native American children from their homes to facilities thousands of miles from their families and communities. The first of these was established in the dungeon within the fortress at St. Augustine Florida, but the most famous became the Carlisle Indian School, near Harrisburg, PA. School reports depict Navajo and Apache boys being outfitted in coats and ties, having their hair cut in contemporary styles and being labeled "Uncivilized" and "Civilized" in the before/after photographs. These policies were imported to Alaska with the first schools, operated by teachers who often also received support from their denominational mission societies. Church and State worked cooperatively to suppress Alaska Native and Native American languages and cultures. Many of Alaska's foremost leaders survived and succeeded in the Boarding School experience, but for every prominent and productive graduate, there are many more depressed, disillusioned, damaged and demoralized survivors, who often constitute an anti-school, anti-teacher constituency in some villages. Newly arrived teachers need to hear with sensitivity some of the "horror stories" this generation can tell about their years at school, in order to relate respectfully and appropriately to these sometimes hurt, sometimes angry parents and elders. For more information see *Must One Way of Life Die for Another to Live?*

Old School, Elim, Alaska (Photo courtesy of Alaska Division of Community and Regional Affairs Community Database, photo © Bill Stokes)

After a century of forced enculturation and assimilation promoted by federally funded schools, Alaska Natives won the right to secondary education through legal action, culminating in the "Molly Hootch Case," in which the Alaska Supreme Court ruled that rural students had a right to be educated in their home villages. Thanks to abundant income from the Prudhoe Bay oil fields, the State constructed and maintained hundreds of new village high schools similar to the one shown. Some continue to argue that village high school programs cannot fully or adequately meet the academic needs of college-bound students, while others maintain that the curricula of rural high schools cannot address the unique interests or needs of the local community. Nevertheless, more Alaska Native students are completing high school today than ever before, and more are continuing their schooling at the post secondary level as well. The typical curriculum prepares students for additional training outside the village, but seldom meets the needs of the majority of the student body who have no desire or ambition to leave home. Despite the end of boarding schools that removed teenagers from their homes and communities geographically for several years, the high school curriculum in most schools remains psychologically assimilationist.

Many of Alaska's rural high schools are extraordinarily well equipped with internet technology that most teachers "outside" would envy. Native communities have made an astonishingly rapid transition from traditional tribal societies to the modern age in the lifetime of today's elders. A child born in 1915, for example, would have been raised in a totally pre-contact world, completely dependent on hunting and gathering, using stone and slate tools, wearing animal skin clothing, eating only the food his ecosystem provided. The first "technology" he might have encountered would have been the written word, books, as first conceived 5000 years ago in the ancient Middle East. Within a decade, this child would have been introduced to guns, rifles, electricity and indoor plumbing at the village school. In his teens he would have seen the first motorized transport, boats and air planes, and in his early adult life, household appliances. During the Second World War, he may have joined the Territorial Guard and learned more about modern weapons and automobiles. By the time his grandchildren were born, he probably would have electric lights and a CB radio in his HUD house, and within a decade television and microwave ovens. In the lifetime of today's elders, rural Alaska has moved from the Stone Age to the Space Age.

Computer Lab, Nondalton (Photo courtesy of Alaska Division of Community and Regional Affairs Community Database, photo © Lake & Peninsula School District)

Aerial view of Aniak (Photo courtesy of Alaska Division of Community and Regional Affairs Community Database, photographer unknown)

Even Alaska's city dwellers have little practical experience of the Bush. Without roads in the northern or western half of a state twice the size of Texas, rural Alaska is accessible by barge only in the few brief summer months, and by small airplanes during the nine or ten months of winter. The two to three week transitional periods between summer and winter, "freeze up" and "break up," are not particularly beautiful or convenient seasons, since travel is greatly hampered by excess water and mud. Wind, low temperatures or snow prevent mail and supplies from landing several times each month. And with groceries and fuel flown into these communities, prices can be double those in the larger cities. The rise in heating costs has prompted a return to wood stoves in many regions, though snow machines and four-wheelers remain the primary means of family transport within and between neighboring communities.

"Teachers, who have themselves been educated to believe that Native Americans lacked a culture of their own and needed to be civilized by the Europeans, are not in a good position-without additional learning-to teach their Native students respectfully or with an appreciation for Native heritages. Teachers with Eurocentric attitudes trying to teach Native students could be compared to the agriculturally untrained trying to raise a crop. At best, such teachers offer condescending sympathy-a response to Native students that can be as stultifying to growth as overt disrespect. Grant & Gillispie, 1993

A Good Teacher: Period?

There exists the naïve belief that a good teacher is a good teacher: period. This is the view reflected in the efforts of the State Mentoring program as well as in the training that is required by the State for educators to work with Native students or to evaluate teachers of Native students. It is certainly in disagreement with Kleinfeld's description in her study, *Effective Teachers of Indian and Eskimo High School Students,* as it is based on my personal experiences teaching and observing educators for three decades.

There is a variety of reasons why a student decides to put forth effort and learn in school. Some children are motivated by grades, others for the desire to gain admission to a college. Some are influenced by parental pressure or by an internal, self-drive. Others are motivated by reward and recognition. Native students tend to be motivated if the material has some relevance, if the language of instruction is matched to their proficiency, and if they have a positive, personal connection with the teacher.

Kleinfeld places educators into four main categories. She creates a profile of these teacher-types by describing their characteristics and attributes and their likelihood of success with Native students. Very briefly, the four teacher-types she provides are:

I. The traditional teacher who exhibits a professional distance whose demandingness and concerns are oriented toward his/her narrow subject matter.

II. The sophisticate who portrays a polite reserve that the students interpret as a distance or coldness. This teacher-type has a low degree of demandingness from his/her students due to excessive concern for cultural differences.

III. The sentimentalist teacher conveys a high degree of personal warmth and personal concern, but this teacher-type has a low degree of academic demandingness due to his/her overwhelming sympathy for Native students ('as stultifying to growth as overt disrespect').
IV. Supportive teachers are described as combining a high degree of personal warmth and concern with a high, active academic demandingness. The atmosphere created by this teacher-type facilitates a higher degree of verbal interaction. The Native students interpret the teacher's high expectations, demands and requests as personal concern for them.

Profile I describes teacher characteristics that are common and usually successful with western students in urban, suburban schools. But they may not be most suitable when working with Native students. The professional distance may translate to the Native student as coldness and indifference. The styles explained in II and III involving low expectations are rarely successful anywhere and success is left up to a student's self-motivation. An educator with a personality that fits Profile IV might not be effective when working with aggressive western students. Some teachers who possibly experienced success when working with Native students in village schools, discovered this same style resulted in difficulties in non-Native classrooms on the road system,

Based on my experiences, Kleinfeld's description of the various teacher types and their likely degree of effectiveness with Native students is accurate in rural as well as urban settings and provides rare and valuable information on a topic that is seldom addressed. Educators need to be enlightened as to her study's merits despite it being a thirty-five year old resource. It flies in the face of the belief that a good teacher is a good teacher: period.

An educator's chances for success are greatly increased if s/he is not a hard-nose person who demands power and control. A sincere person who is truly concerned and interested in each individual, who uses humor, has high and appropriate academic and behavior expectations and does not employ sarcasm, tends to develop positive relationships with many Native students.

Kim-boy has his head down today. It is not usual. Getting in his face and demanding he turn to a certain page like the other kids in the class even though it is clear he is not willing to participate right then is not going to be of any value to anyone. It is not a matter of babying Kim-boy or giving him special treatment. It is a matter of being sensitive to a variety of factors that may be influencing certain behaviors. Kim-boy may be dealing with something (like the loss of his brother) that makes taking part and turning to that page at that time quite irrelevant. A teacher needs to learn to use good judgment to properly read the situation and try and understand the complexities so success can occur and relationships with students are not damaged. An in-tune teacher can tell if the student is dealing with a legitimate issue or is just simply exhibiting inappropriate behavior.

Are those individuals mentoring, evaluating or training teachers aware of the information that exists as to how best work with Native students? In the recently implemented state program, mentors are matched with first and second year teachers in the state to provide assistance and support to these novices. The experience of the mentor is not necessarily matched with the teaching position of the new teacher. An experienced elementary teacher of fifteen years could be mentoring a secondary science teacher for example. A teacher with twenty years of experience in a small urban, non-Native town could be mentoring a person in a two-teacher school who teaches all secondary subjects to Inuit students from twelve to eighteen years of age.

This attitude that a good teacher is a good teacher no matter the locale or the backgrounds of the students is an elitist position. Of course, in many ways kids are just kids the world over. But this does not mean that educators can ignore the fact that children of a culture different than the mainstream school system just might have very different ways of looking at things, possibly possess a very different set of background information, and experienced a very different set of life and language experiences prior to entering the western classroom. By not mentioning or addressing the differences and needs of Native students, educators are encouraged to attach blame inappropriately for the education difficulties many Native students experience.

Three decades ago, John Collier, Jr. wrote, "Blindness to Native history and insensitivity to Native self cut a deep chasm between the White teacher and his Eskimo students, a space that education too often fails to cross." To this day, there exists only haphazard, feeble attempts by the State department of education, educator preparation schools, and school districts to address this chasm.

I have no intention of disparaging the work of the State mentors, a very experienced group of professionals, but when no differences are made within this program between the needs of western students in an urban or suburban classroom and that of isolated aboriginal Alaskans, this chasm is reinforced. The State mentors recently produced a booklet entitled *Ready Set Teach*. This is a booklet of ideas with no mention of and absolutely no distinction made between a new teacher entering a remote, multiage classroom in a small village of Athabaskan students or one entering a regular suburban classroom of highly verbal, competitive western students. These situations are drastically dissimilar. Each has its own challenges and a generic, mainstream-biased approach conflicts with the landscape in rural Alaska.

Many Native students have ways of looking at the world, beliefs, needs, language considerations, and values that are in conflict with the system and the majority of the personnel manning this institution. To ignore this and treat the situations as if these differences do not exist is folly. Ready, set, teach, and it matters not where or whom or how?

What's Wrong with This Picture?

Time: *Not really that long ago*

Setting: *A larger rural Alaskan village school*

Cast: *A K-6 staff. Let's see. That means seven teachers, a special education teacher and one principal: nine adult, certified, professional educators.*

Situation: *This staff creates a discipline plan for the near ninety, five to twelve year old students.*

Summary: *This Discipline Plan stipulates that when a child breaks the School Rules, his/her name is entered on a list of the guilty. This ledger is kept in the principal's office. On the last Friday of each month a popcorn, video party is held in the gymnasium for the student body. The school day is shortened There is a festive air.*

Climax: *Each teacher arrives with his/her charges, and they find their places in the bleachers. The popcorns pop and the video screen awaits. One of the staff then stands with a microphone and proceeds to read the names of the students on The List. These guilty students line up in front of the bleachers and when all names have been called, they file out and ago to sit quietly in a classroom while their classmates enjoy popcorn and the movie.*

Problem: *Can you identify at least two concerns you might have regarding this discipline plan?*

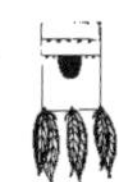

Studying Alaska

At this rural high school, first semester was American government and second semester was Alaska studies. Sara informed her parents of this change and explained to them after her first day of class in Alaska studies, that everyone had a project to complete. It was the same project for each student, and they had four weeks to accomplish this. Four weeks was 44% of the course.

Everyday at the beginning of class the students, boys and girls, entered the room, picked up their materials off a shelf (a tanned hide, a needle, and some leather twine) and spent the class time sewing a pair of sealskin slippers.

Every day Sara went to class, picked up her slippers, sat at her desk and cut and sewed. At the end of each week she brought home a progress report that indicated a grade for that week for each of her classes. Week one in Alaska studies, an A was earned. Week two was the same. Week three, though, the progress report showed a B in Alaska studies.

Sara's mother asked her what was going on and why the change. Sara shrugged and explained that on Wednesday, she was talking with Troy while she sewed. The teacher told her to stop talking, but she continued and completed whatever she was in the middle of telling Troy. Thus, a B in Alaska studies for week three. Simple as that.

Look Out the Window: There's Logic and Common Sense

There often seems to be an abundance of poor logic and a lack of common sense in rural Alaska school districts. It can be seen in the discipline plan and the Alaska studies class examples above. But educators, particularly administrators because they make more far-reaching decisions, often discover a new brand of logic displayed by school board members and parents as well.

Parents, school board and community members have a responsibility to ensure their dealings with school personnel are based on accurate information. There is an onus on them, an obligation, to incorporate fairness, good judgment and logic as well as the need for the school staff to do so. Too often this is not the case. A hard-working, sincere educator may be supported and considered in a very positive light by parents or board members, that is, until he or she makes a decision that negatively affects their children.

Gossip, emotion, partial and distorted information, personality conflicts, and the interests of certain factions all play a very caustic role in the education process. This occurs to some degree in all systems that involve human interaction, but it is of a particular concern in small, isolated places where it becomes intensified, magnified and destructive. The reputations of many educators have been undeservingly damaged by irrational, misdirected dissatisfaction and misinformation enabled by angry individuals operating in self-interest or for some reasons other than what is honest and in the best interest of the kids.

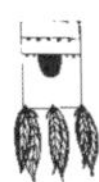

Principal Sal

The staff at the small rural high school seemed to be quite pleased with the new principal. Admittedly it was only mid-September, but things looked hopeful. Right off the bat she set up new avenues to receive input from the teachers and classified personnel, and various changes were already made based on their suggestions. She was a good listener, she truly liked the students and quickly learned all their names, she smiled but she was firm, and the school seemed to be really taking on a new, cheerful look. They were off to a good start.

Moose season was open, and a new school policy had been implemented the prior year. Each student could have four excused absences annually for subsistence activities. It required that one of the child's parents call or meet with the principal ahead of time so the absences could be approved and listed as excused.

The first parent advisory committee meeting of the year was scheduled for Tuesday evening. Principal Sal was excited and anxious to meet the parents and share some of the things going on at the school as well as some of the plans that were in the making. Introductions were made and before the agenda could get underway, a parent asked to speak. He was angry. He demanded to know why his two boys got unexcused absences for the previous Wednesday, Thursday and Friday. He explained gruffly that they were with him hunting moose, and subsistence activities are supposed to be excused.

Principal Sal patiently and kindly asked if he or his wife had called or visited her to get prior approval because she didn't recall talking with them. This began a tirade from the parent that was a bit difficult to follow. The well-prepared principal had the school handbook with her. She waited until he finished talking, and then she politely read aloud the policy that this same committee (including this parent) had adopted the year before. Of course, she was not there the year before, but she explained that she was following the policy as it was written. There was nothing ambiguous about it: for the absences to be considered excused, the principal needed to give prior approval to a parent or guardian.

This parent then began a new diatribe where he accused her of not caring about Native ways, she was just a visitor, and she didn't know Native people. She should go back to from where she came. She was a prejudiced person he declared. Principal Sal was shocked.

No matter the positive changes that were taking place in the school: the appreciative, newly motivated staff, the students who felt cared for, the bright and refreshing new look to the building. This meeting was the beginning of her downfall, and she moved on after the school year ended.

The accusations made by this parent were heard around the community, passed on to others and distorted. The facts were irrelevant. Now when she made a decision, it was looked upon with suspicion by the parents because they heard she didn't respect Native people and she was prejudiced. Many parents argued with her now. The honeymoon was over. Can't blame her for seeking a friendlier place to live and work come May.

I've witnessed similar logic expressed by parents and community members when principals have legitimately disciplined a star basketball player resulting in him/her not being able to play in the game Saturday night. Eggs were thrown at one principal's house and another received repeated obscene phone calls and threats from adults. Such behaviors and attitudes are, of course, destructive and further hamper the development of a positive relationship between the school and the home. There is no reasonable excuse for this type of conduct sanctioned by adults from any culture be they educators, parents, or community members.

Making Informed Decisions

This lack of logic is sometimes reflected in the very manner in which the system is set up. To elect lay people to serve on school boards and have parent members on school advisory committees is generally well and good. Problems become evident, though, when they make decisions and direct efforts in areas that require specific expertise and are made based upon emotion or politics.

Can you imagine the difficulties we would face if hospitals and clinics were run in this manner? It would reflect the same logic if we elected lay people to a hospital board and had them select the temperature for operating rooms or decide the number of nurses assisting with certain operations. Should administrators ask the parents on a village advisory committee, as I have witnessed, how they thought reading should be taught in the school?

A common responsibility of school boards is establishing the school district calendar. This is often done for reasons other than what is educationally sound. This explains such decisions, for example, as having students return to school on a Friday following a lengthy Christmas vacation. From past experience, as one can guess, very few students bother to attend that Friday.

One area that involves decisions by uninformed lay people is bilingual education. Research and information concerning second language acquisition and dual language instruction are usually not a part of the decision-making process. Old-fashioned beliefs often reign. I have heard school members argue that Yup'ik as a second language should not be taught in the school because it would interfere with the students' ability to learn English. Parent committees that decide that all instruction should be in the Native language until the children are eight years old, but at the same time, want their children competent in basic skills may be basing their decision as well on emotion and opinion with no informed analysis of what is educationally sound. In some situations this might be quite appropriate, in others, not. The decision needs to be an informed one.

Much of the world's children learn two and, in some cases, three languages concurrently. There are villages where the situation is conducive to the children successfully acquiring English and the "subordinate" Native language simultaneously. Delaying English an additional three years is certainly not doing the children any favors in some circumstances. The students are quite capable of acquiring two languages without interference. It is not a simple black and white issue to be decided by emotion and politics. There are a variety of factors to take into account in making this decision of what language or languages children receive instruction in at school. Consultation with experts in language acquisition would be more beneficial than emotional opinion.

Some of this same uninformed decision-making occurs when the Native language is taught in schools as a second language. Local people are hired, but they are not provided training in language acquisition, and they often replicate some of the methods they have seen regular classroom teachers use. Thus, maybe flashcards as well as other practices of teaching vocabulary in isolation are modes of instruction. Students can attend such programs over the years and end up with no ability to speak the language except to provide the word for some objects or animals. Teaching the Native language would be honored, respected and far more successful if the instructors were trained in second language acquisition and provided the necessary materials and resources instead of deciding to place them in that position with no guidance and support.

Normalcy Is Wide

In mainstream America, for example, there exists a band that is, say, five of some quantity wide. Behaviors within that measurement of five are considered normal, appropriate behaviors and do not cause attention. It has been said that individuals who are not able or do not want to fit into that band become characters that head to the South Seas or rural Alaska. In these locales the band of normalcy might be eleven on this scale. In other words, behaviors that are clearly outside the band of five can still be within a range of this 'other normalcy'. If an individual is operating in the ranges of six to eleven, sometimes in rural Alaska this doesn't cause too much attention whereas this same behavior in the mainstream would be quite unusual or simply not tolerated. This isn't necessarily a negative characteristic. It can result in an array of very independent and creative individuals. But it can also be a haven for individualism and behaviors of the undesirable sort.

There is a certain percentage of educators in rural Alaska who operate in the six to eleven range. They are able to do so due to the remoteness of some schools, the constant turnover of personnel, and this adjusted scale of what is considered allowable behavior that exists. And they are both of the negative and positive variety. Their numbers increase as school districts experience increased difficulties filling positions. The difference with educators, of course, is that they work with children and their behaviors are of major import and influence.

An Aside

Principal Ralph once told me jokingly that the most dangerous section of roadway in Anchorage, especially January through March, is the first mile or two out of the Anchorage airport. This is when many Bush teachers come to the city after six-seven months of living in a slow-paced village with no car.

They get a rental and as they leave the airport trying to figure out how to turn on the lights, the heater, and the windshield wipers in the strange car, they discover that traveling at thirty-five miles per hour feels like seventy. Cars whiz by, and they get a renewed respect for how dangerous the highway is and how stressful driving can be.

These same educators can be seen in the Carr's parking lot on their way back to the airport. Their blood pressures are high as they keep looking at their watches so they won't miss their flight. Groceries are strewn on the asphalt, ice, snow, or slush as they hurriedly toss into a cardboard box the fruits and vegetables and other items they can't buy in the village. It is raining, snowing, or it is cold and the packaging tape won't stick and the hastily scrawled address smears. Got to make it to the airport post office, return the car, check in, get on the plane and then, exhausted, just look forward to getting home and receiving all the goods in the mail.

Musical Chairs

French poet Charles Baudelaire wrote that, "This life is a hospital where every patient is possessed with the desire to change beds; one man would like to suffer in front of the stove, and another believes that he would recover his health beside the window." It seems many rural educators hold a similar view. Come April and throughout the summer months there is the annual rotation of educators in the State who seek what they hope is a better location to live and work. Some burn bridges or are encouraged or forced to leave. Some want better housing or a different climate. Others are looking for a new set of administrators or simply a different work or living environment.

Some educators decide to leave because of frustration and job dissatisfaction. It is natural that individuals want to succeed at their efforts. If a person has earned a credential as a certified teacher; had a rewarding experience as a teacher in a school near Austin; works hard and is sincere, but still feels unsuccessful as a teacher in a village, one option is to give up and go elsewhere. This lack of success, to some degree, may be of the teacher's doing. But initially the true fault lies in hiring this person and placing him/her in this situation without adequate training, without equipping him/her with the skills and information that would allow success. This person who decides that the situation just is not rewarding and chooses to leave displays more integrity and professionalism than those who get comfortable, remain and continue to teach without self reflection, without searching for answers, and without making any adaptations to their methods even though all indications show they clearly are not working.

There Comes a Time

Mr. Dan had been teaching in the village for going on fifteen years. He taught social studies, Alaska studies, physical education and was a coach. His wife was a teacher also. They lived in a beautiful home. He loved to hunt and fish. The manner in which he taught when he first arrived was the same as when they decided to move back to Nebraska.

He had his world history texts, his United States history texts. He ordered the publisher's workbooks and the accompanying test booklets to go with the texts. His basic mode of instruction (despite all the evidence that exists indicating this is not an educationally sound practice) was to assign a chapter or have the students take turns reading it aloud in class. They were to answer the questions at the end of the chapter and do the workbook pages. He xeroxed the test from the booklet for the chapter quiz on Friday.

The tests the students took on Friday were on his desk on Monday ready to be passed back. This same ritual and results continued his fifteen years of tenure. The first one showed three items correct out of thirty, the next five correct, then four, three, and five out of thirty. These tests received a grade of D.

While the majority of the tests received a D, there were a few C's for those with seven or eight correct and a couple B's with nine and ten right. In looking through the stack, there was a test that showed the highest score, thirteen out of thirty correct! A big A was written on top of the sheet.

It can certainly be said that Mr. Dan did not receive any training as to how to be successful teaching in this situation. Shame on the fact that this is the case. But after a couple years of Mr. Dan seeing clearly that what he was doing was not working, shame on him for not making any efforts to at least try and figure out how his teaching could be improved so student learning could occur.

He was comfortable living and working there. He was going through the motions of holding class, and his students went through the motions of being students.

A Taboo Subject

There are some educators, more than we would like to think, who have breached the Educators' Professional Code of Ethics without losing their certificate. They simply apply and are hired by another district in the State. In some situations, inappropriate educator behavior has been protected by administrators, teachers or board members due to personal relationships or for other unprofessional reasons.

There is no mechanism in place besides the legally shaky reference checks that might or might not occur, in order to protect schools from hiring an incompetent or inappropriate educator, some of whom should not be working around children. A means of accomplishing this would be difficult to establish due to legalities and teacher unions. But in order to do truly what is best for kids, there needs to be a manner in which those who commit gross behaviors are better prevented from continuing to be around children and so easily moving to a different location in the state. Just because the schools are remote and the personnel is largely transient does not mean they should be sanctuaries for incompetence.

This is somewhat of a taboo subject. Discussing the high percentage of incompetent or inappropriate educators found in rural Alaska seems to be politically incorrect. This is probably the case, at least partially, because it so poorly reflects on the hundreds of professionals who deserve positive recognition. Addressing examples of bizarre and improper behaviors of educators is left to informal conversations and are only presented, sadly, as humorous anecdotes. This doesn't mean, though, that this serious issue should be ignored and continue as is.

There are, of course, some very sincere, creative, understanding, and hard working, professional educators who do wonderful things in the schools and classrooms. Even if an excellent teacher or administrator comes into the school, he/she must exist and work within the overall structure of a system that was not designed for these students or this locale. These educators often find a creative way to do their good work independently within this framework, sometimes to the disdain of their more mainstream colleagues.

Generally teachers must work in a system void of established and/or sustained processes and one that is in a constant state of flux with little continuity and largely based on the degree of skills and beliefs held by the individuals currently in positions of authority.

There is a difference, though, between hard working, effective educators and ones that just plain work hard. A person can work really hard loading a dump truck using a teaspoon, but it surely isn't effective. All educators perceive themselves as hard working. This is natural. Longevity and hard work alone, though, are not necessarily the key ingredients leading to student success. Often effectiveness is confused with how well the person is liked and gets along with colleagues, parents and the people in the community. An educator's effectiveness is largely perceived by other educators, parents, and community members through emotion and gut-level opinions and has nothing to do with student learning and success and what goes on in the classroom or the school. It is certainly more valuable in having an effective, positive educator in place for a short time period than a damaging individual who comfortably stays on and lowers the turn over statistics.

More Realistic Education
Native Educators

"One of the major concerns has been the reality that problems do not automatically disappear when the schools are run by Indian people themselves."

— Collier

Just as some people feel that by incorporating readily observable cultural activities in the school, alienation and academic difficulties will be alleviated, others sense that the solution is in lessening teacher turnover or, of course, it is simply a funding issue. To others, the answer lies in having Alaska Native educators working with Alaska Native students.

"Let's examine what Native Teachers bring to a classroom. Regardless of expertise, their presence in the classroom quiets the stress and increases the confidence of Indian children. Even when they emulate White teachers, their roles are acceptable and offer an image of Indian accomplishment that in itself can make education more realistic for many children. But this human accomplishment may not be enough to adequately meet the needs of Native students. " John Collier, Jr.

For the most part, Native educators, as most all educators, are products of the K-12 system, are indoctrinated by university programs that promote this same system and are then hired as a part of this same structure. Despite all the positive ramifications, just in the mere fact that the teacher or administrator is an Alaska Native, the inflexible system generally overshadows many of these benefits. Native educators must fit into a very uncomfortable, unnatural set of boundaries. They are required to become more westernized in order to take part and succeed in this western organization. It takes more than Native educators replicating how they have seen non-Natives hold school and how they have been trained as to the way school is.

It has never been easy for Native people living in rural Alaska to obtain education degrees. To do so requires leaving their homes and culture then dealing with an unfamiliar bureaucracy and operating in a very alien environment. There have been various university programs that have attempted to assist in the process, but they are generally grant-driven and short-lived (e.g. XCED, REPP). The PITAAS program (Preparing Indigenous Teachers and Administrators for Alaska Schools) at the University of Alaska/Juneau is a grant-funded program that targets Southeast Alaska Natives and has been in place since 2000. It is a positive attempt at fulfilling this need.

But there is no permanent, suitable avenue available for Alaska Natives throughout the state to earn their teaching certificate without extreme sacrifice and clear deference to western requirements. There is no program that is an integral part of the Alaska State university system that is specifically designed to accommodate the needs of Alaska Natives seeking a teaching degree. Alaska State universities are not "user-friendly" places for some Alaska Natives seeking education certificates or for those wanting to learn how best teach Alaska Native children.

Future teacher clubs have been established in villages over recent years to encourage and support Alaska Native high school students to become teachers. Participation in these clubs has grown and they are a positive attempt at increasing the number of Native educators. Grants have been the funding source so their continuance, once more, is tentative.

The concerns, though, are two fold: one is to provide an avenue for certification that is conducive to Alaska Native success, with a balance between high expectations and institutional understanding of the unique situation and needs of adult Native students; and the second aspect is to ensure the graduates simply do not become another cog in the western system and, thus, replicate the same methods and practices as the conventional western teacher. The second concern relates to all educators.

"Consciously or unconsciously they operate from the belief that the only road to success lies in emulating the system in which they received their training. Such Native graduates retain their Native physical characteristics but employ the same debilitating teaching methods by which they were taught years earlier. They, too, adopt rigid schedules and harsh disciplinary practices and, perhaps un-wittingly, give the impression that the old ways and culture are best forgotten." Grant & Gillispie, 1993

A new, welcoming, less alienating place called school could be created by incorporating cultural activities in schooling efforts; altering the school system to meet the particular needs and characteristics of Native students; providing appropriate training for all educators; in conjunction with increasing the number of Alaska Native teachers and administrators.

"The value of a teacher from the child's own culture cannot be overestimated" Grant & Gillispie, 1993. This is true despite the current incongruity between the system the Native educator must fit into and the Native students themselves.

If the K-12 system is retooled to better match the needs of Native students and the educators are adequately trained to contribute to the goals of a new model, more confident and academically proficient Native graduates will result. This must be coupled with establishing an appropriate, lasting, culturally responsive avenue at Alaskan State universities for those Native high school graduates interested in acquiring training and certification in education. Such a revised system would certainly be more inviting to Native people to want to participate in and, thus, the much-needed Alaska Native teaching corps would be enlarged. The significance and import of Native educators will be then truly realized.

"Training the 'Native' teacher to return constructively to the village school will require new guidelines and a radically changed philosophical approach to educating the culturally different child. Unless this takes place, the value of the Native teacher is often destroyed by the *White backlash* of conventional teacher training." Collier, p.119, 1973

CHAPTER 8

But Kids Are Just Kids (Aren't They?)

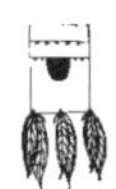

Lapp Game as Metaphor

There was a field outside my classroom window and, particularly in the spring, I would be working at my desk after school and hear the screams and laughter of Yup'ik boys and girls playing Lapp Game. The rules were pretty loose and somewhat ambiguous, boundaries were vague but the result was kids running and giggling and screaming and laughing. There was constant action as someone hit a ball with a stick, someone grabbed the ball and, in one variant of the rules, tried to hit one of the kids in a frenzied group running from one side to reach the safe line on the other side.

There are different ways to play and names for this game. It is also called Aleut, Native or Eskimo baseball. Any number of people can play and there are no teams. Most players are, at any give point, fielders. There is a pitcher, batter and first baseman. The pitcher pitches without intending to strike the batter out, but to allow the batter to hit the ball.

The batter tries to hit the ball far enough to make it to the one and only base safely. If the ball is caught on a fly, or if the fielder is able to throw it to the base before the batter can run there, the batter is out and joins the fielders. The pitcher then bats, the first baseman pitches, someone from the outfield becomes the first baseman and the game resumes.

If there is a runner on base, he or she can run home and "score," but the point does not matter, except maybe to the successful base runner. "Homeruns" are possible, running to base and then home, but with so many fielders they are quite rare. Everyone bats. Everybody runs the bases. Everyone pitches. There are no winners or losers. Families and neighborhoods could join because there are no limits to the number of players. Lapp ball can be played with as few as five or six players, or as many as two dozen. Men and women, elders and kids have played this game together for generations in rural Alaska.

The first couple of years there might have been a non-Native kid or two playing in the game after school outside my window. As years passed and the ethnic make-up of the town shifted, there reached a critical mass of non-Yup'iks playing Lapp Game, and I began to hear different sounds outside my classroom in the spring. I heard arguing and yelling and, thus, frequent stops in the action. The non-Native kids were not content with a loosely run game for the sole sake of steady fun.

Cultural differences were evident in the classroom and Lapp Game clearly illustrated these differences. It isn't a question of good and bad, better or worse, right and wrong. It is a matter of recognizing differences and what they can mean to educators.

The non-Native students wanted the game to be competitive. They wanted to keep score, and they wanted stricter rules. And they wanted to win. The nature of the game, though, is such that it is impossible to keep score. Their attempt to turn this very random abstract game of fun into a concrete sequential game of competition resulted in arguments and a stop to the screams and giggles and laughter and, eventually, the field outside my classroom was empty in the spring.

"Native children come from homes and communities where the cultural expectations and values are different from, and discontinuous with, those held by mainstream society, according to studies conducted by Fuchs and Havighurst (1983). Our own experience and observations as teachers and teacher educators are consistent with this conclusion. Native students confront a dilemma. They must decide to which cultural belief system they will pledge their allegiance:

the one they have learned from their community or the one promoted by the public school system. Choosing the former usually means falling further and further behind and eventually leaving school. Choosing the latter can lead to serious self-destructive behaviors of chemical addiction, violence, abuse-all typical responses of a societal group coping with cultural discontinuity (York, 1989)."

Teach Who? Where?

Of course Native groups vary greatly and there are always individuals who do not fall into categories of tendencies. Just when one reads that "Native people" have a very different view of how dogs should be treated (not as pampered pets), a tough Native male walks in holding a Chihuahua cooing kind words in its ear. There are always exceptions. This is not about stereotyping. It is about tendencies.

Well, What Are the Kids Like?

After a few years of interviewing educators for positions in rural schools, I became aware of a certain phenomena to which I subsequently paid particular attention. Each candidate was always provided the opportunity to ask any questions he/she would like concerning the position in question. After nearly two decades of interviewing hundreds of teachers, I am still somewhat taken aback that only one teacher amongst all of those applicants ever asked a question about the very students she would be teaching if she were offered the job (this teacher was hired and proved to be a superb teacher in a village school). One would think that someone like Dave or Debbie from Michigan might have at least one question about the Yup'ik students they would be teaching in a sub-Arctic village come fall. But, no, my experience was that applicants' questions were 'me' questions mainly concerned with salary, hunting, fishing, housing and benefits.

Native students tend to have certain unique characteristics that are necessary for educators to be aware of and know what it means to the classroom. The school system, as one would expect, reflects the same qualities as the western students tend to possess. The tendencies of Native students are incongruous with the system itself.

Example Tendencies

Indigenous Students	Western Students
Global, holistic, reflective, visual, tactile, group good, learning as a process, learning via observation, personalism, skilled in non-verbal communication, high spatial and perceptual skills, long wait time, low discourse, present, external locus control.	Sequential, linear, auditory, competitive, individual good, learning as a product, learning via verbal explanation & text, professionalism, fast paced, short wait time, highly verbal, past-future, internal locus of control.

The Language of Berry Picking

The Yup'ik mother and her two daughters were in their front yard as I worked on my four-wheeler next door. Amid the foliage alongside their house berries grew, and her young daughters were picking them and filling the little bowls they carried. The mother stood nearby and watched them.

One little girl said, "Mama, berries so juicy!"

"Uhmmmum," the mother warmly replied, acknowledging her daughter's comment.

The other daughter then said, "So sticky!"

The mother smiled and, again, said, "Uhmmmum."

It remained quiet as they continued filling their little bowls. Now, if this occurred in suburbia with a Sesame Street raised Yuppie mother, you can rest assured that the daughters would have received a lengthy reply full of information from comments regarding the textures and the color variations of the berries to maybe even their Latin name. A deluge of language would likely have been what each daughter received from their mother in reply to any comment they made.

This isn't a criticism of either style of interaction. It is about differences. It is easy to see that the daughters experiencing all the language usage would have a clear advantage when attending a school system that is based on language ability.

It is not necessarily a matter of attempting to change the manner in which the Yup'ik mother communicates with her daughters. It is a matter of the school system recognizing the difference in purposes of language, the differences in language experiences and, thus, ensure instruction is developmentally appropriate for children with limited exposure to the language of the school. The school system, though, marches on seemingly oblivious to these disparities, and school readiness efforts are limited or nonexistent or simply replicate generic attempts to prepare kids for school anywhere.

"Access is key. In both oral language acquisition and learning to read, access is the critical component. Children with access to rich and responsive language interactions about their experiences in the first three years of life develop power over language even as they learn to talk. Their orientation to the world around them is one of agency and curiosity. They acquire ever larger vocabularies as they notice, talk about, and receive adult feedback on experiences. These children come to school ready to continue that quest for knowledge and to make their own the words that name it." Building a Knowledge Base in Reading, Braunger, Lewis, 1997, p.61

School Language:
The Centerpiece of School Learning

The following comes from an essay that I wrote a number of years ago. The content is as true today as it was then, the sources referenced just as valid.

The western education system is one that honors verbal ability. "Verbal ability has long been regarded as the best single predictor of academic success" (Stodolsky and Lesser, 1967, p. 33). As Ernest Boyer writes, "language is the center piece of learning. It's not just another subject but the means by which all subjects are perceived". There is ample evidence that verbal ability in the language of the school is the weakest area for many of our Alaska Native students. Various studies show that Eskimos are low in abstract verbal abilities (Lipinski 1990, More 1984, Kleinfeld 1978, Bock and Feldman 1970). Brown (1991) explains that "Native students rank far below norms in reading, language arts, and language arts related subjects." As Bock and Feldman found, Eskimo children scored significantly below the norms on all test items in the English vocabulary tests. Streiff's study (1980) showed that the nearly 3,000 Eskimo children of western Alaska are almost three grade levels below their ages in reading comprehension.

It must be emphasized, as Olsen wrote in 1971, "verbal deficiencies of the culturally different are not related to low intelligence or emotional immaturity" (p. 68). Salisbury echoes this in writing "Eskimos' communication problems stem from conflicting cross-cultural values, not from any lack of intelligence" (1969. p. 27). The Eskimos are of a culture and environment where there is little experience with the purpose of literacy and little exposure to reading and writing behavior, linguistic concepts or language usage. The education system must take this into consideration.

Rural Native students do not live in a world of print. There are few signs, billboards or written communication in village life. I have been to numerous villages where the only visible print in the community is the name on the school building. There often are no books in the homes and parents seldom model reading and writing behavior. Many basic concepts about print are not held by our rural students when they enter our schools.

Along with this is the cultural trait of emphasizing learning via observation, not by verbal explanations. As Collier points out "the information procedure amongst the Eskimos was terse in verbal explanation and highly non-verbal in demonstration." Kleinfeld (1973) echoes this in suggesting that Eskimo children learn more by watching adults than by receiving verbal instruction. They were educated by example, not by verbal command. They did not use tongue-lashings. They employed ostracism. Florey (1986) shares findings that "the learning and behavorial characteristics of Native Americans as being different than the predominant culture in that they have a reliance on non-verbal communication and use undetailed verbal accounts". It is evident that the Eskimos'situation clearly coincides with the results of research that attempt to explain the causes of reading disabilities and poor "school language" skills.

From a home and village environment that does not emphasize reading and writing behavior and a culture that is strong on learning by observation and non-verbal communication, a Native student enters the school environment, a language-saturated institution. Short concrete verbal exchanges with friends and family are now replaced with the fast-paced "school language" of abstractions, concepts and long decontextualized verbal explanations in the classroom, an unfamiliar world full of print and talk. Without making adaptations for these students, our schools follow the standard school model. Before these students develop an adequate foundation of listening and speaking skills of this school language, we generally try to teach them to read and write and to communicate decontextually.

Moore (1976) states "oral language development is the single most important factor in determining readiness for reading." Buckley (1993, p. 7) explains, "a child's mastery of oral language determines his/her future mastery of reading and writing." Simpson-Tyson (1977 and 1978) reports "the study of oral language of Native American children indicates that many are not proficient enough in English to learn to read." It is not likely that a successful reading and writing program can be built on an inadequate base of oral language.

Some Irony

It is ironic that the converse is true: a school system that allows success and positively rewards students with strength in communication skills is the same system that seldom provides opportunities for many Alaska Native students to demonstrate the special strengths they possess.

Let us say there is a boy named Caruso who gets up and dresses himself every day and heads off to school. The school he attends is a ballet school. Caruso is not very coordinated and every day he stumbles around and tries to do the things he is told to do. The ballet teacher's kids are in the class, and they seem to glide around and do pirouettes with ease. Caruso can sing like a bird but there are no opportunities for singing in the school day. One can only guess that after not too many months or years of attending an institution that focuses on the things he is not good at and provides no outlet for or recognition of the talents he does possess, that he could possibly become dispirited and maybe even give up.

More (1984) found, "Eskimos are significantly higher in perceptual skills, visiospatial abilities and imaginal decoding than other students." Kleinfeld (1973), Bock and Feldman, and Kaulbeck (1984) support this as well, and I have verified these findings with school pyschologists who have tested hundreds of Native students on the Yukon-Kuskokwim Delta and in the mid-Kuskokwim region in the 70's, 80's and 90's.

Kleinfeld suggests that Eskimos possess superior perceptual skills and spatial abilities. Florey also describes the "superior visual discrimination and fine motor skills of Native Americans". The abilities of Eskimos to envision the workings of complex machinery and make repairs are legendary.

These skills, though, are not valued by the standard western school system. The system concentrates on verbal ability and, for the most part, the transfer of abstract information to students via lecture and text.

He Did It

It was a village high school of about eighty students. Students who were tardy, skipped classes, misbehaved, fought and otherwise broke some rule had to serve time in detention after school was out for the day. When they entered the room the students had to sign in and, next to their name, explain why they were sent to detention. In a review of this logbook with entries over two school years, not one student indicated that the reason he/she was in detention was because of something he or she did. The reason always indicated someone or something else as the cause.

Cause and Effect

An individual's locus of control is his/her perception of causality. If outcomes are attributed to something outside the person, the locus of control is external. An external locus of control negatively affects motivation to learn in school. In the classroom, a student has a clear advantage with an internal locus of control. This means the student believes he/she is in control and that results or achievements are due to his/her own efforts.

Research concerning locus of control indicates that people in traditional societies, hunters and gatherers, and people of a lower socio-economic class who are welfare dependent tend to possess an external locus of control. The crops were good because the weather cooperated. A moose was harvested because he gave himself to the hunter. She got an A on the test because she was lucky. In days past some results that occurred were attributed to witches and sorcerers by some cultures, or they were predetermined by fate.

If a family exists on welfare, a check periodically appears, but there is no connection between effort and reward. A child can lose or break a pair of expensive eyeglasses, and they may be replaced with no charge. Obtaining the product required no visible effort on the individual's or anyone's part. A young man might not change the oil in the engine, and it breaks down. The cause is attributed maybe to his uncle who borrowed the machine the week before: there is no connection between action or lack of action and result. It is not clear nor intuited that individual effort or action is directly related to the outcome.

Children are raised seeing parents working hard, picking crops all day but the family remains poor. The connection between the work done and benefits derived is not made. In groups where outside forces such as weather and abundance of game had so much to do with success or lack of success this tendency for developing and possessing an external locus of control is reinforced.

It is very natural for all people to blame problems, difficulties, and occurrences on someone or something other than themselves. It is human nature. This is a different matter, though, than individuals tending to possess an external locus of control that has developed in a population over generations of living certain life styles. And this can effect students in the classroom.

There are various strategies that can be incorporated in the curricula to assist students in making this connection between effort and action and results. Attribution Theory and Imagery (RSI) Procedures are examples of techniques designed to modify locus of control. The goal is to have students better understand that their own efforts in school directly relate to learning and academic success. It is not by chance a good grade is earned. It is not a matter of luck that someone did well on a test. One's actions, decisions, efforts produce positive or negative results. It is a matter of knowing when those results are due to one's own efforts or are out of one's control. It is recognizing and determining, being aware that this good thing or bad thing that happened was or was not due to one's own efforts. It would be valuable to Native students if schools assisted in modifying locus of control to be more internal. Educators could continually reinforce with their students the link between cause and effect.

Ain't Fair

Back by the pencil sharpener was Mr. C's Comment, Suggestion, Idea Box available for students to slip in the "coin slot" any note they wanted to pass on to their teacher. Very interesting writings were found in that box over the years.

Just as the playing of Lapp Game was influenced by the changing ethnic make-up of the town, so were the dynamics in the classroom. The Kleinfeld article mentioned earlier describes how personal concern and warmth can positively affect requests made of Native students by the teacher.

Mr. C would say in a normal voice to two kids in class who were fooling around, "Hey, c'mon, don't do that. I can't do my job with that horsing around goin' on." They would stop because they didn't want to bother Mr. C.

But as the number of non-Native kids increased in the class, disciplining inappropriate behavior resulted in new dynamics. It didn't really matter to Brandon from Portland if his behavior was bothering Mr. C or not. Mr C had to aggressively and authoritatively deal with the Brandons. The Native kids had never seen Mr. C act like that before. It was confusing.

Mr. C found himself in the situation where he could just frown, shake his head back and forth or simply ask the Native students to stop doing whatever needed to be stopped. But since some of the non-Native kids didn't respond to that mode of discipline, Mr. C had to change character and exhibit displeasure in a very stern and unusually angry manner.

This was a bit bewildering to the students, and it is easy to see how the teacher's behavior might be misconstrued. This misinterpretation was evident one day after school when he looked through the comments in his Comment, Suggestion, Idea Box.

"Why do you take it easy on the eskomos (sic) and pick on us?"

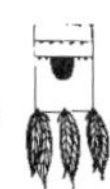

Dynamics

Native students are affected by the ethnic make-up of the school and classroom situation in which they find themselves. In a grade level classroom, a teacher might have a few teachers' children who are very verbal, high achievers who jump at the chance to answer questions and do whatever the teacher requests. The rest of the class might consist of Native students with a very wide range of abilitics, low and high achievers, possibly two or three special education students and maybe a few FAE/FAS children. The same situation can be found in smaller village classrooms but the students are also of varying ages. There is an array of proficiencies in this group of kids. It is quite challenging for the teacher to meet the needs of each student. The needs largely relate to each student's proficiency in listening, speaking, reading and writing the language of the school.

Even by casual observation it is sometimes easy to see the disproportionate amount of time the teacher spends with the students who are most verbal while somewhat ignoring the quiet, well-behaved Native students. This can be the case in urban and suburban schools also where the Native students, since they seldom cause a disturbance, are not provided with the same attention as their more aggressive and verbal classmates.

Urban and suburban school environments can be very stressful and uninviting to the village student. The stereotypical quiet Native can get lost in the shuffle in the large, crowded, loud, fast paced, talkative, confusing and seemingly unfriendly place. Some schools and some teachers just don't know quite what to do with the Native students. Since behavior problems are generally not an issue, they can easily be overlooked. And because some students are quiet and/or they are having difficulties related to language, this is often misinterpreted as something other than what it is.

This is usually what occurs when there are teachers new to a rural school district: there is a spike in the number of special education referrals. The difficulties many Native students face in the language of the school are taken to mean something else by new teachers who recommend special education testing for some children who appear non-communicative or show little comprehension. More often it is a language issue, not one of intelligence or disability.

Despite the conclusions in the late 1990's of the largest evaluation ever done on a federal education program (Chapter I/Title I), that the pullout model of teaching at-risk kids is not effective, the practice is still in use. I recently visited a mostly non-Native, suburban elementary school where I saw a group of Native children at a table in a cubbyhole working with an instructional aide checking boxes under a paragraph on a worksheet. Another group of five students sat at a table outside the library with an aide doing the same thing. This might help the classroom teacher create a more homogenous group of students to work with, but it is questionable how helpful this is for the Native students who have been pulled out and kept busy with a person untrained in reading instruction. No diagnostic assessments had been done; there was no prescription to meet identified individual needs. The amount and effectiveness of the reading instruction that occurred was questionable.

Educators working with Native students in urban and suburban schools must also be apprised of the cross-cultural concerns, language issues and various factors related to making school a positive experience. Many Alaska Native students find themselves attending an institution be it rural, urban, or suburban that concentrates on their area of weakness, the abstract, verbose language of the school, but virtually ignores their unique powers of observation and strengths in spatial, perceptual skills. The characteristics of Native students are largely in direct discord to the attributes of most of their teachers, their non-Native classmates, and to the very school system itself. These same dynamics occur for many Native students at the university level as well.

CHAPTER 9

System As It Is

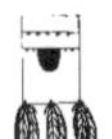

As It Is and Has Been

Schools are not factories or businesses and students are not widgets or products, but this analogy is an alternative attempt at illustrating the situation as it is and has been. The prototype of Maple Widget Factories was established in 1850 in Prussia. The United States took this model under its wing and designed its widget factories quite similarly. Individuals were trained around the U.S. to work in these factories. Maple was the material available and, thus, the factory equipment was set up for making maple widgets. The factory workers lived in areas where, for the most part, individuals very much like themselves lived, raised families and worked at various occupations. Most factory equipment came to be designed in the state of Texas for some reason.

Some workers were interested in specific stages of the widget making process, so they concentrated their training on those stages. There are thirteen steps in making maple widgets. The early, middle and ending phases are quite different from each other and each requires a special training program.

There came a time about a hundred years ago when the federal government decided to make widgets in rural Alaska. Maple Widget Factories were packed and hauled up to the remotest areas of this Great Land. Of course Maple Widget Factory workers went along to man the machinery and manage the operations.

The widget workers quickly discovered that maple wasn't an available material. The wood in rural Alaska was uqvik. Its characteristics are very different, not better, not worse, just different than maple. Every type of wood has its own strengths, weaknesses and unique attributes. The tolerances, the weight requirements, the bearings and blades, lathe settings and all aspects of the factory machinery were designed and set for maple. And the employees were trained to work in a Maple Widget factory. Problems soon became apparent. Widgets were not turning out according to Maple Widget Factory expectations.

But the management and workers were paid well and the factories were in very adventurous locations. Lots of great fishing, hunting, and scenery. Lots of freedom. Due to their remoteness, regulations were often slack. Factory workers trained in certain aspects of widget making were not necessarily assigned to their area of expertise. So rural Alaska was an interesting place to go for a while, make some widgets, hunt and fish, have an adventure, earn some money and then return to the Lower Forty Eight with some quaint and unique stories to tell at parties and to relatives and friends.

These factories operated with well-established processes, standard equipment and methodologies that, over time, became accepted as a given. They continued cranking out widgets made of uqvik that did not fit maple widget specifications. A steady stream of Maple Widget Factory managers and workers came from Maine, Michigan, Montana, Minnesota, and other states for stints which lasted varying numbers of years. During their holiday and summer breaks from factory work they generally returned to their home area. It was understood that no matter how long they worked in the Maple Widget factories in rural Alaska, they would eventually head back from whence they came. Management came and went. Workers came and went.

Uqvik widgets that didn't have the specifications of those made out of maple at the different stages were just passed on to the next stage. Hopes were that whatever imperfections found in stage one, for example, would be corrected by the workers in stage two or stage three. Workers in the later stages of widget making usually pointed their fingers at the incompetence of those workers in the earlier stages as to why the widgets that came to them were flawed.

In some Asian countries when you first meet someone new, you need to find out the person's age so you know how to appropriately interact with that person. Rural Alaska widget factory employees are similar. When meeting a new worker, they find out as soon as possible how many years the person has spent making widgets out of uqvik. A widely held, unsubstantiated belief, is that the longer the individual has been at it, the more of a skilled widget maker he or she probably is.

Some workers spend long hours and put forth great efforts in trying to make their uqvik widgets look just like those of maple. But their sincere hard work doesn't seem to have a direct positive effect on the end product. Some workers dedicate many years of their life trying to create the desired widgets. Based on the characteristics of the finished uqvik widgets, though, it is obvious there is no correlation between the number of years spent working with the material and the quality of the widgets. Sincere effort or longevity is not the key to ensuring successful uqvik widgets are produced in these maple widget factories. Some uqvik widgets turn out wonderful (just like ones of maple) and some of the workers are not sure why.

The training opportunities that specifically address the characteristics of working with uqvik have been, for the most part, anecdotal. There have been some things written down here and there but these handbooks seldom fall in the hands of the factory workers. Even some college classes dealing with the subject are offered. Occasionally a curious factory worker seeks out such information. But all in all, employees are firmly ingrained in maple widget making, and they continue trying to make maple widgets out of uqvik. If how to work with uqvik is specifically addressed in training the factory workers, it is still done so in the context of the Maple Widget Factory.

Various costly programs are purchased by the uqvik widget management in hopes they will increase the quality of their end product. Programs come in and out of vogue. Each one is initially thought to be the panacea. Workers are sent to conferences and training opportunities all over the country, and trainers travel to the factories and give presentations regarding the current new program. The fact that the factories work with uqvik and not maple is not addressed by whatever program is fashionable.

The general consensus, spoken or implied, is that maybe uqvik just isn't up to snuff as far as what is needed to make the desired widgets. Some of the workers blame the factory management, some blame not having the most advanced, up-to-date equipment. Some, of course, blame uqvik while others believe the problems are due to the environment in which uqvik grows.

Often newcomers would quickly determine what they thought the problems were in making uqvik widgets. After a short tenure of working with the wood they would return to their home state holding on to their naïve conclusions about widget making in rural Alaska. If they did stay on for a length of time, they generally joined others with similar beliefs as to what or whom to blame for the factory's poor success.

Occasionally workers are employed who are from the region and are quite familiar with working with uqvik. They must successfully attend training schools in order to be hired. The training they receive, as all factory workers, is geared toward making maple widgets. Thus, their familiarity with uqvik is overshadowed by their attempts to follow the principles they learned which really pertain to maple.

After all these years of producing widgets in rural Alaska that often do not possess the desired characteristics according to maple specifications, may it be realized that these factories are equipped, designed and outfitted to make widgets out of maple. May it be realized that the factory equipment and employee training require some significant adjustments and alterations due to the unique characteristics of uqvik and the environment in which it grows.

All over the United States, businesses that buy widgets became very concerned the last few years about the diminishing quality of widgets all factories seemed to be producing. Alaska, like many states, declared that widgets of wishy-washy quality were no longer wanted no matter what wood was worked with. It became a law that in order for a widget to get a certificate stating it is complete and ready to be sold, it must pass a set of standards established by the state government based on the original <u>maple</u> specifications.

So now the factories all over the U.S. are gearing up to ensure their widgets will meet the required standards. Some of those ingrained factory processes that were once accepted as the way things are, are now being questioned and altered to a system that is based on these state standards.

Many uqvik factories in rural Alaska are following suit. They are reforming their factories to Standards-Based Maple Widget Factories with some following the Quality Maple Factory Model.

Basic Factory Settings for *Maple*

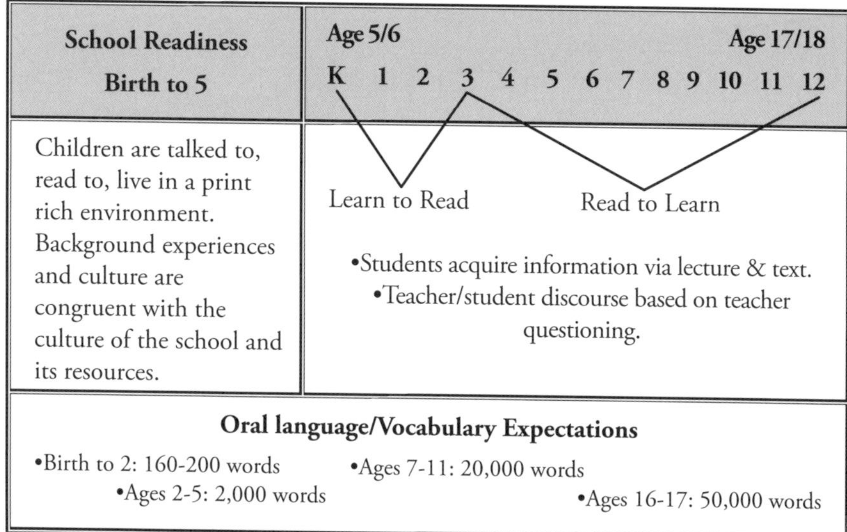

These factory settings require that all students and employees heed this particular pattern that was determined long ago to be the right, the correct pattern. It matters not if the students are aboriginal children in a mid-Kuskokwim village that has acquired telephones, electricity and cable television in the last two decades or if they are sons and daughters of legislators raised in Juneau in a western family with radically different values, beliefs, environment, goals, experiences and school readiness skills. There is no question which landscapes are in accord, which children more easily fit into this long established pattern.

Due to historical, cultural, environmental, social and experiential concerns; due to limited exposure to print, literacy behaviors and the language of the school; and because Native students are often unaccustomed to the purpose and use of decontextualized communication: the factory settings of the western school system clearly must be adjusted.

Texts and other reading materials, grade level and teaching resources reflect the maple factory specifications. Concepts and skills are introduced according to the schedule established long ago for a different clientele.

Betty Hart and Todd Risley, researchers from the University of Iowa, completed a two and a half year study a decade ago concerning the power of spoken words on brain development in infants. They found that, in their homes, children of professional parents heard, on average, 2,100 words per hour; children of working class parents heard 1,200 words; children of parents on welfare heard about 600 words per hour. I suggest a high percentage of Native children are exposed to a good deal less than 600 words per hour in their homes. When these same children in the study were in third grade, their school performance was measured. The results showed that by far the greatest predictor of school success was how much the children were talked to before age three. This type of information clearly gives cause for making adjustments to the school program and ensuring school readiness skills are a part of a district's education efforts.

The standard western system, though, is so ingrained and reinforced by the steady stream of like-minded educators that, in reality, it is very difficult to tell any differences between what village classrooms looked like in 1977, 1987, 1997 or currently. Classrooms, today, are likely to have a poster of the Alaska State Standards on the wall. The necessary adjustments, though, have not been made.

In the introduction to the Alaska State Performance Standards it is explained that the standards "define what it is students should know and be able to do". This happens to be one definition of curriculum. It is the course of study and students in the schools are expected to demonstrate that they know and are able to do certain things at various stages along the K-12 continuum. Since the standards define what students should know and be able to do, and because students are required to take tests regarding these standards as well as pass a final exam to obtain a diploma, we have what is actually a state mandated curriculum.

Basic understanding of literacy development, though, is being ignored when the same competencies are expected in all children at the same time. Students get on the literacy train at different ages. There are no set stages that occur at particular times. Some students enter school reading and writing while some students are not reading until ages six, seven, or eight. Many Native students experience reading difficulties throughout the entire K-12 program. So much depends on what literacy/language experiences a child has prior to entering the school. Basic tenets of literacy development such as the impact of the first five years of a child's life on school readiness are virtually ignored by the system's design and in training teachers.

How Well?

Example data from a rural school district regarding a state norm referenced, group test administered about six years ago showed that:

- *17% of the students received an NCE of 1 or it was indicated they did not finish the reading section. 24% of the students taking the math test were affected by either the administration of the wrong test, they received an NCE of 1 or they did not complete this section. This disqualifies any attempt to average scores or analyze group results.*

- *three sites were not aware of the test dates despite repeated communications and did not do any planning or preparation for test day.*

- *wrong tests were administered to two secondary classrooms.*

- *in at least four classrooms a substitute teacher administered the test.*

- *several sites administered additional test sections that were not required.*

- *several students filled out the wrong sections of the answer sheet.*

- *of the over four hundred test information sheets turned in to the district test coordinator, not one was filled out correctly. At least one error was found on every sheet.*

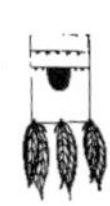

Assessment Concerns
Good Teacher? Good Student? What Can Be Said?

The entire realm of testing and assessments is often the most neglected part of teacher training programs and the educational process. Generally teachers' exposure to the subject relates to classroom tests and quizzes and state mandated assessments. Elementary teachers are usually more apprised of the critical role of testing as it relates to guiding instruction; as it concerns diagnosing individual strengths and weaknesses; and its function in monitoring the growth of a student or a group of students.

It would be extremely valuable to schooling if we could move our thinking concerning assessments to a different perspective. We want to know what does and does not work when it comes to methodologies and the use of particular resources. We want to diagnose with some degree of reliability each student's proficiency in reading, writing and mathematics and determine a plan to address the student's needs. We want to know if the diagnosis and prescription worked. Did the student learn; did he/she progress?

Say a diagnostic reading test was administered to Charley, and it is learned that he is reading on a low level as suspected. The test tells us, for one thing, that he pronounces all vowels long. Thus, he cannot provide a synonym for 'pal' because he pronounces it 'pale'. It is easy to see how this can affect comprehension. Without this information and if Charley is in a regular sixth grade reading program, his needs might be met or they might not be addressed. It is left somewhat to happenstance. If, though, his problem is identified, then his needs can be met by design instead of by chance. It isn't that during reading class every day Charley is taught how to pronounce vowels all period. But it does mean that Charley definitely receives help in this area. And assessments along the way will tell us if his problem is corrected over time.

The use of such assessments shouldn't end in the early elementary years. It is critical that all teachers working with a student are aware of his/her reading proficiency in order to ensure assignments and tasks are matched appropriately. This is particularly true when working with Native students who often have a great deal of difficulty in this area. Classroom tests and quizzes are usually given to help determine grades. Group assessments are the state mandated performance-based and norm referenced achievement tests. They are not designed to help diagnose a student's particular reading difficulties and provide information to address specific needs and to guide instruction.

Very important decisions are made based on the results of the state required tests. Schools, teachers, and students are judged as to their worth, their success or lack of success. School district efforts must reflect the importance of these tests despite the common concerns related to their inappropriateness. In order to obtain more reliable and useful assessment results the administration of district and state tests must be made a clear priority and proper procedures followed. This is of particular concern in Native communities.

Since high-stake tests are a reality, special efforts must be included in the school curricula regarding the administration of district and state assessments. Practice tests must be provided and test-taking strategies taught to students on an ongoing basis throughout the school year. Special and continual efforts need to be made to try and motivate students to do their best on these tests. The purpose of the tests and the test results and their meaning must be provided in a clear and understandable way to parents and students. It cannot be assumed that all students understand the mechanics of test taking such as appropriately filling in answer bubbles. The use of the answer sheet and all aspects of test taking need to be taught and reviewed. It is not a matter of teaching to any test. It is a matter of teaching students how to take tests, teaching useful strategies and techniques, how to infer and interpret, and ensuring optimal test taking conditions.

Some districts, of course, do some of the items mentioned above. But not all districts make sure that teachers present testing as important and valuable and explain the purpose of the tests to the students. Not all schools encourage students to perform optimally on the tests so we can assist them with learning. Students need to be encouraged to not mark answers at random and to not complete a few items then stop. Not all schools create a positive test-taking environment when these group tests are held. A testing schedule and an appropriate testing atmosphere need to be established. Testing notices, signs posted in schools and the post office can be set up. Motivational activities can be planned and incorporated on test-taking day. Parents need to be informed and there are many ways they can take part in the process besides encouraging their children to get the necessary rest and do well on the tests. There are many things districts can do to give value to the testing and promote more positive participation.

These high-stake tests are a reality. They are administered and used to make important decisions. They do not assess the whole child, they greatly affect the curriculum of the schools, and they are questionable as to their validity, their content and purpose. But they are a fact and schools can experience more reliable and useful results if they are administered and managed more correctly and if students are better prepared.

Suggestive Test Results

I take Louis off to the side and, in a one-on-one situation, I ask him to please raise his right hand, and he does so. Louis returns to a classroom of students, and I ask everyone to raise their right hand. Louis doesn't do so. He has already shown me that he is quite capable of understanding and carrying out this request. Something in the group situation interferes, and he doesn't raise his right hand. I found this to often be the case when I would ask my class as a whole to do something. A smattering of correct responses might occur. But if I made this same request to each individual student comprehension seemed to be no problem.

This is a peculiarity that was evident when noticing the large disparity between how many Native students performed on one-on-one diagnostic tests and how the same students achieved on group tests. In situations where one-on-one diagnostics tests such as the Woodcock Diagnostic Reading Battery and Running Records (or the Quality Reading Inventory for older students) were administered to the same student, the results were often in accord. They were generally at odds, though, with the results shown in a group achievement test for this same student.

Students A, B, C, and D are fairly typical examples. These are actual test results for four upper elementary Native students. The one-on-one diagnostic test administered was the Woodcock Diagnostic Reading Battery. The group achievement test was the Gates-McGinitie Reading Test. Both tests are norm-referenced. Findings were similar for the twenty-three students in a rural high school, grades nine and ten. Two of the students were non-Native (#2 and #14) and there is little discrepancy in their scores. The majority of the Native students have incongruous test results. The better performance on the one-on-one test may possibly relate to the Native student's tendency for personalism and being better motivated to do well for that individual test-giver.

Discrepancy Between One-on-One and Group Tests

Student	Reading Comp.	Vocab.	Reading Comp.	Vocab.
		Upper Elementary		
A	93%	94%	52%	32%
B	56%	84%	4%	33%
C	95%	93%	25%	40%
D	48%	48%	16%	13%
		Students Grade 9 and 10		
1	33		8	
2*	87		89	
3	94		68	
4	37		3	
5	41		9	
6	67		31	
7	32		13	
8	82		38	
9	59		41	
10	25		27	
11	28		22	
12	24		4	
13	92		70	
14*	86		90	
15	14		5	
16	75		4	
17	6		1	
18	94		52	
19	26		13	
20	45		70	
21	39		17	
22	54		47	
23	74		40	

Since the ramifications of test scores are so far reaching, this information raises serious questions and, if nothing else, gives cause for further study. But this significance could also be very important to the classroom teacher. Benchmark tests and other group test results are questionable as to their value and reliability in diagnosing student proficiency and in guiding instruction. There are so many factors affecting the validity and usefulness of test results, it can be stated summarily that, despite its common practice, it is simply unwise to make important decisions based on the results of any one assessment.

But According to This Test

In late August I was getting my homeroom class of twenty-eight village students underway when a messenger came into my room with an envelope. I glanced at it, saw that it was from the district office, set it on my desk and continued on with my students.

About ten minutes into the period there was this commotion at the door. I went over and there was an older Yup'ik man in hip boots. He wore a coat in the manner done on a hot day with his arms through the sleeves, but with the back pulled down off his shoulders hanging loosely from near his waist. He was sun darkened, and it was likely that he had just left his boat on the nearby riverbank and walked up to the school.

He said to me his son's name, and I motioned for him to come on in. The man saw his boy, remained by the door and spoke to him at his desk at length in Yup'ik. The son stood, looked through his pockets and supplied an extensive response in Yup'ik to his father. They continued with several more lengthy exchanges, then the father smiled at me, said "quyana," and he left. We continued on with class.

After the period was over, I opened up the envelope. It contained some test results for this very boy that indicated he is "English Only" and is not a Yup'ik speaker.

Good Or Bad, Who Is To Say?

Just as making decisions regarding a student based on the results of one narrow assessment instrument is folly, judging school and educator effectiveness on these same results is equally so. Important and life altering decisions are often made based on the results of these extremely limited exams.

Teachers are also evaluated by a video: don't take education courses, take acting classes! Teachers in a remote village school with indigenous students will be judged by "expert" educators who have not necessarily been trained as to how to work effectively with Native students.

Do they know about wait time? Posture? Proximity? Are the evaluators aware of the appropriate tempo required in a village classroom? Do they know that sometimes it is best to leave a student alone and not force him or her to turn to the page asked? Do these evaluators know the ineffectiveness of long verbal explanations of abstract, decontextualized material or asking some students to independently acquire information from grade level texts?

Have these evaluators ever faced and solved the difficulties of teaching in a remote, multi-aged classroom of aboriginal students with extreme differences in proficiency, maturity, and home life? Does the evaluator understand that the surly, longhaired boy who came into the class fifteen minutes into the video and put his head down on his desk has an extremely difficult living situation? The teacher knows him well and doesn't force him to participate because 1) The teacher is really happy that he has come to class and 2) The teacher has learned how to positively interact with this student by giving him space and time when he knows he needs it in order to prevent a disruption and further alienation. Even if this is attempted to be explained in the narrative accompanying the video, the evaluator may not understand and view this as inappropriate behavior on the teacher's part.

Many of the skills required to successfully deal with the dynamics and complexities of a village classroom are unique to that extremely challenging situation. It is far more complicated than meets the eye and even if an "expert" evaluator once taught in these circumstances, it doesn't mean that it was a successful experience and that he/she is capable of watching a video and judging another teacher's effectiveness and worth in this snapshot of a movie.

Thus, we have teachers who may or may not have had experience in village schools, who have not been trained in cross-cultural and Native education issues, mentoring new teachers. We have similar educators evaluating the worth of teachers teaching in village classrooms by watching a video. And we make important decisions about children and schools based on the results of tests with highly questionable reliability and worth.

Full of Questions

When I first moved to rural Alaska I overheard an elder Yup'ik woman tell her friend how "Kass'aqs are just full of questions." Westerners are often uncomfortable with silence in social situations. Many Native people are just the opposite. To fill the silence, westerners tend to ask questions. That keeps the conversation going and occupies the awkward quiet.

At this time many of my students were from surrounding villages. They would come and go frequently. It was not unusual to have a new student several times a week. Since I had large classes I put together an information sheet for these new students to try get to know them a bit, as well as to give them something to do while I got the other thirty-some students in the class engaged.

On the paper the student was asked a series of questions. What village are you from? What do you like most about school? What are two of your favorite things to do away from school? etc. Invariably I would get the form back from the student and find that he or she wrote their name at the top in the blank and that was about it.

After several unsuccessful tries I received one from a new girl who filled out her name and then wrote in big letters diagonally across the page, "So nosey!!" It dawned on me that I was another Kass'aq full of questions.

I went back to the drawing board and eliminated all the questions and, instead, left blanks for the student to complete a sentence (the Cloze technique). This is what it took. There seemed to be no problem with new students filling out my information sheet now. It was no longer an interrogation. I carried this concept into other areas of teaching and began limiting my questions in class discussions and on tests and found other ways to get "answers" to see if comprehension was taking place.

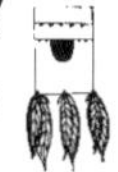

What Works? What Doesn't?
Pass It On
How?

Whether informal discoveries such as in the anecdote above, the results of an individual educator's personal classroom research, or full-fledged, serious academic study, there is no organized means to inform the educators in need of such information regarding what does and doesn't work.

Ms. REI goes to a village and unintentionally commits blunder after blunder. By the time she figures it out to some degree, she moves on. Mr. Hunter arrives and commits some of the same blunders along with maybe a few new ones. Mr. Hunter might stay on for six or maybe fifteen years. That he is committing errors may never dawn on him. He establishes a comfort zone and digs in and the students just have to adapt to his way of doing things.

There are no means, no overlap in place designed to rectify the blunders that occur or that identifies what is working and what is not in order for the next educators in line to learn from the past. Some new teachers begin in August with no information available as to what went on in the school even during the last year. Assessment information on individual students may not be readily available. How tight or loose the ship was run by the previous teachers and administration is not known. If it was loose with low academic and behavioral demands, new staff will have difficulties for a while in developing a new structure, a new routine with new expectations.

There is also no mechanism to evaluate the effectiveness of the various teaching resources so that the information can be shared with other schools or districts and, thus, prevent wasted monies. The acquisition of teacher resources in the schools is often reflective of the likes and dislikes of those educators who come and go. This is why in many rural districts there are school basements, attics, and storage sheds full of various texts and instructional resources that became out of favor.

Some districts have procedures for reviewing and selecting new resources. Some do not. Mrs. Dee comes from Tennessee where she taught world history for several years using a certain text. Now she is in the village of Kavik and wants to use that same book she is accustomed to; student copies are ordered and used for the two years she is there; they are placed in a storage shed when she leaves because Mr. Max prefers a different text. Some resources are purchased due to grant requirements. Many are culturally irrelevant and some have too difficult of a reading level. Some texts, no matter their appropriateness, are simply used unsuccessfully because teachers ask students who are not yet capable, to independently acquire information from them.

Decisions need to be made concerning resource acquisition based on factors other than what is convenient for teachers due to them being comfortable and familiar with the materials because they have used them in the past. But there appears to be no one home to review assessments, discuss the resources with teachers and students, and analyze the effectiveness and value of the texts and materials in use. Say Phonics X is the adopted district program and is used in the classrooms. Looking at the reading assessment results it is evident that the majority of the students are having substantial difficulties with word attack skills. This resource and the manner in which decoding skills are taught need to be reviewed, questioned and possibly altered.

Some resources are certainly more effective than others. It would be tremendously valuable to discover what works, what doesn't work, and then communicate this information to other schools and districts. Currently there is no organized means of determining what resources are most successful when working with Native students. This results in wasted monies, wasted efforts.

Read All About It!

So, where do people like Dave and Debbie go to prepare themselves to live and teach in a remote village school since they do not receive this preparation from anywhere else? They are probably not even aware of the need. They have credentials that confirm they are trained, certified teachers. They are, naturally, more concerned about housing, purchasing proper clothing, deciding what to pack, and how they are going to obtain groceries. If they need some additional training and information, they assume the district or the state will supply it.

There is a multitude of publications related to Alaska Natives, Native education, and teaching in Alaska. There is a slew of pamphlets and resources that have been published over the years. Some are quite valuable and would be very useful to Dave and Debbie. At casual glance at my bookshelf I see issues of *Promising Practices*, and *The Wisdom of Practice for Rural Schools*, *Profiles of Exemplary School-Based Programs for At-Risk Youth*, *Village Science*, and numerous other such sources. There are dozens of resources available from the Alaska Native Knowledge Network.

The problem for Dave and Debbie and others like them is that it is a jumble of information. The resources are not consolidated, and there is no easy access or way of determining the usefulness of all that is available. The ability to make sense of all this information and to determine just what it means to a classroom teacher in Hoonah or a principal in Kiana is overwhelming, particularly for new educators. Most often new educators simply don't have the time to seek out and familiarize themselves with such materials.

The purpose here is not to provide even a partial bibliography of useful and relevant resources. In the 1960's and 70's several very pertinent resources were made available. They seemed to have influenced positively some individuals, but did not become a part of any concerted or lasting effort to train and prepare educators regarding cross-cultural issues and Native education. They remain on library shelves. Some are as appropriate now as they were decades ago.

One example is ***Alaskan Eskimo Education, A Film Analysis of Cultural Confrontation in the Schools*** by John Collier. Jr. (concerning Indian and Eskimo students). This booklet is a thoughtful and informative work. It specifically addresses cross-cultural concerns and provides historical context in a manner that is rare to find. Another is the Kleinfeld article referred to previously, *Effective Teachers of Indian and Eskimo High School Students*. These resources contain the kinds of information that would be quite valuable to Dave and Debbie, State mentors, and those evaluating village teachers. But it is left to individual educators, when they can find the time, to seek out on their own such knowledge, and to read and synthesize what the contents mean to their teaching situation.

Many useful resources are not necessarily directly concerned with education. The information provided, though, can be most beneficial in learning the history of an area and its people. An example would be ***Bashful No Longer, An Alaskan Eskimo Anthology, 1778-1981*** by Wendall H. Oswalt. This book gives an interesting and valuable understanding of the mid-Kuskokwim area. It is not explicitly explained within just what this means to an educator. Individuals who have discovered this resource, just like many other important sources, must determine its usefulness and applications for the classroom themselves. An individual moving from a Tlingit village in Southeast Alaska might find it valuable information to read Oswalt's explanation as to some reasons why the Native people in the mid-Kuskokwim are so unlike the students he/she was teaching previously. The history of the area was greatly affected by the manner in which westerners interacted with the indigenous population due to access to the region. The degree of Westernization has been more limited and more recent than what has taken place in other locations in Alaska. Books such as this provide the visiting educator with a background and better understanding of the students and people in the community.

The impact of missionaries and entrepreneurs, of flu epidemics and tuberculosis are documented and important for educators to know prior to entering the homeland of the students they are to teach. Some villages were actually bombed by the United States military. There was forced internment of hundreds of Native people in Alaska during World War II. It is obvious that an educator informed of the history of the place and the people will have a greater respect and understanding of his/her temporary home and his/her minor role in the larger picture. Further discussion on this topic as well as other important, relevant resources are mentioned elsewhere in this text.

Since there is no organized manner in which educators new to the state are supplied useful and valuable resources, it is left up to the diligence, determination and inquisitiveness of individuals to seek out such information. Dave and Debbie have no idea what resources are available, appropriate, useful, or disingenuous.

The one hundred and sixty-six page section on Eskimos in Coles' book, ***Children In Crisis*** is an example of a resource Dave and Debbie might run across. It is based on his observations of four boys and four girls during his summer visits to their homes in Noorvik and a coastal village. This book has been used as a text for some university Native education courses. Not all the information he writes is invalid. But the majority of it should not be accepted as reality or necessarily considered useful. It can be deceptive.

He explains the writing resulting from this method of information gathering as being "in the tradition of the social essay" (p. 59). It is his reactions and opinions that are made into a narrative-type of, supposedly, non-fiction. The problem is that it is presented as fact, and undoubtedly generally read as a description of the way things are. The author explains that he would be the last to deny the subjective element in his work (p. 59). But it doesn't do Dave and Debbie or anyone else any favors when a group of people is romanticized and opinions are published and presented as fact.

It seems that Coles is partially aware of the reasons that some of his conclusions and comments should be questioned and accepted cautiously. His observations took place in the summer, and he mentions that "he will never know whether the particularly relaxed, thoughtful, gentle attitude of the children during the summer months was the result of his familiarity with them or had a great deal to do with the season itself" (p. 51).

The summer months are short and vastly different from the long winter. The wintertime is one of extremes. The area becomes a dark, windy, extremely cold, remote area of snow and ice. An understanding of winter's influence on the psychology and behavior of the inhabitants can only be acquired by being a part of it. Coles writes that, during the winter, "the whole world bears down on Eskimo homes, on the villages, for long months of the year" (p. 194). He is not writing this from personal experience. He would have to live there during this time to actually observe the attitudes, feelings, and the results of this environment on the people. They cannot be experienced through brief visits during the winter, let alone just the summer. It takes a day-to-day, month on month endurance of this very odd and powerful environment to be able to write of it truly. One of the major experiences and influences on these children's lives is not even a part of his essay.

Several times he writes of how friendly and kind the Eskimos are, and how they smile at him. Then he explains, too, in another section that an Eskimo "will feel inclined to welcome strangers, however arrogant, and smile at them, no matter what they say or do" (p. 123). He mentions, also, that the Eskimo will agree with white people, listen to what they say, "say yes, yes, and they keep moving their heads up and down. Later when they are alone, they will laugh and shake their heads back and forth instead of up and down" (p. 120). He writes that Eskimos feel the white people are often "full of themselves and, really, quite ignorant" (p. 118). But Coles isn't immune to this: he is non-Native, an outsider, and possibly was considered and treated in the very manner he describes above.

Coles intellectualizes and reads into the children's behavior to such a high degree that somehow he is able to interpret what the children think and feel. He writes that Eskimo children, even those far up river, "regard the ice and snow around them as ultimately the ocean's property" (p. 27). Coles explains that while one child was drawing, she was thinking of how "the machine is no match for the world in all its threatening, awesome and occasionally quite beckoning presence" (p. 75). He credits them, too, with "knowing enough to not get hypnotized and fooled by Western industrialism" (p. 75). As a group of children walk towards the river, he interprets it as a "religious procession" (p. 197). He continues by saying that "white people don't know how to thank the wind or smile gratefully at the river" (p. 200).

Are children as conscious and capable of such abstract poetic thought and feeling? He writes that, "to many white outsiders, the Eskimo has become a romanticized reproof to all other human beings" (p. 223). Coles perpetuates this notion and further romanticizes the Eskimo people with his imaginings.

Coles explains that when the Eskimos drink a lot "they usually don't let loose, show a truculent, nasty, mean side. They seem as quiet and considerate as ever: still courtly, a touch different, a touch amused at the world's ups and downs... " (p. 205). This is an absurd statement to anyone who is aware of the statistics and the degree that alcohol abuse threatens the Native culture. Close to one hundred per cent of all crimes that Eskimos are involved in are alcohol related. Many of these are quite violent and horrendous crimes.

Coles does make some observations that would be valuable to Dave and Debbie as teachers. It is evident to him that the Eskimos do not "take issues directly and vocally with outsiders" (p. 119). This often includes the teacher or an administrator. Some Native school board members are quick to accept whatever the superintendent suggests without any challenge or question.

Especially important to the classroom is the evident low amount of verbal interaction, "one word can take the place of dozens of sentences" (p. 191). Also it could be observed how Eskimos "do not make a lot of inquiries, not to ask one why or what or how after another" (p. 197). He describes that there is rarely any shouting done. Sharp words are seldom used. Also, the children "rarely play alone, they are not solitary" (p. 210). Their cooperating behavior is obvious to Coles. These are the kind of observations that are valuable for educators to consider.

If Dave and Debbie managed to read Coles' book in preparation for their new position as village teachers, they would not know which observations and comments are valid and useful. It illustrates how finding appropriate and valuable resources for uninformed educators is difficult and that, sometimes, they can be misleading.

As It Is

There is no process in place that ensures educators have access to or are provided the much-needed information to assist them in successfully working with Native students. This means it is up to an individual educator's integrity, priorities, sense of responsibility and initiative to educate one's self by whatever means possible.

Whether it concerns educator-student interactions, teaching methodologies, instructional resources, educator training and preparation, or the use and administration of state, district and individual student assessments, the system that is and has been in place to educate

Alaska Natives is sorely wanting. To coordinate and make available what is appropriate and inappropriate and what is educationally sound practice in village schools, and to prevent the chaos and lack of continuity, a means must be established to progress and escape from the status quo for the sake of indigenous people however inconvenient that might be for educators. But as the adage explains, most people are more comfortable with old problems than with new solutions. By allowing Native education to continue in the manner it is and has been, schooling perpetuates the antisocial, destructive behaviors and poor academic performances exhibited by much or our indigenous youth.

Clif Bates

SECTION II: AS IT COULD BE

A Different View of Culturally Responsive Schools

CHAPTER 10

Considerations for Policy Makers, School Board Members, Educators, Parents and Other Interested Folk by Clifton Bates

"The challenge of Indian education is that we generally agree on why it has failed, but remain confused on its practical solution. Its failure is in the destructive impact of white education on Native children. This culture shock appears to divide children from self and it degrades children's most formative years of environment and family. But even more threateningly, it can distract and destroy cognition. The affect of this "jangling" is sluggish thinking, lowered achievement in school and later in adult life. This disfigurement has been seen for many years and has obscured further causes of failure which may impede the educational emergence of many Native peoples." Collier J.

Neither the traditional schooling system nor the Quality Schools Initiative model take into consideration the specific needs of Native students in regards to educator training, language considerations, and cross-cultural issues nor do they involve altering curriculum, instruction and assessments specifically for Native children. Incorporating culturally relevant activities and resources in the curriculum are certainly integral to positive changes. The considerations mentioned here do not negate the efforts made by the Alaska Rural Systemic Initiative, the Alaska Native Knowledge Network or other such programs attempting to improve indigenous education. All these resources along with increasing the number of Alaska Native educators can act in concert with this new discussion on other practical means for making our schools truly culturally responsive.

Educators, dedicated to the success of their Native students, will have to begin by acknowledging their current failure. They will have to decide to do things differently. Grant & Gillispie, 1993

The recommendations provided here are not exhaustive; they are intertwined but fall into three main areas. They relate to:

A. Curriculum, Instruction, and Assessment
B. Establishing/Implementing Researched-based Structures
C. Mandatory Educator Training: The Development of Training Centers

Examples of Training Curricula:
Cross-cultural Concerns Regarding History
Cross-cultural Concerns Regarding Communication

A. CURRICULUM, INSTRUCTION, ASSESSMENT
Practical Proposals

Due to state and some grant requirements as well as district procedures, school districts annually obtain opinions, attitudes, recommendations and various input from students, parents and community members regarding different aspects of the local schools. Hands down the results in rural districts are nearly identical year after year. Parents want their children to be competent in basic skills, and they want their culture reflected in and respected by the school and by educators.

There is nothing wrong with assessing and ensuring each student graduating possesses basic skills in English. And, unless there is a disability, Native students are quite capable of acquiring and demonstrating competence in these areas as anyone else. But the manner in which the education system is and has been operating, does not allow the majority of them to do so. This first set of proposals relates to making adaptations in curriculum, instruction and assessment.

The western education system is designed for students who *tend* to be linear, sequential, auditory, and competitive. They relate to the past and the future and are individually oriented. There is more of a professional relationship between self and educators. They are highly verbal, operate with a fast-paced dialogue and interaction, learn via long verbal explanations and text material, possess an internal locus of control and feel that learning is a product of effort. They have a rich set of literacy experiences and have acquired a similar wide range of background information prior to entering the school.

But Native children tend to possess characteristics that are at polar opposites. Not only are the schools staffed mostly with individuals who are at home with the descriptors just mentioned, but student success is largely dependent upon possessing those characteristics. For the student who is reflective, holistic; learns though observation; is skilled in non-verbal communication; relies on a personal relationship with educators; is strong in spatial ability and perceptual skills; is weak in school language ability and has difficulties comprehending lengthy verbal explanations and text material; is comfortable with long wait time and slow-paced activities; has an external locus of control; and whose language experiences and background knowledge are so unlike that of the school, the disparity is clear. One would think so, but the school marches on, oblivious to this mismatch and cultural discontinuity results.

"It appears that cultural mismatching between home and school often starts a cycle of failure for Native students, which is hard to break once begun... Studies have shown that instructional styles resembling the learning contexts of the home and community are more effective with Native learners than the pedagogical strategy of teachers calling on students to elicit verbal responses." (Erikson, 1963; Krashen, 1982. Grant & Gillispie, 1993

There are various generic educational sound practices identified as being characteristic of effective classrooms, effective schools, and effective school districts anywhere. But there are practices that are known to be particularly effective or ineffective when teaching Alaska Native children. Hands-on and cooperative learning; concerns regarding wait time, pacing, and relevancy are a few of the strategies and issues found in most resources that speak to teaching Native children. My intent is not to delineate all these characteristics here, but to bring attention to a few specific areas that are usually ignored when it comes to discussing education and Alaska Natives and in creating more comprehensive culturally responsive schools.

The example instructional strategies mentioned herein are only used to illustrate a point or a concept that could be included as a part of more comprehensive efforts. There are educators who have developed tremendously creative programs (such as what Mike Hull was able to accomplish in Russian Mission a few years ago. See *http://www.adn.com/front/story/4746155p-4692841c.html).* They can offer all kinds of specific examples of entire cultural units, approaches, and ways of revamping the school day in a new, relevant and effective manner. A means of bringing together the successful work that has been accomplished is needed so badly in order to construct sustained efforts that can be assessed, adjusted, and that do not disappear when the energetic, perceptive creators move away or retire.

Oral Language

The reading difficulties of many Native students are evident in test scores and classroom lessons. The natural tendency then to correct this is to teach more reading. If we do not make the necessary changes, students will continue experiencing cognitive confusion at the integration level resulting in reading disabilities. The oral tradition of many Native cultures should not be confused with the concerns related to oral language proficiency in the language of the school.

"The way to literacy does not lie through literacy. An early immersion in literacy in fact only blocks the way. As teachers and parents become more and more nervous about their children's ability to read and write, they need to back off from the natural desire to increase the pressure for more literacy instruction. Take youngsters out of the current linguistic limbo they find themselves in and move them back into the key experience they have missed--orality." ***A Is for Ox*, Barry Sanders**

Of the near one hundred Native children ages six through eight who were tested by the one-on-one Woodcock Diagnostic Reading Battery in the late nineties, the oral language component indicated that English language spoken at their age level was difficult, extremely difficult or impossible for them to comprehend. Teachers who are experienced working with Native children are familiar with the one or two word reply, the raise of the eyebrows, or the shrug of the shoulders instead of any lengthy verbal responses. Assessments, over time, clearly show that oral language proficiency in the language of the school is nowhere near being adequately developed in the majority of Native children in order for them to fit into the demands of the current school model.

As Coles (1977) writes, "young boys and girls often avoid sentences because their parents are quite content to use one word or two, rather than make a statement or ask a question or give a command" (p. 193). He explains, too, that one word may take the place of dozens of sentences (p. 192), that the Eskimo has no tradition of formal schools, and that learning has been done through experience and observing demonstration".

Some Native cultures tend to not only have a very low degree of verbal interaction, but the verbal interaction that does take place is highly contextualized in nature. Collier (1973) succinctly explains:

"The impact of White schools on Eskimo learning affected not only style and content but also the method and focus of learning. Traditional Eskimo learning was fundamentally a training in observation and the analysis of this sensory reception. Content was frequently nonverbal and ecological in experience—weather prediction, ice prediction, warnings of blizzards, the drift of game. White learning shifted attention to the verbal and the literate, which had survival value in abstract circumstances usually unrelated to the natural world surrounding the school. Humanly, the instructor's role was shifted from village men to strangers teaching content administered from Seattle and Washington D.C." (p. 39).

The purpose of oral communication "in the village culture was for maintenance of day-to-day transactions in village life. It was not regarded as a means of manipulating the environment, influencing others or as a tool for making way in the world" Salisbury, 1969, (p. 27). With the arrival of White traders, missionaries, teachers and government agencies, the purpose of speaking English was "to communicate with a paternalistic establishment. It was for dealing with authority that was there to help the Eskimo because it knew what was best for him" (Salisbury, p. 30). Speaking English for the Eskimo has always been done from a subordinate role.

"Oral language is the foundation upon which the written language system is built. If that foundation is shaky, we can expect a significant impact on the child's performance of written language tasks such as reading, writing, and spelling." The Language Deficient Child, Zirkelbach, Blakesley, Academic Therapy, 1985, page 605

But what about all the television the children watch nowadays in the villages? TV is always on; they hear all kinds of language. Doesn't this translate to increased English listening and speaking skills? This is a gut-level opinion frequently mentioned to counter comments regarding the need for extraordinary efforts toward developing oral language proficiency in Native students.

Television, though, does not provide the necessary interaction between humans. Participation is not required. There is no need for a child to indicate comprehension when watching TV. It does not provide practice with language usage nor any assistance in conversing.

"Television stands several steps from orality... (it) kills the human voice... images pass by too fast for young minds to consider or analyze them." (P. 38). TV viewers are passive recipients who are unable to take part in any real language usage or reciprocal dialogue. Instead "it reduces the complexity of living to a simple set of equations. It projects conflict and the most serious of social problems as entertainment" (Page 48). The Native child can disengage with ease to the TV language, tune in, tune out at will; just as when a teacher explains mitosis or the causes of the Korean War.

Oral language instruction needs to be a purposeful, sequential, definite part of the curriculum and not merely isolated activities that occur sporadically. Otherwise we will continue creating what Dr. David Elkind refers to as the curriculum disabled child: a child who fails in school because we introduced too much, too soon, and in the wrong way.

"In children with low English proficiency, "spoken language must come before written language; it is extremely hard to read a language that is still incomprehensible... In this case, the initial instructional priority should be developing the children's oral proficiency in English. Print materials may be used to support the development of English language skills. But formal reading instruction in English should be postponed until an adequate level of oral proficiency in English has been established." *Starting Out Right: A Guide to Promoting Children's Reading Success*, National Research Council, 1999, pp. 131-132.

Our schools in general tend to give listening and speaking skill development a very limited amount of attention. In our rural schools evidence shows us that we must emphasize oral language development in our Alaska Native students. We have to ensure that an adequate foundation of listening and speaking skills in the school language is established before and as we ask these children to read and write. Head Start, preschools and a district's school readiness efforts must reflect these needs and not simply replicate such programs that are found anywhere else.

There are adequate, exemplary resources available to help in teaching these skills. Oral language development needs to be a definite strand that runs through the K-12 curriculum, but it must particularly be a significant part of school readiness activities and the first five years of schooling.

"One major task is to continue including expressive oral language activities amid requirements for more and more written-language activities. *The second major task* is to develop oral language curricula; that is, a thoughtfully organized, sequential set of experiences leading logically through the grades. The cumulative effect of such a coherent program of activities will be greater than the now-too-common random assortment of experiences." J. Stewig, 1988

Educators need to stop over-emphasizing teaching Native children to read and write before they are cognitively ready, before they possess adequate listening and speaking skills in this school setting and before they have acquired basic concepts about print. We cannot assume students know such concepts as 'letter' and 'word' or that print moves from left to right.

Inadequate oral language proficiency not only inhibits literacy development, but all areas of the education process. Individuals require oral language facility and an adequate reservoir of vocabulary to employ inner dialogue for problem solving as well as identifying and interpreting emotions and feelings. It is difficult to have meaningful, detailed conversations within one's own mind if there is limited vocabulary to draw from to label and describe such abstractions.

Our rural schools do not take into account what is developmentally appropriate school language-wise. An adequate oral language foundation in English is not established in village students; there are reading difficulties, so more reading is taught; then the system proceeds as it is accustomed and students are asked to read to learn before they have learned to read.

This proposal requires the school model to take into account the environmental and cultural factors affecting Native students' school language abilities. Thus, the standard curriculum, instruction and assessment are altered by:

• ensuring school readiness skills (with an emphasis on oral language development) are a definite part of the school district's efforts;

• including a definite, purposeful, sequential oral language curriculum that is far more than sporadic, random oral language activities;

• training educators as to the critical role of oral language proficiency as it relates to Native students' situation, its relationship to literacy and to problem solving;

• training educators in oral language instructional activities in order to carry across the oral language curriculum:

• assessing students regularly in oral language proficiency with the goal of students at least reaching and maintaining age-level proficiency in the school language:

• training educators in interpreting assessments and how the assessment results effect and help guide instruction.

Currently the Dibels is probably the most commonly used assessment that has an oral language component. Each section of this test takes about one minute to administer to elementary students. It does not test listening comprehension, and it provides no information that will monitor growth or provide any guidance for instruction concerning oral language proficiencies. It is not adequate for determining the oral language competencies of Native students, and it does not provide any diagnosis that will assist a teacher beyond letter sound identification information. The State's interest in Dibel's assessment results focuses on the two subtests concerning phonics.

The other program that contains an oral language component is the one developed by Linda Mood-Bell. Some districts have adopted this approach but it does not come close to meeting the needs outlined in the bullet points above.

"Without significant, numerous, and to-some-degree standardized assessment measures, oral language will not be included systematically in the curriculum." Stewig, 1988. Oral Language: A Place in the Curriculum? The Clearing House, p. 173

Incorporate Strengths
Spatial Ability and Perceptual Skills

As previously stated, the education system concentrates on the weakness of many Native students: verbal ability in the language of the school. This same system does not provide adequate opportunity for Native students to demonstrate their unique cognitive strengths: observation, perceptual skills and spatial ability. The school day particularly emphasizes abstract verbal tasks (listening, speaking, reading and writing) in the school language. Other than sports, extracurricular offerings are usually such activities as Battle of the Books, Academic Decathlon, and Spelling Bees, all concentrating on verbal abilities.

Spatial ability and perceptual skills can be included in the curriculum in a variety of ways: mapping, geometry, mechanics, drawing, carving, and model building are some examples. The Vocational Industrial Club of America (VICA) provides some opportunities in these areas, but it is not something that is available in many village schools. Ensuring the inclusion of activities involving these other intelligences cannot help but assist in developing positive self-esteem and a more favorable attitude toward school in students who are experiencing negative rewards in an academic verbal world.

We cannot continue concentrating on the weaknesses of these students, expecting them to fit into this model and, at the same time, ignore their unique strengths. Tasks that involve or rely on such skills could be made a part of school competitions such as Academic Decathlon. Schools can use the students' special cognitive strengths to assist in developing proficiency in their area of weakness.

This would be particularly helpful beginning around age eight. Third grade is often the time when content area information is being taught to these students via teacher explanations and text. It is when they begin to be asked to read to learn. But a good percentage has not yet learned to read sufficiently. Many students, especially male students, begin to sense that this place called school is not as enjoyable as they had hoped. Doesn't seem to be much there they are very good at except play and sports. The rest is a lot of fast-paced, irrelevant, abstract language and confusing demands and questioning being made upon them. Caruso's growing lack of motivation over time is understandable.

Build the Bridge
Contextualized and Decontextualized
Oral and Written Material

There are a variety of known techniques that teachers can incorporate to assist all students having difficulties comprehending text material. Familiarizing students with how texts are written and organized, pre-reading activities, previewing vocabulary, rewriting text passages, and various guided reading strategies are some valuable methods teachers can utilize.

But just as tasks that relate to spatial ability and perceptual skills can be incorporated to help Native students gain proficiency in verbal skills, their area of weakness, contextualized material can be used to assist them in comprehending decontextualized lecture and text. Special efforts must be made to assist students in making the bridge between contextualized oral and written language and decontextualized oral and written language. If we do not do make such changes, students will continue experiencing comprehension difficulties and continue developing negative attitudes toward themselves and school.

Contextualized oral language is face-to-face conversation involving clarification words such as here, there, me, you, etc. The language is used in context with facial expressions, body language, hand gestures and known information. The circumstances within which the discourse takes place assist in understanding. Contextualized written language is a step removed from oral discourse. It is communication such as used in the language experience approach, in letters, e-mails, and notes. It is personalized, familiar and circumstances and known information still assist in comprehension.

Decontextualized communication is several steps removed from contextualized oral or written discourse. Lectures, reading aloud, and certain story telling are examples of decontextualized oral communication. Text material, novels, and subject area content are examples of decontextualized written communication. The western school system's means of knowledge transfer emphasizes lecture and text.

Before students have adequately acquired the skills to communicate in contextualized oral language in the school setting in "school language", we ask them to demonstrate abilities in decontextualized oral and written discourse dealing with unfamiliar abstracts and concepts. There is a leap that must take place from comprehending face-to-face dialogue to understanding text materials. This is a particularly significant leap for students with the environmental and experiential backgrounds and cultural traits as those of Native students in village Alaska. There are many strategies available to help students make this leap to comprehending decontextualized written and oral communication.

There is a variety of ways to adapt the school model to better assist Native students in bridging contextualized oral language to decontextualized written language and to develop proficiencies in all areas of literacy. A very real goal, as with all students, is that Native students will acquire information and knowledge by listening to long verbal explanations in English and by independently reading texts. This is another example of it not being a matter of Native students being unable do these things, but more a matter of them not learning how to by repetitively asking them to do so.

Communication	Oral	Written
Contextualized	Face-to-face conversation, local story-telling, telephone, CB radio	Letters, notes, emails, personal communications
Decontextualized	Lecture, some story-telling	Text, novels, content/ subject information

Nagy, W.

An Assignment

Read the following passage. Let us call it Chapter Three. After you finish reading it, please answer the questions at the end of the chapter. The reason you are being asked to read this and if all the content is or is not of equal importance will remain a mystery until you are tested on the material on Friday.

Chapter Three

"Except as explained in the succeeding paragraphs of this section, the Federal share of the property shall be the same percentage as the Federal share of the acquiring party's total costs under the grant during the grant or subgrant year (or other funding period) to which the acquisition cost of the property was charged. For this purpose, "cost under the grant" means allowable costs which are either borne by the grant or counted towards satisfying a cost-sharing or matching requirement of the grant. Only costs are to be counted—not the value of third-party in-kind contributions. Moreover, if the property was acquired by a grantee that awarded subgrants, costs incurred by its subgrantees shall be included only to the extent borne by the subgrants."

— Federal Grant Register

End of the Chapter Question--Due before the test on Friday:
1. Is the Federal share of the property always the same percentage as the Federal share of the property of the acquiring party's total cost under the grant during the subgrant year of the property charged? If yes: Why? If not: Why not? Explain.

This type of assignment, to one degree or another and despite its ineffectiveness, is still used as a mode of instruction in some village classrooms. Students are asked to get information on their own by reading decontextualized text. Then they are to respond to questions concerning that material, and then they are tested to see if comprehension took place. Often it isn't clarified at the outset just what the teacher wants the students to know and be able to do. The students approach the assignment under the assumption that all that is written is of equal importance, and they may even try to read it as if it is a story.

What you felt upon reading Chapter Three is possibly similar to the reaction many Native students experience when asked to read some content area information. They are usually asked to do so beginning in grade three. Over time some Native students simply reject the text and do not even attempt to read the assignment. They have learned that such reading material is meaningless to them. It is irrelevant, uninteresting, frustrating, and certainly unrewarding.

Reading specialists explain that the knowledge and experience a person brings to the reading material largely determines his/her ability to comprehend what is written. If you have been employed as a grant writer, Chapter Three might make perfect sense to you. You are familiar with grant language and have had experience that helps you accept and have access to what is written. There is reduced interference in allowing you to understand this passage.

But to a reader with no experiences related to federal grant writing, there is nothing within the text in this assignment that assists in comprehension. It is decontextualized written material. Would this be interesting to you at twelve? At eighteen? Now? Is it applicable to your life at all? Is there anything in that section of writing that means anything, is relevant or is of any interest to you? The information in health, science, and social studies that Kim-boy was being asked to read was not only heavily decontextualized, but it was also undoubtedly written on a higher reading level than his proficiency in reading English: thus, no wrestling for Kim-boy. The eligibility issue in rural Alaska has always been built on a false premise. The one thing that Kim-boy has found he can do well, the one thing that is keeping him in school, he is not allowed to participate in because the academic tasks he is asked to do are simply beyond his capabilities.

Your high achieving, western student might read the decontextualized text that is assigned and try hard to understand and maybe even arrive at a correct response to the "chapter question". His or her purpose in completing this assignment is likely to be an attempt at being correct in order to get a good grade and/or parental praise. But such material is likely to be immediately rejected by Kim-boy in village Alaska. There is nothing to which he can relate. There is no purpose in dealing with this jumble of meaningless, irrelevant words. He learned that much long ago and, at this point, he doesn't even waste his time trying.

The goal, though, is to teach Kim-boy so that he is capable of independently reading and comprehending decontextualized material. But he needs to be assisted in reaching this goal. Again, by continually asking him to do such a task, does not teach him how. Appendices 1 and 2 provide examples of activities that illustrate the use of context to assist students in making the transition so decontextualized oral and written communication can be better comprehended.

Cart Before the Horse

It was new computer software designed to teach the local Native language. The teachers, all elderly Native ladies from the surrounding villages, were gathered to attend this training so they could use this program with their students at their school back home. The trainer was well versed in computers and software, was a former classroom teacher, and he was prepared to show these language instructors how to use this new resource.

His computer screen was projected on the wall so all could see. He explained how the program progressed from basic to more complex language usage, and that it was set up to replicate the Total Physical Response method of teaching. He clicked on an image, talked some more, and went on to the next step in his presentation.

Eventually he looked over and saw that all his students were watching one woman who was standing and had moved as far as her mouse wire would let her as she tried to get the cursor to go where she wanted. She had her hand over her mouth and was giggling quietly.
It dawned on him then. They had never used a computer

before. He was progressing through his Power Points when he realized that his students were quite far from being prepared for even his very beginning.

Models and False Assumptions

It was Fred Astaire who said something along the lines that a difficult task for kids to face in these modern times is learning good manners since they seldom get to witness what good manners look like in this often, rude society. It is the same in village schools where it is difficult to ask many students to do certain tasks that they have no experience witnessing. Teachers often try in vain to get students to discuss a book, a piece of writing or a controversial topic assuming the students know what such a discussion or a debate looks like.

Asking students to take part in a classroom discussion is like asking students to obtain information independently from a textbook: the skill or ability cannot be taught merely by continually requesting that the students do this. It is not necessarily that the students are unwilling to do what the teacher asks. It is more likely they simply do not know what to do because, for example, they have never seen such a discussion.

If short, scripted videos as models of Native student "actors" effectively discussing a book or debating an issue were available for teachers to show their students, they could then see what such a task they are being asked to do looks like. Since such videos are not available, a teacher could script a discussion or a debate for a group of students. This would serve as a model that could lead to the students independently, with no prompts, participating.

Teachers often proceed with the teaching of reading as the computer trainer did with the Native language instructors. He was teaching how to use the software program before they knew basic computer usage. Teachers sometimes teach Native students to read before they have developed concepts about print, can identify letters and sounds, and before they have acquired an adequate oral language proficiency. Upper elementary and secondary teachers, usually unaware of each student's reading level, ask the students to read to learn before they have sufficiently learned to read.

Certain C&I/Assessment Suggestions in Sum

There are various ways to adapt the school system in the areas of curriculum, instruction and assessment to better meet the needs and characteristics of Alaska Native students. A few that are mentioned are:

•the need for a substantial oral language curriculum, sequential, meaningful oral language instruction with regular diagnostic assessments;

•including activities in the curriculum that allow students to demonstrate their unique cognitive strengths in spatial ability and perceptual skills and to use these skills to assist in developing their school language proficiency;

•consciously assisting students in making the transition from contextualized oral and written language to comprehending decontextualized oral and written language;

•using context to teach concepts and abstracts;

•assisting students in developing a stronger internal locus of control;

•providing models and examples of what it is students are being asked to do and not just assume students possess the knowledge and understanding;

•ensuring each teacher who works with the student is aware of his/her language proficiency to ensure tasks are matched with abilities;

•one-on-one assessments are used to diagnose student needs; prescriptions are created to address those needs in a variety of ways by design so it is not left to chance.

B. POLITICALLY INCORRECT? NO MATTER
Impose Structures

A Revolving Door

Superintendent Kay was hired to lead this district of several village schools of Native students following the retirement of an administration that had been in place for fifteen years. The previous supervisors had kept good records, innovations had been implemented, and district procedures had been established. Assessments were organized and filed so at least some information was available as to what was and wasn't working.

A great deal of money and effort was spent the spring prior to Superintendent Kay taking reins on articulating a detailed strategic plan for the district. Input was gathered and an expensive, experienced consultant was hired and all interests in the district contributed to this plan during a series of costly meetings of educators, parents, and community members.

Committees were established over the previous five to six years to review research and examine the various teaching resources available that might be appropriate for these students. A few hundred thousand dollars were spent acquiring new language arts, mathematics, social studies and other programs.

Superintendent Kay was hired by the school district board and came on the scene with her own agenda. It was evident from the word go. Assessment results, the recently created strategic plan, the new resources as well everything that had been going on in this district including the various procedures (that took a great deal of time and effort to establish) were ignored. She had her own ideas.

She immediately implemented a totally new program. She had her way of hiring, selecting teachers for training, acquiring resources, and running this school district. She immediately erased the past. Whether it worked or not was irrelevant. She had her own plan.

All the efforts of the previous administration were ignored. Some were actually quite successful, and they cost huge sums of money. The texts and other resources were stored in sheds, basements and attics. Assessment results were shuffled away and lost.

Native people's interaction with non-Natives has a history of being in a subordinate role: fish and game, state troopers, doctors, teachers, social workers and missionaries. And Native school board members often act subservient to the non-Native superintendent. They listen to him or her and commonly accept the information and recommendations provided without any aggressive questioning or resistance.

The school board abided by whatever Superintendent Kay requested. They bought into this "new direction". It was not even four months into this superintendent's contract when she learned there was an opening in another school district in Alaska on the road system. It was a non-Native school district. She applied, was interviewed but not offered a contract. So much for her commitment to this Native school district that she just put on a totally new course after wiping out its past efforts. Included in her plans was her personal agenda that involved receiving new feathers in her cap to assist her future professional aspirations. This would be fine except it is accomplished at the expense of the parents and students whose home this is.

She ended up staying two years before she returned to Nevada.

"Next!"

Why Structures?

It is often a revolving door of ineffectiveness in our village schools. Efforts are personnel dependent, thus, chaotic, short lived, and wasteful. All is based on the whim, views and preferences of whatever commissioner, superintendent, principal, or teacher is in place. Soon as someone new comes aboard, directions change, efforts are shifted, new resources are purchased and a new ballgame with different rules begins. The classified personnel at the school who are residents of the community have a front row seat. The Native parents and students must adapt to this parade of educators. They have grown accustomed to this constant change and chaos at the school. It is just the way things are and have been.

A plan or structure can help extinguish this chaos. Here is an analogy: there is a group of students on board a boat that the crew is trying to get to a certain island. It usually takes about thirteen years to row there. Some crewmembers get off at different ports of call and decide to leave their position; new ones take their place.

New rowers are trained and a written explanation as to how the boat is going to get to their destination is provided before they sit down and pick up an oar. They row together, they communicate; the rowers and the coxswain have the same map. If there is a new coxswain, he/she is provided training regarding all aspects of this map *that is already in place.* The coxswain ensures the written explanation that is provided to the crew is followed. It is a map devised by experienced individuals who have incorporated known, effective practices concerning this boat and these waters. Through research and investigation, they have determined the best ways to reach the goal.

When at some port of call the crew gathers and talks, they might identify some area that needs improvement to help them on their journey. Calluses and other indications are brought to light, and it is determined that a specific adjustment is needed. A decision is made to alter the material where the rowers grip the oar so their hands won't be injured and, thus, better progress could be made. The Plan was improved based on reflection, evidence, and dialogue.

The identified destination is far more likely to be reached under this scenario than if each rower did his own thing, had his own vision of where he was headed, used his own idea as to how to row, or if a new map or plan was provided each time there was a new coxswain. A great deal of time, effort and money would be saved not to mention the benefits to the students on board.

Catering to the plans and ideas of individual educators who come and go is folly when it comes to quality Native education. These educators are not trained and skilled in Native history, cultures, learning styles, and appropriate methodologies and resources. Their personal agendas too often interfere. What is convenient for them is not necessarily what is best for Native students.

By establishing researched-based structures in these school districts that require the educators to do the adapting instead of the kids and parents would be of monumental benefit. The example of Superintendent Kay is common. Whether a superintendent stays in the position one or fifteen years, a structure that remains would prevent the disjointed, short-lived, changes in direction and the wasteful spending that results from personnel dependent efforts. It prevents teachers coming into a classroom and operating independently using their own methods, ideas, and resources that may or not be appropriate but have no connection to the district's efforts. It also hinders new, uninformed school board members from illogically steering a district in a direction that is educationally unsound.

The structures need to be researched-based and continually evaluated, monitored and adjusted according to a regular examination of the various components. An array of assessments is used to determine the degree of effectiveness of methodologies, resources, curriculum, and hiring practices.

The immediate reaction to imposing structures on rural school districts will be that "it stifles creativity; it infringes on educators' individualism and professionalism". This is a politically incorrect proposal, but it is likely what is best for Native kids despite its inconvenience to educators. We don't need to receive input on how to best teach Native kids in a village on the Koyuk from Jay who just arrived from Nebraska. Jay needs to be willing to listen, learn, change his comfortable ways so he can contribute to the goals articulated in these imposed structures: structures that will remain long after he is back in Omaha. Educators that come and then go, must come and agree to fit into the established structures and work within the identified ways and means to reach the goals (in a manner they may not be used to) then they can return from whence they came.

The structures must be devised through consultation with educators and Native people who are versed in cross-cultural issues; aware of needs specific to Alaska Native students and Native school districts; and knowledgeable of developmentally appropriate practices, methodologies, resources and Native education concerns. Alaska Native educators, parents and board members assist in articulating education goals and training educators. The structures must be written, readily available and used as a basis for staff development and all district decisions. They do not impede educator creativity or the ability to make choices. They are not in concrete. They are monitored and adjusted on a continual basis according to assessment results, observations and dialogue.

Structures would ensure stability over time. As it is and has been, it is difficult to near impossible for researchers to have the opportunity for any long-range studies. School systems are so chaotic, in such a state of flux, with transient personnel; they do not provide any consistency conducive to any longitudinal studies.

For example, intuitively it is felt that a culturally based curriculum, an increased number of Native educators, reduced teacher turnover, relevant resources, more money, and array of other recommendations would result in improved education for Native students. Due to the circumstances, though, it is extremely difficult to study issues over time and acquire hard data that indicates what is and isn't working. Educators are in dire need of reliable findings that would provide a basis for decision-making and directions for what is truly best for Native students.

Structuring Literacy Instruction

A few years ago I looked closely at thirteen Alaskan schools to determine their efforts and what occurred in the classrooms regarding literacy instruction. Teachers completed a lengthy survey and answered various questions, and I observed dozens of classes and teachers.

One of the schools (K-2) actually had an articulated procedure to address literacy. There was consistency from teacher to teacher, the same assessments were used and a profile of each student's proficiency was collected and passed on to his/her next teacher. The principal of this school recently left this position, so it is uncertain if or for how long the literacy plan will remain in place.

At one school consistency existed due to having adopted a canned reading program. The program, including its own assessments, was the 'literacy plan' for the K-6 students. These canned programs (Success for All, Open Court for example) are not specifically designed for the Native students' needs in rural Alaska. They do not have a definite oral language strand.

Reading material in programs like Open Court, Success for All and basal readers is decontextualized. It is not relevant to the lives of Alaska Native children, "it is chosen for a generic audience. It may be that any program that spends extra time and money on reading will tend to have positive results... the promoters of these programs tend to evaluate them with tests from that program that focus on the particular skills their program teaches, and students usually show good progress, especially early on. However, results tend to be less positive on more general standardized achievement tests and, while students do better, they usually don't match up with national averages." Reyhner, J. P.

One K-12 school used one of these canned reading programs in grades K-6. The administration was gung ho for the program. It was a sacred cow. The Native students, though, showed identical problems related to reading in their 7-12 classes as such students in any other similar school.

The other eleven schools' lack of any literacy plan resulted in "every man for himself". There was no consistency, no shared efforts, no organized means of determining student proficiency. Communication between teachers was informal and left to happenstance. Whatever literacy efforts occurred in the classroom concerning instruction, resources, and assessment depended upon that particular teacher. Some incorporated more whole language methodology while others used basal readers. Some used Running Records and a variety of leveled books. Time specifically allotted to direct literacy instruction varied tremendously from class-to-class, school-to-school.

After elementary school, reading instruction generally does not take place. Secondary teachers are usually trained in teaching literature and literary devices such as plot, conflict, and irony and but not in diagnosing reading difficulties and teaching reading skills and comprehension. Many Native students of all ages require such instruction. Continually asking them to read to learn when they have not adequately learned to read; asking the students to comprehend information that is written or spoken on a level that is beyond their proficiency simply doesn't work.

Student materials, teacher resources, assessments, specific considerations, time allotments, and recommended methodologies need to be delineated in such a plan that addresses literacy. The superintendent, principals, teachers, instructional aides, school board members, and parents must be made aware of this structure and their particular role and, over time, a new communication can exist. Over time assessments, experience, observations and dialogue continually assist in improving the components of the plan. Educators come and go; the students and parents remain along with this structure to improve listening, speaking, reading and writing proficiencies.

Appendix 3 contains a condensed plan to address literacy in village schools that is an example of a researched-based system, a structure that can be established in a Native school district. This is just an example. It is a possibility. It is one model.

The plan is not personnel dependent in that it remains in place. Educators adapt and receive additional training in order to fit into this system. Educators (school board members, superintendents, principals, and teachers) contribute to carrying out this plan's mission. The plan is a permanent structure that provides continuity, focuses efforts, and is regularly adjusted based on various input and assessments. It prevents a Superintendent Kay from arriving with her own agenda, changing a district's directions, wasting monies, and then heading off when she decides to seek new pastures.

Since the majority of the educators in Native school districts are non-Native and unfamiliar in ways best to educate Alaska Natives, it is time for them to do the adapting. Educators, due to their own school experiences and university training, acquire a comfort zone regarding methodologies, resources, ways of interacting with students and parents, what is developmentally appropriate, and "how to hold school". It is time for the educators to be inconvenienced instead of Native students constantly being required to fit into a system that wasn't designed for them in the first place.

The details and specific content of this example plan is not necessarily of main importance. What is important, is the concept of there being a research-based plan that is a structure that remains, and is adjusted based on informed decisions. Educators coming into the school system join the plan's efforts to reach its goals. They do not enter and carry out their own agenda.

Besides a Plan to Address Literacy (the most important issue), one can be developed for math, history, and all subjects. It is not a curriculum guide. It is not a list of objectives or student outcomes. It is an articulation of a district's approach to dealing with an issue. It could be a hiring plan, a staff development plan or a plan for acquiring instructional resources (and, of course, all efforts are related and support each other). The point is, that a research-based structure designed for the specific student population is in place, remains in place and the personnel are required to fit into that structure. A superintendent's role is to ensure the district implements and carries out the structures and makes possible a continuing adjustment to improve the plans over time based on a variety of information. The next superintendent is charged with the same role.

Structures will provide continuity. They will allow opportunity for study and improvement. They will provide a record of the district's efforts and an end to constantly having to reinvent the wheel. They will prevent wasteful spending and lessen the chaos of disjointed efforts. They will provide the one constant that is missing in rural education. The educators that come and go (95% non-Native) will need to adapt to the plan and do their part in helping achieve the goals identified in the structure. Structures would require the educators to adapt to a system instead of the indigenous students being forced to fit into an inflexible program that was intended for students with far different traits, school language proficiency and life experiences.

Structures must be research-based and developed by knowledgeable, experienced individuals. It may take a few years to establish and implement such structures. It will be no easy task. The alternative, though, is to continue with the status quo, a system that is far more convenient for educators than it is for the Native students and parents: entire cultural groups of people. Maybe an innovative, understanding, bold, foresighted school district will adopt this concept and prove its worth.

C. MANDATORY EDUCATOR TRAINING
More Than the Requirement of Three Multicultural Credits

Truly culturally responsive schools would employ educators well prepared and adequately trained for the cross-cultural issues they face in Native classrooms and the village environment. If the goal of the usual three month intensive Peace Corps training is to allow the volunteer to "hit the ground running" and to be as effective as possible during the two year stint in a particular foreign country, we should be able to do something likewise for the educators working with "our" indigenous people. Peace Corps training involves a generic curricula for all volunteers no matter where they are going. It also includes training specific for the particular location.

There is a variety of ways training can be provided in Alaska for educators working with indigenous students. As it is and has been, efforts are non-existent or sporadic at best. Some districts provide brief, and usually one-shot, workshops dealing with some aspect of the topic at the beginning of the school year. They vary greatly in value. But the impact of even ones of quality is short-lived and quickly overshadowed by the demands of the ingrained system. The State requiring three nebulous credits of course work dealing with multicultural education is an insult to its aboriginal population. There are close to seventy different courses to choose from that fulfill the multicultural requirement. This includes such courses as Alaska Natives in Film; Geography of Alaska; Education and Socioeconomic Change; Alaska Native Politics; Philosophical and Social Context of American Education; Elders in Residence; Rural Alaska Natives in the Alaska Press. It is questionable how many of these approved courses would be of much value in providing the information and skills in which Dave and Debbie are in need.

The initial hurdle to cross is recognizing that substantial training is critical and, thus, making it a requirement for all educators (*all* teachers and *all* administrators as well as the Commissioner) working with Alaska Native students. The training curricula, like that of the Peace Corps, would include a generic component regarding Alaska Native education, as well as training specific to the different locations and cultural groups in the state.

The basic tenets in preparing educators that have been in place in the State would have to be changed. It must be recognized that a good teacher is not necessarily a good teacher period and that all kids are not really the same when it comes to their schooling needs. There are certain teaching practices that are more effective when working with Native children, and there are particular adaptations the school system must make in order to meet the particular needs and characteristics of Native students. What makes a teacher effective in a fifth grade classroom in Petersburg or Palmer is not the same criteria required to be successful when teaching and living in Kwigillingok or Aleknagik.

Training centers could be established in the main cultural regions of the state, located in the large cities of Juneau, Anchorage, and Fairbanks, or one large center could exist. Centers would be open year around. They would be staffed by carefully selected educators who successfully completed an intensive series of trainings similar in scope to the two year long academy that our state mentors attend to prepare them for their position working with first and second year teachers. That academy consisted of about eight weeklong sessions. The preparation for those individuals managing the Area Training Centers could be condensed but rigorous and held over a shorter time span.

Training centers would have a variety of purposes besides preparing educators to successfully live and work with indigenous people. Native educators would take part as trainees related to curriculum, instruction and assessment, but would be utilized as a resource in acclimating non-Native educators as well as other Natives who may not be familiar with their own culture.

"Educators have typically attempted to teach Natives according to the single, prescribed method presumably applicable to everyone-a practice that has resulted in failure for many Native (and non-Native) students. This approach to instruction appears to regard all Natives (all persons) as indistinguishable from one another. However, perceptive people exposed to different Native

groups soon observe great differences among them, including differences in physical features and life ways" (Wax, Wax, & Dumont Jr., 1989). Grant & Gillispie, 1993

A training curriculum would be implemented at each center; a portion would address Alaska Native education in general, statewide issues, and history. Another aspect would deal with issues particular to the region the center covers. A certificate would be earned by each educator successfully completing the program. But if he/she moved to a new region, the person would need to complete the section pertaining to that area of the State at the designated center.

Centers would become clearinghouses of information within their region. They would be the memory. All information regarding assessments, resources, and programs would be held and accessible here. Information would be housed so that it doesn't disappear as personnel changes. As it is and has been, there is no memory, no avenue or mechanism that one can tap to learn what has occurred or what works and what doesn't. There really is no definitive place to go to obtain assistance and learn specifically about how to succeed when working with Alaska Native students.

They could be avenues for educators, university professors and other researchers to perform longitudinal studies. They would be vehicles for sharing what the districts in the region are doing. They would prevent the wheel having to be continually reinvented as people come and go in various positions taking districts in new directions with no awareness of what has occurred. The monies saved by preventing the wasteful expense caused by individuals making unilateral decisions based on uninformed personal beliefs would be substantial enough to cover a good part of the training center concept.

It is critical that the people responsible for developing the curricula for such centers are the most knowledgeable and experienced people available. The typical university professor is not the type of person in mind. There must be an intensive and comprehensive training for the individuals manning these centers. The university system has not and does not provide what is needed. Individuals with doctorates espousing demagoguery is not who are needed training educators as to how best work with indigenous Alaskans and positively dwell in their communities.

The purpose here is not to provide a detailed listing of the training center contents, but to propose that their creation would be an answer to many of the problems that exist. It is the concept that is important. No other practical, valid solution has been offered that doesn't merely perpetuate the status quo.

Example curriculum topics for centers:

- Overview of each of the five main cultural groups
- History, culture, and other information and concerns regarding the specific area the center or certificate covers
- History from Native and non-Native perspectives of the area, the people, the school, the state
- Cross-cultural issues in the classroom, the school, the district, the community
- Appropriate methodologies
- Use of assessments, diagnostic instruments
- Multi-level, multi-graded instruction, meeting the needs of a wide range of proficiencies and ages while teaching multiple subjects
- Oral language instruction and assessment
- Use of particular resources
- Components designed specifically for school board members, administrators, teachers, instructional aides, and parents
- Making academic content relevant
- Developing positive communication between the school, the child, the home, the community
- Incorporating local knowledge, local resources, community members, parents into the school program
- cross-cultural concerns regarding history
- cross-cultural concerns regarding communication

An educator should be able to request specific training if he/she determines the need. Administrators evaluating staff can suggest or require teachers to attend the center for specific training or retraining. Training centers would house reference libraries specific to the region they represent. They would bring an end to the temporary fiefdoms established by the superintendents who come and go and who have limited vested interest in the Native communities.

Clif Bates

-Examples of Training Curricula-

CROSS-CULTURAL CONCERNS REGARDING HISTORY AND COMMUNICATION

by Michael J. Oleksa

If the State of Alaska's Department of Education and the University of Alaska's School of Education were to reconsider the requirements for teacher certification, I would propose, in addition to all that has been recommend up to this point, specifically mandating courses in Alaska Native History and Cross Cultural Communications with a focus on particular Native Alaskan concerns and issues. In these concluding sections, I present my arguments in favor of the inclusion of this particular reform whether as university courses or as a portion of the curricula for the training centers we suggest establishing.

CROSS-CULTURAL CONCERNS REGARDING HISTORY

Any History and Alaska History

History, in the European tradition, is the written record of what certain important people have done, at particular critical points in the past. It is not everything that ever happened, or anything that anyone ever did, since that would make history "everything." In a sense, of course, it is. Any person or event from the past is "history." So officially history must be written and published by scholars called "historians" whose duty it is to discern what events and which people were significant to be included in their authorized and permanent records. Obviously, history, just like beauty, is in the eye of the beholder, or perhaps, more realistically today, the owners and editors of the publishing house.

The Historian's Perspective

An historian seldom has any significant problem finding material. The historian can consider, as history, anything anyone ever said or did, and that would be too much information. So the real task of the historian is to separate the irrelevant from the pertinent, the insignificant from the important. To do this, the historian must necessarily approach the task with certain criteria. These may be conscious or not, but there must be some way to distinguish what a scholar considers relevant or not. And this means all histories arise from a certain personal and cultural perspective. This is unavoidable. It cannot be otherwise. Someone must choose who will be the heroes and villains in a particular story and present it in those terms. Otherwise, no one would bother to read it. There must, necessarily, be "lessons" and "meaning" in the story or there is no use to preserve, publish or repeat it.

The History of Alaska, therefore, is just like all others. The texts that have been produced over a century ago are now rare and out of print, but the "truths" they revealed, the basic story they told, has not been altered very much in the last hundred years or more. In the 1880's, readers interested in Alaska's past were mostly Anglo-American history buffs. Writers came from this same social group, approaching the subject with their particular point of view. They were mostly interested in recording the contributions and accomplishments of their own people, those who had come as "pioneers" to the last frontier. They were eager to learn of the prospectors and miners, the teachers and missionaries, the soldiers and the whalers who braved the dangers of the remote north to make their fortunes, instruct and save the souls of Indians, establish law and order, or just gave up and came home.

Missing from the story as it has been told for generations are the original people of this land. In none of the established history texts are the Native peoples accorded more than a few paragraphs per cultural group. Although they were here for ten thousand years, their story was not important, not interesting, not relevant to the history as those writing and reading it preferred. So what we call "Alaskan History" is almost totally the story of what European-Americans have done in Alaska over the past 250 years.

The Russian period of Alaska lasted 127 years. But this, for English-speaking Americans, is also rather irrelevant. They are interested in their own story, not someone else's. During the half-century of Cold War between the USA and USSR, "Russian" also meant "communist" and "enemy," so any mention of anyone or anything "Russian" assumed a very negative connotation. Since thousands of Native Alaskans also claim Slavic ancestry, this prejudice against mentioning anything positive about the Russian Era also meant neglecting any mention of their ancestor's heroic or remarkable deeds. The "point of view" in the official texts disparaged or disregarded the contributions made by Native and Creole teachers, preachers, linguists, artists, explorers, seamen and military leaders as if they had not existed.

History always has a point of view. The author must be literally "sitting" somewhere, and that place will effect the criteria used to discern the outlines of the published story. For example, someone writing a "history of Alaska" sitting on the campus of the University of Alaska's main campus in Fairbanks, might survey the landscape outside the office window and ask the pertinent question, "What happened out there that my students should know, in order to make better sense of the world in which they live today?" And with this basic question in mind, one might prepare a list of names, dates and events as the format for a new history. Sitting in Bethel, or Attu, another scholar might consider the same question, but the list of names and dates each would produce would necessarily be different. It is not a matter of one being more correct or truthful than the other. It will depend on perspective, focus and interest. Heroes in one volume may play no significant role in another. Major events in one might be marginal in another. The Historian makes these determinations without realizing that intrinsic to all histories is inescapably a way of seeing a culture. There is no such thing as "unbiased" history. The best historians can do is admit to theirs, not deny them. No one writes decontextualized "truth." The facts don't fall out of the sky. Someone had to discover, choose and publish them. And that process is necessarily affected by the historians themselves.

The Traditional History Curriculum

When American History became a mandatory subject in school curricula over a century ago, in the heyday of the assimilationist policies out of which public schools arose, the texts approved were essentially an invitation for minority children of various immigrant backgrounds to identify with and "melt" into the Anglo-American "pot." As early as kindergarten, five year olds were dressing as Mayflower pilgrims and delighting their family and friends with skits about the coming of the Pilgrims. Real Americans were there, at the Beginnings at Plymouth Rock, and if one's ancestors immigrated somewhat later, that would be acceptable, as long as one accept these English exiles as one's own cultural predecessor, the one with whom each identifies and emulates. These paradigms then multiply to include Washington, Adams, Jefferson, John Paul Jones, Patrick Henry, Abraham Lincoln (or Robert E. Lee), and Teddy Roosevelt. The purpose of teaching history at all was, like everything else in the curriculum, assimilationist. White Anglo-Saxon men are the heroes in our histories and the entire citizenry should admire, respect, honor and emulate them. All our presidents to date have been elected from this group, which since the founding of the Republic constituted the majority of the population and for most of that period, its sole electorate. (An exception to this generalization might be made in the case of John F. Kennedy who was Irish Catholic, but he had to prove his WASP cultural identity in order to gain acceptance even then).

A More Inclusive History

The entire curriculum was very consciously designed to fulfill the mission of public education, which was primarily to assimilate immigrant children from southern and eastern Europe into Anglo-American culture and society. And since this is precisely what immigrant families desired, the program succeeded. Only much later in the 20th century did the assimilationist policies and curriculum come under attack from millions of parents and hundreds of communities who could not or would not identify with the established histories, because these excluded them. Black, Hispanic, Asian and Native Americans could not pretend they had come on the Mayflower. That was not their story, and even if they had been willing to pretend it was, no one could have seriously believed them. Central as the Pilgrim saga might be, there are other, equally authentically "American" stories. And various history departments have devoted much of the last forty years to researching, publishing and teaching these in Black, Women's, Asian, Hispanic and Native American Studies programs across the USA. Until these are "digested" and a more inclusive national history promulgated, we still have no single text to present as authentic and representative of the richness of cultural diversity that makes the United States truly unique.

This is also true of Alaska. Over the last three decades, greater attention has been given the Russian era, and competent scholars have been researching the archival treasures in both Washington DC and St. Petersburg for additional information about the heroes, villains and main characters of the period. Hundreds of Native Alaskans were, not surprisingly, involved. They were, of course, the vast majority of the resident population, there never having been more than 800 citizens of the Russian Empire in the territory at any given time. There were hundreds of marriages between Siberians and Alaskans, producing thousands of offspring, bi-cultural and multi-lingual. More than a century after the transfer of Alaska to American rule, I met Elders on Kodiak Island and the Kenai Peninsula still fluent and literate in Russian, as well as their Native language and English too. But nothing of this cultural legacy was mentioned in the established history texts.

This may be only an error of omission, but I believe it serious. Not telling the stories of Alaskan Natives who retained their cultural identity and yet participated in the development of the territory leaves the false and unchallenged impression that Native Alaskans contributed nothing. They appear in the histories as the innocent victims or the passive bystanders in the story instead of active, courageous, intelligent participants. If we fail to include their names and accomplishments we use history, even unintentionally, to perpetuate not only ignorance, but negative stereotypes, prejudice and racism. As an historian myself, I object to my discipline being misused for such dishonorable purposes.

Alaskan Native History

All Alaskans, I believe, should graduate from high school with some knowledge of Alaska's rich cultural and historical past. But this must include much more than a vague notion that we have Aleuts, Eskimos and Indians here, somewhere. They should have a positive appreciation for these tribal societies and a determination that these should continue, survive and prosper, in centuries to come. They should be aware that Alaskan Natives have for centuries been active players on the stage, as the adventure, tragedy or comedy of the Alaskan script has been written. They should be familiar with Russian, Creole and Native American leaders, artists, explorers, educators and authors who laid the foundations for so much of what we enjoy today. Unless history becomes truly inclusive, it can be misused to do more harm than good.

This means that in preparing teachers to teach in Alaska about Alaska, they will need substantial post-secondary courses in this field. We require them to study math before teaching arithmetic, and grammar before teaching English. Should they know something about history before attempting to teach history? And even the history of history, so they can become aware of the prejudices and distortions of past writers who had their own assimilationist agendas to advance under the guise of writing "the Truth."

Besides teacher training, an entire curriculum needs to be developed for elementary and secondary programs so that teachers will have appropriate materials at their disposal for telling a more inclusive history of Alaska and its peoples. Documentary films of quality equal to that available for the teaching of US History need to be produced and edited according to grade level. Maps, textbooks, illustrations and activities need to be developed as well.

Re-writing history is always a challenge. Questioning established "facts" and critiquing yesterday's "heroes" can be dangerous as well as exciting. But that is the historical quest, to question, to challenge, to debate and to prioritize, to wrestle with difficult questions as detectives trying to discern the pertinent facts, the reliable witnesses, the basic evidence to substantiate a particular "case." Alaska's rich and diverse history offers many points of view, and only by considering seriously each of these can we, as investigators at the scene of a crime, arrive at any tentative understanding of "the facts."

Alaska is a "last frontier" not only because the land itself is remote from so much of the inhabited world, but because there is so much about the place and its people that remains unexplored. Our history has yet to be researched, discovered, written. There is much we can learn, so many questions still to be researched, discussed, debated and resolved. The stories do not "fall out of the sky" ready-made. They are always the product of human analysis, human understanding, human perspective. That is what I would hope all our students, both Native and not, would gain from their examination of Alaska's amazing history. Anything less is merely the promulgation of propaganda, the foisting of one point of view as the whole truth, when it may not be, in fact, true at all. Only research, discussion and debate over time will resolve and ultimately produce our history. I would hope our students might be invited to join in that exciting enterprise.

It is a relatively simple exercise to assign students several readings, preferably from several eyewitness accounts, of the same event. Bering's Voyages, the entire Prommyshlenik Era (1742-1791), the Battles at Sitka (1802 and 1804), the role of Creoles, the Orthodox Mission (bilingual) schools (contrasted with the BIA/Mission schools under US rule (1884 onward), Ethnographic art, Trade, Exploration and mapping, the careers of Sophia Vlasov, Philip Kashevarov, Jacob Netsvetov, Alexander Kashevarov, Ilarion Archimandritov, the lives of Innocent Veniaminov and the Elder Herman, the Martyrdom of Hieromonk Juvenaly and his Alaskan Native companion (Alaska's longest-standing "murder mystery"), the significance of Alexander Baranov, Nicholai Rezanov and Ivan Kuskov—all these remain controversial topics and themes. Sheldon Jackson, Mike Healey, Territorial Governors Swineford and Brady, the naval bombardments of Kake and Angoon, William Duncan and the founding of Metlakatla, S. Hall Young, the Jesuit Missions, John Kilbuck, "Sinrock" Mary and the Reindeer, the Revenue Cutter "Bear," The Jesse Lee Home—all these offer tremendous insights into the life and times during the transition from Russian to American rule.

New Resources

Russians in Alaska by Dr. Lydia T. Black provides the best overall survey of this era, together with Barbara Sweetland Smith's ***Russian Orthodoxy in Alaska***, and her museum exhibit, video production and catalog ***Russian America: The Forgotten Frontier***. The bibliographies in these two volumes provide a wealth of material for including more Native and Russia-era history, bringing the overview of Alaska's past into better balance. Dr. Richard Dauenhauer's monograph "Conflicting Visions in Alaskan Education," is, in my opinion, required introductory reading for anyone teaching in the state or interested in the philosophical foundations of Native education. And ***Haa Kustiyee***, which both Richard and his wife Nora have compiled, is a tremendous resource for the teaching of Tlingit History in Southeast. More than a decade ago, the City School District of Kake contracted myself and the Dauenhauers to prepare curricula in Tlingit history, language arts, social studies and the Tlingit language itself. The volume we produced was substantial. It included newspaper coverage and government reports involving Kake far back to the early and mid-1800's, Kake's participation in the attacks on Sitka and Baranov's retribution, the US Navy's bombardment of the village in retaliation for the killing of Col. John Eaby on Whidbey Island in Puget Sound fifty years later, the renunciation of traditional customs and the "driving of the silver spike" are all uniquely part of the history of that village, but also of the Tlingit nation and all Southeast Alaska. Yet none of this receives mention in our "established" histories, written from another point of view. We can do better.

Because of a change in district administration, this curriculum was, as far as I know, never implemented. (Institutional amnesia, however, is a problem discussed elsewhere in this text). This can change, and it should.

My own ***Alaskan Missionary Spirituality*** and ***Orthodox Alaska*** provide additional material for exploring these issues. Despite the "religious bias" of these titles, both printed by ecclesiastical publishers, the bulk of the material in these focuses on Alaskan Natives. Of particular importance are the petitions for redress, composed by literate Aleuts and Tlingits, submitted to the President of the United

States, asking for relief from what they considered oppression and persecution at the hands of government officials stationed at Sitka in the late nineteenth century. How many Alaskans know that Tlingit chiefs addressed a petition to President William McKinley in 1898, begging for him to forbid the territory's appointed governor from building roads through their village, desecrating the graves of their ancestors, to limit the canneries use of traditional fishing sites, which the chiefs fear are being depleted, and to close liquor stores and bars? How many realize that Alaskan Natives fought for the citizenship the 1867 Treaty guaranteed them, not just by writing letters to the Russian ambassador but by suing in court?

For that matter, how many know that the literacy rate among Aleuts in 1867 was higher than parts of European Russia? Or that there were Native teachers, writers, translators, missionaries, cartographers and seamen? How many could name the Aleut who became a Major General in the Russian military? Or the Native sea captains who mapped the Arctic coastline from Point Hope to Point Barrow? Who can name the Siberian genius who learned Unangan Aleut, Tlingit, and later Yakut, devised grammars and alphabets for these tribal languages and opened schools in these regions during his 40 year career in the "bush"? Or his colleague, born on the Pribilofs, educated in Irkutsk, who spent 20 years teaching and translating at Atka and then another 18 at Ikogmiut, on the Yukon River, where he learned Yup'ik Eskimo and published the first books there, before 1870? Who can name the first Native school teacher and the dates when she was active? Shouldn't we all know this stuff?

My "*Alaska Native Women: Pre-Statehood,*" includes the biographies of seven amazing ladies, for one of whom, (Elizabeth Peratrovich), the State has established an annual (February 16) holiday. Certainly every Alaskan should know about her life and accomplishments. But there is no guarantee now that they will. We can do a better job, meaning we can approach history more fairly, acknowledging these people and events, but only if the teachers have been trained and the materials are available. We can do this.

Hubert George Bancroft compiled the first ***History of Alaska*** in English with the dishonest support of Ivan Petroff, who provided Bancroft with "translations" of non-existent Russian material. Entire chapters of Bancroft's volume have been proven erroneous, the product of Mr. Petrov's fertile imagination. Most twentieth century descriptions of Alaska under Russian rule are derived from Bancroft, so that all of Hector Chevigny's popular works, as well as more scholarly treatises by Governor Ernest Gruening, and even the more recent ***Alaska: A History of the Forty-Ninth State,*** are tainted with Petrovian fiction. Issues of Alaska Geographic repeat many of Bancroft's errors, so that the same misinformation, after more than a century, has been widely disseminated. But there is enough new scholarly research available today so that we don't have to continue repeating lies and myths under the banner of Alaska History.

History: The Last Frontier

Fortunately, Dr. Richard Pierce founded Limestone Press some decades ago and began publishing primary source material, translated from Russian archival sources. Dr. Sergei Kan's ***Symbolic Immoratality*** and ***Memory Eternal***, as well as Dr. Andrei Znamenny's ***Through Orthodox Eyes*** open new vistas for scholars of both Tlingit and Athabaskan cultures in the early historical period. Kurt Vitt's work in the Moravian Church archives and all of Dr. Anne Fiunup-Riordon's research, substantially broaden and deepen our understanding of the Yup'ik region.

Alaskan Natives themselves are writing their own biographies, providing us with another perspective to add to the rich diversity of materials potentially useful for an exploration of our past. Raising Ourselves, for example, and Paul John's volume, ***Stories for Future Generations***, are excellent examples of this new genre. For a statement on assimilation and a collective Yup'ik response to it, the eloquent "*Must One Way of Life Die for Another to Live?*" Published in Bethel remains a classic. It should also be required reading for teachers in the Yukon-Kuskokwim Delta and beyond.

I realize that it is impractical to recommend that all teachers of Alaska History absorb this much information in their leisure time and then design a series of instructional units themselves, on their own time. To teach this subject well will require a great deal of preparation, first for the instructors themselves and then for the development of a curriculum that does not trivialize or oversimplify or worse, ignore or belittle the accomplishments and contributions of Alaskan Natives.

There is, as always, plenty of material "out there," both published and electronic, but there are no criteria, no guidelines, for even suggesting what should be included and what can be without regret left out. Teachers now are left, each to their own resources, to find, however haphazardly, their own materials and to prepare their course however they choose. Some, as I have witnessed at Anchorage's Dimond High School, do extraordinarily work. But I have little confidence that this excellence is the norm. I cannot fathom how teachers can invent a course, without clear instructional goals, without any particular focus, with many questionable and few substantial resources available, and with no extra time (or pay) to do any of this. Time and energy are limited, and interest levels vary widely.

Teachers can currently meet the Alaska Studies requirement, which the Department of Education has established for teachers in Alaska's schools in such a wide variety of ways, that there is no guarantee a particular teacher will confront any of these issues. Thus, through ignorance and neglect the current style, the "teach whatever you like as Alaska History" free-for-all, will continue, and in the name of "history" our schools will perpetuate negative stereotypes and lies that only further depress and demean Native students and their communities.

The DOE requirement is useful. It is already in place. I am only arguing here that it should be a substantial course, requiring teachers to become familiar with the issues in Alaska's past that remain with us today. I would go a step further, and define "Alaska Studies" as Alaska History, now that the state legislature has added this subject to the list of required courses for high school graduation. If we are forcing everyone to take this class, it should be taught well, by teachers who are familiar and enthusiastic about it, and who actually know a lot about Alaska's history and can include a significant unit on the active and creative role Native Alaskans have played. This is, I believe, as it should and can be.

CROSS-CULTURAL CONCERNS REGARDING COMMUNICATION
Can We Talk?

Let's suppose that we have teachers prepared, culturally and historically informed, educated in intercultural issues, appropriate teaching methodologies, and Alaska Native cultures and history. Are we ready to open a new, happier and more academically rewarding chapter in the story of schooling in rural Alaska? Even if all the certified staff embraces this vision and with the best of intentions applies all they have learned to their programs, there are still obstacles.

Inescapable Miscommunication

People from different parts of the country talk differently. Linguists have long ago identified the varieties of accent and dialect across the United States, but with good will most Americans manage to communicate fairly well despite these differences. For the most part, they share a common worldview, play the ballgame of life according to implicit and unstated rules in more or less the same way, and are, with some regional differences, part of the same national story. Alaskan Natives do not share the same view of the world, are not necessarily playing the same ballgame of life, and certainly were born into a different story. The probability of miscommunication across these cultural boundaries is much higher. In fact, it is almost unavoidable. And the universal rule about communication applies: when miscommunication happens in a hierarchy, whoever has less power suffers the consequences.

Unfortunately, goodwill will not in itself suffice. "The road to hell," a medieval Spanish mystic, St. Theresa of Avila, emphasized, "is paved with good intentions." Knowledge and therefore training in interpersonal communications is also essential to the success of parent-teacher and teacher-student relationships.

The same words mean different things to different people. This is a theme developed in ***Another Culture/Another World*** that I will not repeat here. People only approximately say what they mean and their partners only approximately grasp what the speaker meant. Perfect communication virtually never happens. People often advise,

"Don't jump to conclusions," but if we didn't we would not be able to communicate much at all. All conversations happen within personal and cultural contexts. These, as much as the lexical (dictionary) definition of the words, determine how we understand each other.

I say "school", and with it comes all that I associate with school and schooling, my entire personal history of being in school, my teachers, and classmates, the bully on the fourth grade playground, the applause at the sixth grade operetta, the success of the football team, the defeat on the wrestling mat, the state championship for our senior club. "School" invokes memories and stories, some from my parents and siblings, some from grandparents. School may be a particular building or a "herd" of fish or a particular style of architecture or philosophy. The word itself has too many connotations and associations, but context will imply which meaning I intend, maybe.

As recounted elsewhere, school can be a glorious and exalted institution that illiterate immigrants felt unworthy to enter, or the chamber of horrors where a contemporary generation was subjected to humiliation and physical punishment for being who they were. The story of schooling in a particular community defines the word "school" more than Webster. In ***Another Culture/Another World*** I used "on time" as a culturally defined concept about which my parents disagreed for over six decades. The dictionary was useless in resolving this conflict. Their respective attitudes were based on culture. But this is the tip of the proverbial iceberg.

The "Iceberg"

The words we use and how we mean them or interpret them can be recorded, transcribed, reproduced and analyzed on film or audio recordings. But communication runs deeper. Language is but one of the ways we communicate, however inefficiently, but the words are not the only factor. There are other behaviors each human being learns in infancy and early childhood from care providers, parents, neighbors, relatives and older siblings that effect the way each communicates and is perceived by others for the rest of their lives. But we are seldom consciously aware that we ourselves have these patterns indelibly on the "hard drive" of our own mental "computer," and we are even less aware that others have the same patterns on theirs and that these behaviors impact the way we speak and the way our words are received.

Tempo

During the first three months of life, researchers tell us, we picked up a tempo, a drum beat, the pace at which we comfortably and unconsciously operate. Like a ticking metronome, we walk, talk, chew our food and physiologically function at a certain pace City people tend to have fairly rapid beats, walking, talking, eating and working faster than most rural people. City folks are usually in a hurry, or worse, behind schedule, trying to catch up. Rural people tend to have slower tempos, and the further south one travels the slower the pace becomes. One-syllable words elongate into two or even three. A southern friend once told me that sermons in the South (pronounced Sigh-yowth) are longer (pronounced) lown-gah because Gah-yah-owd (God) is a three-syllable woowd. This is more than a difference in pronunciation.

Silence is necessarily a part of every conversation. Speakers pause to indicate that they are done. They are relinquishing the floor to other speakers. The pause time, however, varies cross-culturally. People tend to wait one beat on their "ticker" for a response. But a Yankee's pause will be relatively brief, since one tick on their metronome will be rather short compared to a Southern belle's. This difference in tempo causes confusion and conflict. The faster talker wonders why the slower one can't just "spit it out," and the slower talker wonders why the other guy never shuts up, never offers the floor to anyone else. The slower talker comes across as disinterested, uncommunicative, deceitful, passive aggressive or just stupid. The faster talker comes across as imposing, domineering, pushy, arrogant and unreceptive to any other viewpoint. This difference in tempo accounts for many jokes and negative stereotypes these groups have about each other. It is a hidden form of miscommunication.

In the rural Alaskan classroom, differences in tempo can be devastating. The faster talking city teacher asks a question and calls on a particular student. The teacher waits a tick on her internal "metronome" but hears no response. The instantaneous and unconscious assumption is that this student was not paying attention, did not understand the question or did not know the answer. So the teacher goes on to the next student. This child is waiting for a signal that the teacher is finished speaking and expects the student to reply, but the pause time has not been long enough for that signal to register. The teacher goes to a third pupil who answers because by now the message "I'm done and now it's your turn" has been transmitted—not by words but by the interval of silence between question and answer. Silence is part of the message. And the different durations of silence mean different things to different people.

How fast is "fast" and how slow is "slow" depends almost entirely on the metronome setting each person invisibly and unconsciously carries within, but differences in the tempo translate into differences of interpretation and assessment of the other person's competence, sincerity, honesty, intelligence and politeness. The faster talker can come across as rude, bossy, intimidating, arrogant, proud or simply insensitive and uncaring. The slower talker can come across as uncommunicative, shy, withdrawn, unassertive, passive-aggressive, deceitful or just stupid. These misassessments of other people's attitudes, integrity and qualifications can be devastating in a classroom setting.

Decades ago I wondered why so many teachers in rural Alaska originated in the rural south. Their upbringing in a much warmer climate seemed to conflict with the need to adjust to Alaska's much cooler climate. But I discovered that they were more attuned to Native communities, both parents and students because of their rural background and the slower tempo at which they operated, giving students that extra moment of pause-time to respond. Less hurried meant better communication and therefore greater student satisfaction and success. It helps to be synchronized.

Slow Sam

I had a ten-year old boy in my Special Education class back in the 1970's who clearly did not belong there. His IQ was above average, he was bright and cheerful, respectful, polite, charming. But he had a tempo problem. He moved slower, worked slower, spoke slower than his peers or instructors.

When given the last few minutes of class time to finish an assignment, the rest of the class would hurriedly complete the worksheet and avoid having homework in that subject. Sam always needed more time. He'd stay after school each day to complete the exercises everyone else had finished earlier, just so he did not have to lug his heavy textbooks home and back each day.

Our school welcomed several new administrators during these years. The new principal, spotting Sam at his desk, ventured into the classroom and asked, "Are you on detention? Why are you still here?" Sam looked somewhat mystified. It was obvious what he was doing, so he said nothing to the gentleman who ambled over toward his desk. "Multiplying fractions!" After a moment of silence, the educator continued, "I don't know why you're working so hard, Sam. You're only going to grow up to be just one more drunken Native." And he walked away.

Sam today is a college graduate. And he never drinks.

Tone

Besides tempo, tone of voice, the music we use to "sing" our language also impacts the way people understand and relate to each other. English-speaking parents and family members provide a wide range of musical notes when speaking to infants, toddlers and young children. The tinier the child the higher the notes used to address the baby. Newborns are spoken to in a squeal. One can see adult males raising the tone of their voice to notes far above the treble musical staff, smiling, cuddling and addressing the new arrival on notes that they would never use for any of their peers. The tendency then is to gloss downward rapidly to notes far below, on the bass clef, and end with a groveling tone and a few kisses. The purpose of this otherwise rather strange behavior is to "program" this child to speak English on the wide range of notes on which it is spoken by native speakers. We use the music of the language to send indirect messages, to introduce irony or sarcasm into our speech, to alter slightly or significantly the meaning of the actual words. The music not only influences the way a message is heard. The music can be the message.

For example, if one says, "I didn't forget my tickets," it can mean "I've got the tickets right here in my pocket." But singing this line different completely changes the message. If it is sung as "I didn't forget MY tickets," where the pronoun MY is said on a higher pitch and held an extra beat, the implication is that someone else forgot theirs, and that this was a silly, foolish and almost unforgivable mistake. What is simply a reassuring statement of fact can be transformed into a hurtful accusation by "singing" the words differently.

When have children learned the "music" of their first language? Before their first birthday would be the answer most scholars have concluded. But not all parents squeal at their babies. Hispanics, Native Americans and many East Asians do not use tone of voice to alter the meaning of their words. In fact, in most of these languages, such a change in pitch does not alter the communication significantly. Sarcasm as expressed in a change of tone does not exist in these languages, in these cultures. Their tonal range is much narrower, rising or falling only one or two notes on the musical staff. Adults speak to children on the same notes they use with adults and everyone else. There is no special high-pitched, singsong voice to use with babies and small children.

Kids from such cultures may be confused when their kindergarten instructor greets them with a smile and a pitched, singsongy "GOOD Morning BOYS and GIRLS!" Accustomed to the adults in their life speaking to them on the notes G A and B in the middle of the treble staff, they are confused or even terrified by this strange person speaking to them in such an extraordinary high pitch. This person is clearly losing his mind! The children's reaction is clearly apprehensive, even fearful. Who wants to remain trapped in a classroom with a crazy teacher?

Do these instructors intend to terrify the minority kids in their classrooms? No. Of course not. Do they realize they are intimidating them? No, almost certainly not. Do these students feel welcome at school? Probably not. Do they want to return tomorrow? Not with that crazy person shouting at them, "ringing the fire alarm" every eight minutes! Tone of voice can be a significant aspect of the miscommunication that regularly occurs between teacher and rural Alaskan students.

Teachers whose first or only language is English use tone of voice to convey what linguists call "meta-messages," the context in which the spoken message is to be received. Both sarcasm and sincerity can be conveyed, depending on the way the speaker uses pitch, higher or lower notes on the musical scale. But for Native students for whom tone is irrelevant, these nuances bear no significance. By paying no attention to them, they miss certain aspects of the communication that are "obvious" to native speakers of English. On the other hand, teachers may expect students to use tone of voice to express sincerity, regret, politeness, emphasis or indifference, and perceive that the students are being insubordinate disrespectful, insincere or uncommitted from their indifferent sounding monotone. How many minority teens are disciplined or criticized because they failed to "sing" English on the expected notes!

Women tend to focus on the tone more than men do. This explains why so often it is the female who turns to her male companion with an accusatory tone and asks, "What did you mean by that, dear?" The man, having failed to notice that he had inadvertently communicated any particular metamessage will usually repeat what he just said, exactly as he first said it. This will result in a controversy in which neither party actually can pinpoint what they are upset about. Miscommunication is everywhere. It is everyone's problem. But in the multicultural classroom it affects minorities, Native children more negatively.

Distance and Volume

Besides tempo and music, distance and volume can also be factors. Most Anglo-Americans and Native adults stand approximately at arm's length from each other when talking. Frenchmen stand at about sleeve-length, and Italians generally at elbow length. These "settings" are also established in early childhood. Everyone has them but no one remembers learning them. We follow the patterns our parents and care providers established, inherited from their Elders when they were quite young. There is no absolute right or wrong in these matters, but whenever one's own boundaries are violated, metamessages abound. A person standing closer than one is accustomed seems intrusive, overbearing, and confrontational. A person standing further back seems unfriendly, unwelcoming, cold. Native students, for example in math class, when offered some personal assistance by a well-meaning instructor, may unconsciously shut down completely, refusing to respond to a person "in their space." And those whose volume dial is set louder come across as belligerent, intimidating, domineering or aggressive, while those who speak softer than a particular cultural norm seem passive, indifferent, uncommunicative or withdrawn. All these standards are cultural and relative, but when people of another culture violate the norms of another culture, they inevitably miscommunicate, sending metamessages they did not realize they were sending.

Politeness

Politeness is another system each child learns primarily by observing the way adults interact. Most cultures have at least two systems, one for dealing with relatives, close friends and social peers, and another for relating to strangers, officials and people of higher social rank. And the way one system is applied and the other abandoned differs from one culture to the next.

Showing respect to those of superior status requires the use of titles. Assuming that some people enjoy more prominent positions of power or rank, those in the inferior class address their betters as "Sir," "Madame," "Your Honor" "Your Grace," "My Lord," and ultimately "your Majesty." This form of politeness is known generally as "deferential." In certain parts of the USA children are taught that all adults outrank all youngsters. Children should speak to adult strangers as "Sir" and "Ma'am'" and address those whom they as know as "Mister" and "Misses." Politeness demands that those of inferior rank *defer* to those superior.

In the USA, over the past forty years, *deference* style has been supplanted by *solidarity.* In this system, people in a democracy assume that all citizens are equal. They are basically the same, think the same, enjoy the same rights and accept the same responsibilities. In such an egalitarian society, strangers meet and address one another by their first names. Two British doctors, using deference politeness may be introduced and greet each other as "Dr. Smith" and "Dr. Brown," while two American doctors may shake hand saying "Happy to meet you Jim," and "Glad to meet you Bob." Inevitable miscommunication occurs when the Yank meets the Brit. One uses deference "A pleasure to meet you Dr. Jones," while the other says, "Yeah, nice to meet you Dan." Both go away unsatisfied with the encounter, the English finding the American presumptuous and rude for addressing him in such familiar terms, and the American put off by the cold formality of his English counterpart. One man's politeness can be another man's rudeness.

Most Native people find these various styles of etiquette confusing. They have met schoolteachers who insist on being addressed as Mr. and Mrs. and others who introduce themselves to the community as Dave and Debbie. It never seems particularly clear what the appropriate form is, and few newcomers think of clarifying this. Different ballgames are played by different rules, but who ever realizes they are playing by their own rules and secretly critiquing others for violating them?

Rituals

Most societies also have ritual behaviors that most children have learned by observing the adults around during the first two or three years of life. They have watched grownups answer the telephone, for example with scripted greetings, or begin conversations with the expected "Hi! How are you?" This, in English, Spanish and French, is an established ritual introduction. The reply is always "Hello! Fine thanks!" This applies in all situations, no matter how incongruous. As a pastor I often visit patients in the hospital. Without thinking much about it, I can greet them with these same usual phrases, and get the same scripted answer, "Fine thanks" even where it is blatantly (as in the Intensive Care Unit) untrue. But this ritual beginning is not intended as a sincere inquiry into anyone's actual health. It is just the ritual we perform to start a conversation.

We usually require two hellos to start an interaction, and also two farewells to end one. The fastest anyone can terminate a telephone call might be an abrupt, "Wow! I've gotta be going," to which the other party says, "Well, okay!" and the first person then says "Bye!" and the second "Bye." One farewell will not suffice.

"I've got to go" Click, would be considered rude, too abrupt. The other party will almost certainly feel slighted, and in many cases, call the first back, to find out what the problem was, for there is no excuse for "hanging up on someone," unless there is a life-threatening emergency, or the first person felt insulted. We generally expect and demand our two goodbyes!

Few rural Alaskans realize this. Telephones are a new technology and villages have adapted them to their own purposes, without the alien ritual forms that European-Americans usually expect. Villagers generally know each other very well and have little need for identifying themselves. Without any ritual greetings, many tend just to start the conversation, rather abruptly compared to the Anglo American style. This can come across as impolite, abrupt, even intrusive.

Moving to a small village of 212 Yup'ik people almost a decade ago, I received telephone invitations that I could not accept because of this difference in local protocol. The phone rings. I answer "Hello, Father Michael," the caller says, "Please come over for dinner," and hangs up. I have no idea who that was or where they live, but I am the only person residing in the town who would not know. Sometimes miscommunication is hilarious.

My family did things in threes. At any gathering of our clan, there would inevitably be more food than the entire assembly could possibly consume at one sitting. The cooks had to store bowls and platters of food on adjoining tables or back in the kitchen, but they were also attentive to their guests. As soon as one finished his or her first helping of say, mashed potatoes or chicken, one of the hosts would rush to bring quantities of both to this hungry cousin. "Would you like some more?" they would ask. The guest would refuse. "Oh, no thank you. I've had so much already!" Unwilling to take no for an answer, the auntie then tries to persuade the reluctant guest, "Yes, but there is so much more, and I'm sure you have a little room for a second helping, don't you?" The guest answers, "Well, I don't know…" and the host insists "Here! Have a little! And the cousin capitulates with "Well, all right." That is the ritual. And if children did not learn this by observing their Elders refuse emphatically the first time, waiver the second and surrender on the third, they distinctly recall being reprimanded on the way home, with their mother scolding "You took the chicken on the first offer! You act like you are starving to death, like we never feed you at home!" So one way or another, kids learn the rules of the game.

But the rituals differ cross-culturally. There is virtually no way to know ahead of time where the boundaries are, what is expected as polite ritual behavior and what is perceived as substantial. Many of my Russian students at the university ask why Americans use the greeting "How are you?" when they don't mean it. This is not a ritual question in Russian, so when an American asks, a Russian hears it not as form of greeting but a sincere question, "How ARE you?" (In English the sincerity would be communicated by emphasis and tone of voice, emphasizing the verb.) The Slavic students were both confused and offended by what they perceived as the inherent hypocrisy of this encounter. "If they don't care, why do they ask?"

Even terms of gratitude are used differently in different Alaskan cultures. Yup'iks tend to express their thanks at the end of a meal, once with conviction. It is not necessary to say "Quyana" for every individual favor done at the table, the passing of the butter dish or the sugar bowl. Tlingits, on the other hand, express their gratitude for formal recognition, shouting *Gunalchéesh* whenever a speaker mentions their clan or personal names in appreciation for the respect that has been officially rendered, acknowledged and accepted. Englishmen may seem to overdo their thanks, expressing their gratitude in exaggerated phrases such as "Oh thank you so very much indeed" for minor courtesies. One wonders how they would express truly deep, sincere gratitude for a truly generous gesture. Even "thank yous" can be a problem.

Recommendations and Strategies

What can we learn from this survey of some of the inevitable pitfalls one encounters interculturally on a personal basis? First, one should not expect communication to go smoothly. Full complete reception of the speaker's message, exactly as intended, virtually never happens. What the speaker meant and what the listener received are never completely congruent. The fault lies in the system. Language is imprecise, but it is the only method we have. Miscommunication is no one's fault. It is inescapably part of every communication to some degree. So one must expect it, anticipate it and blame no one for it.

When miscommunication occurs, then, one need not become upset or angry. When a person from another cultural background violates some cultural norm you thought to be universal, realize that he or she probably did not mean to insult, confuse, or frustrate you. They did not mean to appear as dishonest, rude, incompetent or ignorant. If that is how they seemed, it was probably not their wish, and they may not have realized that they did so. They were unaware of the ballgame rules by which you play the game of life and they inadvertently violated them. But they did not even know your game existed. They were playing theirs with the best of intentions. So in principle, we should give each other the benefit of a doubt. They did not consciously send the metamessage we received.

If this same sort of breakdown occurs repeatedly with someone with whom we interact regularly, there must be a way of discussing the problem without arousing conflict or making the situation worse. In conflict resolution the technique is called "making an I statement." It entails stating as clearly and succinctly what the issue is. When a contingent of Nigerian men attended a college in Anchorage, we discovered that they intimidated and even frightened Native students by standing closer and talking louder than Alaskans were used to. The Africans felt slighted and socially ostracized, believing this was due to racism, while the Alaskans shunned the Nigerians because they found them intimidating. Standing closer and talking louder sent the metamessage "We are one bunch of angry, bossy, Black men." The solution was to compose an "I" statement that named the real issue. "I feel intimidated when you stand that close and talk that loud because it makes me think that you are angry." The formula is "I feel ____when you ___because it makes me feel ____." This way the real issue is put on the table for review, reflection discussion and potentially resolution.

Finally, whoever has superior status, rank or power, needs to say "Forgive me." I specifically recommend these words, perhaps preceded with "Please." This differs from the conventional "I'm sorry," which expresses regret for the breakdown in communication but assumes no responsibility for it. "Forgive me" expresses both an acknowledgement that the problem arose and that the speaker bares some responsibility for it, and then demands a reply. *Forgive me* is in the imperative mood. The offended party needs to respond. And he/she now has two choices. They can forgive, wipe the slate clean and begin again, or they can refuse to forgive, thereby deciding to retain their indignation. Forgiveness is an invitation to throw the anger away, but refusing to forgive amounts to keeping it, taking it home, and possibly dumping it out on the kitchen floor. Forgiveness is what the offended person does for his own emotional and psychological well being. It does not impact the offender nearly so much. In fact, the offender is not much impacted, whether or not forgiveness is rendered. Forgiveness is what we do for ourselves, rather than becoming a more resentful, angry person.

In a multicultural society we are going to miscommunicate. We will never do it perfectly, but we can learn to spot the predictable forms that miscommunication takes and be prepared to deal with them. We can learn not to assign blame for breakdowns in miscommunication. We can learn to expect breakdowns at predictable points and situations. And we can learn to repair the damage after the fact and go on.

I am convinced that Alaska is one of the most suitable places in which people of many diverse cultures can come together and work these things out. It will take commitment and perseverance. It will take time and energy. But the benefits will be tremendous and empowering. What we need is the vision and tenacity to implement positive change. And in that process I believe we will all gradually become Real People, and as we do, we will make the Great Land even greater.

This is our potential, as Alaska could be, if we are willing to change, adapt, to listen and to learn from each other, to open the channels of authentic, sincere, continuous communication across the cultural boundaries that, instead of dividing us, can enrich and empower us all.

— Michael J. Oleksa

CHAPTER 11

BUT WHAT ABOUT NOW?
by Clifton Bates

"Mainstream teachers are often surprised and hurt to find that in spite of their good intentions, they may be a part of the problem. Some react in anger." Grant & Gillispie, 1993

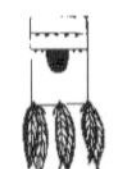

Welcoming, Accepting, Adapting

Since Mr. Ad was not a supervisor or evaluator of this staff, a principal requested his assistance. He was asked to speak to a faculty of a small village high school because the student and staff morale were exceptionally low. The majority of the students were not succeeding. The negativity was evident upon walking through the door of this dysfunctional school. The principal thought that maybe the teachers would open up to a neutral person and a discussion could begin for improvement.

When the teachers entered the meeting room following an early dismissal, they sat away from each other. There was no camaraderie. It was quiet and there was an air of hostility.

It was difficult to get a discussion going. Options of possible subjects were provided to them. Finally one teacher selected the topic concerning reading and the difficulties the students had in this area. He mentioned he couldn't do his job in his content area because the kids couldn't read. Mr. Ad attempted to suggest the value in identifying each student's reading level so that we could assure they had access to the material, and that students were not being asked to try and read information that was impossible for them to comprehend.

This was enough to widen the trickle of water that was beginning to seep through the dam. A couple more comments and the dam broke and the teachers openly expressed anger at the whole school situation. The staff became united in their frustration and resentment. Comments spewed forth about the parents not caring, the lazy, unmotivated kids who stayed up all night with no supervision and were too sleepy to attend or remain awake in classes, no one turned in homework, etc.

They were very unhappy people and if he tried to mention any possible direction or considerations, the anger escalated and became almost tangible. Mr. Ad listened, tried to be patient, and rationalized that this venting was hopefully beneficial. They were now united in their misery. But the more they vented, the more they became comfortable doing so until, as far as he was concerned, they crossed the line.

His role as an ambassador evaporated. Mr. Ad threw diplomacy out the window. Quite aggravated, he took a chance and, without considering the consequences, he climbed on a soapbox with righteous indignation.

"Here is what I hear you are saying. You don't seem to really like the kids coming through your classroom doors. I hear that you wish they were different kids. You want eager, verbal, motivated students who happily parrot back what you want, who excitingly raise their hands and immediately turn to the page asked. You want different kids.

Instead of welcoming the students you have and investigating ways to meet their needs and liking them for who they are, you have become bitter. The kids are not responding to your way of holding school. You are operating class just like the classes you attended when you were in school. You put forth no effort to figure out how you can change your ways and learn and try new methods, different ways of helping these particular students succeed.

Yes, there are many issues that effect them negatively. Yes, there is substance abuse, troubled families. So many major changes have occurred here in such a very short time. It is up to us to make the school a positive place with high and appropriate expectations, where students can succeed, be welcomed and accepted and not a place that contributes to the confusion and alienation many of them are dealing with every day."

The group was quiet and appeared somewhat baffled as Mr. Ad walked out of the room quite visibly upset. 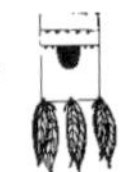

So, In the Meantime

Over the last three decades I have attended a multitude of work sessions, conferences and focus group discussions that address concerns about Alaska Native education. The failures and problems are rehashed and bantered about and each get-together seems to be a reflection of the others.

When it comes to the point in the meeting where recommendations and possible directions and solutions are presented, the content tends to be lofty, general, abstract and, at any moment, I always expect the group to burst into a chorus from John Lennon's *Imagine*. "Differentiation is the key, we need to deal with the whole child" and other such platitudes are expressed, and the group nods in agreement to the well meaning but actually meaningless comments. (I venture to say that it is impossible for schools to educate the "whole" child in any situation. But it is especially true when there is such a tremendous disparity between the "culture" of the system and those manning it and the culture of the indigenous child).

This writing is not exhaustive, not a detailed listing of methods and lessons or lofty abstracts. It is, hopefully, a beginning of a new discussion on real, possible, and specific alterations (some that are systemic, others that are up to individuals in a variety of roles) to improve Alaska Native education. The considerations are practical and provide a direction in order to abandon and progress from the status quo. Simply providing state money for nicer facilities, additional teaching resources, and increased educator pay is not the solution to the academic and social difficulties Native children experience resulting from this schooling.

Some of the recommendations contained in this document are systemic changes that are extremely difficult to make happen and are not likely to be a reality any time soon. In the meantime, what can a school district or Dave and Debbie and others do ***now*** within this current school system that exists?

New and Current Educators

"This action view includes changing the structures that perpetuate negative (Native) schooling... Certainly, in the overall view, this is a long-range revolution that frustrates many teachers absorbed in their daily schoolroom world!" Collier, p.126 1973

A concrete sequential personality, one who wants the ducks in a row, can become quite frustrated when newly placed as an educator in some village schools. Processes, systems, and organization may seem to be sorely lacking. It appears all is chaotic, there are no clear guidelines, and there is certainly no handbook spelling out the steps that need to be taken. The situation is exacerbated by the long history of educators and programs that have come and gone. It is like there is nobody home. Dave and Debbie are fortunate to have each other for support and counsel.

Trying to figure out how to cope and successfully deal with the situation requires a great deal of patience and perseverance. Attempting to get control, to create order, and to make things "normal" can be exhausting and upsetting. Dave and Debbie's situation is a real one.

With pressures from the district administration, real or imagined; the various State requirements; all the bureaucratic paperwork; all that is involved in simply operating a school, it is easy for the true purpose for being there to become lost in the confusion and stress. One might even be so distracted that the reality there are real live kids at the school to learn becomes obscured.

There is an early dismissal and the staff is attending a workshop in the school in order to articulate another slew of student outcomes and design more forms on the computer to record more data. They figuratively step over the bodies of lost students in order to get to the meeting held in some classroom where the walls are crumbling down. In seems that in some situations, everyone: principals, teachers, and students have come to a tacit agreement to just go through the motions of holding school. Too many of the schools and classrooms are simply not the happy, positive, functioning places they could and should be.

To themselves, the educators say, "I really don't know how to teach these kids. Nothing I do seems to work. They are not interested, and they just don't care. But I know I am a good teacher and I work hard, so it isn't *my* fault! And I've got enough of a handle on the situation so it looks like I'm doing my job."

The students tell themselves, "There's nothing here for me. Most of the teachers just talk and talk. We're supposed to read this and read that. But I got to be here. No place else to go anyway. At least I get to be around my friends, and it looks like I am going to school."

Of course there are and have been educators who concentrated their efforts and, on their own, figured out ways to create a unique, successful learning environment. A mechanism is needed so that such knowledge and information can be tapped for others to benefit from and allow the successes to continue when the individuals responsible for the good work have moved on. No such connection exists.

Dave and Debbie best realize that they are just another set of educators in a long line who come and go. The history of the village and school did not begin upon their arrival. They must accept certain things as a "given" in the school district's questionable procedures and not waste time and energy trying to "fix" everything all at one time. It is a matter of priorities, and the kids are truly why they are there. They are there to teach, to interact in a positive manner as the visitors that they are, and do what is best for the children in the school. Dave and Debbie need to listen, learn and realize their students, the parents and community members do not necessarily look at things in the same manner that they do and may possess different goals and views as to what is important and how to go about doing things. The values and beliefs that Dave and Debbie bring with them are not correct or superior; they are likely, though, to be quite different than their students and the parents.

Amidst all the chaos, frustration and confusion of an inappropriate system that is not likely to change any time soon, Dave and Debbie must do what they can to create a positive, safe place for the students to learn. They must welcome all the students who enter their classrooms and respect them for who they are. As professionals they must take it upon themselves to try and learn what works and what doesn't in their classrooms. They must maintain high and appropriate academic expectations for their students and avoid the influence of naysayers and negative colleagues. They need to actively seek information on their own because there is no one that is going to hand it to them. They have to self-reflect on their teaching and become classroom researchers. If a methodology isn't working, they must try and figure out why and then try other approaches. They need to investigate ideas and information on the Internet, in libraries, and with colleagues and incorporate their findings in their teaching repertoire. They need to develop a network of like-minded educators and, together, become advocates for systemic change; advocates for truly culturally responsive schools.

School Boards and Superintendents

A progressive school board and superintendent could incorporate policies within its district that reflect the proposals outlined herein regarding: curriculum, instruction, assessments; the implementation of researched-based, carefully designed structures; and the requirement that existing personnel and new hires attend an intensive training program and their charge would be to work within these structures and contribute to achieving the goals outlined therein. They would be taking an unselfish, long-range view of the district by establishing lasting processes and a means for district stability that will outlast their tenure.

A training center could be established in the hub village in the school district (e.g. Unalakleet, Mountain Village, Tok, Fort Yukon, Aniak, McGrath, Dillingham) and have the same function as the regional training centers described earlier. Individual educators identified (by evidence, not opinion) as being versed and effective regarding specific components of the structures in place could be utilized as trainers. Some training may require the expertise of consultants from elsewhere.

A menu of the training modules offered by the center would be available to all district educators. An evaluator could recommend an educator attend for a particular need that was identified through observation. A teacher or administrator may recognize a need through self-reflection and request certain training themselves. The use of the designated district resources could be modeled at this location. The center becomes the district's memory. It is where all assessment information is housed and analyzed so that what works and what doesn't can be identified and made available. Information and data could be viewed over an extended time period. The center provides focus and continuity pertaining to the district's efforts. It becomes the stabilizing force as educators come and go. It is the means for continual staff development and assists in ensuring the district structures are monitored and adjusted based on a variety of input. Such a training center pertaining to a literacy plan is outlined in Appendix 3. Training centers would be the catalyst for implementing structures and changes in curriculum, instruction and assessment.

Native Organizations

Native organizations such as the First Alaskans Institute, Alaska Federation of Natives, and the various Native corporations around the state could unite in their insistence that changes such as the ones outlined herein are implemented. They are a powerful political block that could get the needed attention and exert the necessary pressure, greatly increasing the chances that systemic change occurs and moves our approach to Native schooling in an appropriate direction and away from how it is and has been. The State department of education, universities and school districts promote and maintain the status quo, Native organizations could assist and insist in the creation of truly culturally responsive schools that are well-designed, positive places for Native children to learn.

Think how valuable it would be if Native organizations in Alaska united in their financial support of a half hour or hour television show designed for Native children in rural Alaska. It could be a Native Alaskan Sesame Street/Mr. Rogers for two to six year olds. Individuals from the various Native groups around the state would be guests and, as positive role models, share lessons in history and cultural activities at the appropriate level. I can envision someone such as Ina Bouker hosting this show and teaching concepts about print, letter-sound identification, and developing oral language proficiency in the language of the school in a very contextualized, culturally and environmentally relevant manner. Her story telling and reading aloud would be an inspiration to Native children and of monumental help in school readiness efforts. There are many very creative people who could actually make this a reality. The funding would truly be an investment in the future for Alaska's indigenous people: its youth.

If we do not prepare educators properly as to ways to effectively work with Native students and live and interact successfully in their communities; if we continue to address literacy education without taking into account relevancy and the specific needs and characteristics of the village student; if we don't make appropriate adjustments to curriculum and instruction in village schools; if we do not establish research-based, monitored structures that are not dependent on untrained educators who come and go, we will continue with the revolving door of ineffectiveness. For the most part, the funding is there. That is not the issue. But it requires a major re-allocation and re-prioritizing of efforts. To use the earlier analogy, let us put the money toward repairing the leak in the main gas line instead of on designing gas masks and other peripherals to outfit a chaotic system with transient, untrained personnel. Native students' "successfulness" will continue to be due to their increased westernization and accomplished in spite of the school system. The more remote and traditional the Native student, the more difficulties he/she experiences with school academics. The more westernized the student, the better he/she performs in the western school system.

Western culture and values, consumerism and modernization, continue to encroach upon and change traditional cultures the world over. Along with the western education system, these forces have the capacity to extinguish intangible attributes of an indigenous people such as their own unique wisdom and perspectives on existence: irretrievable elements once they are lost. Just like a language.

"Consumerism works hand in hand with the modern education system to encourage cleverness without wisdom. It teaches people to look down on their own indigenous, self-reliant culture in the name of progress and modernization." Sulak Siveraksha

Whether it is a people on an atoll in Micronesia, in the deserts of the Kalahari, or along the Amazon or Koyukuk Rivers, every generation possesses less traditional knowledge. But unhealthy diets, substance abuse, materialism, the trash of consumerism, and other ills of modern society do not have to prevail and extinguish indigenous cultures. For some places in the world it is simply too late. Responsibility in preventing or lessening such negative impact lies on many shoulders: government officials, the legal system, entrepreneurs, tourists and sportsmen, educators, medical practitioners, social workers, and the Native people themselves. Cable television, movies, pop music, and fashion are to what many of the youth are drawn and aspire. But these products of the society at large do not provide the self-respect or the respect for their culture, their Elders and ancestors, and their history that is needed to keep traditions alive and vibrant. And the dominance of schools in the lives of Native youth that, subtly or not so subtly, require their westernization do not and have not provided this respect either.

It is the 21st century. It is still not too late in Alaska. By now we should be able to interact positively with indigenous people without continuing to damage psyches and without student "success" requiring the abandonment of traditional ways and the loss of one's cultural self.

"Psychological healing is unlikely until those working with Alaska Native people come to respect and accept the Native perspective on conditions and events affecting the lives of Native people, and to understand that continuing to view these conditions and events from a Eurocentric perspective only fosters misunderstanding and inequity" (Duran & Duran, 1995).

And I Remember When

Everything was new for my wife and me when we moved to rural Alaska in 1977. As far as we knew, we had never been around a single Yup'ik Eskimo our whole lives up to this point. We had never been in this type of environment:

a windy land of flat, near-treeless tundra accessible only by air. Our sub-standard housing was an eight by twenty foot converted army horse trailer that had no running water, a honey-bucket, and was below freezing inside in the winter despite the heat from the struggling oil cook stove. The dwelling was tilted to one side and the only windows were some small portholes just below the ceiling that were covered with ice most of the year and could not be opened.

In addition to now living in a new land and new culture and in a strange shelter, I was a full-fledged teacher for the first time. Like most educators new to the scene, I was definitely overwhelmed but excited and intrigued. And like the other educators, I was provided no information about my students or what I could do to be successful in the classroom or how to live and positively interact in this community.

I was first hired as an English teacher in western Alaska. I taught seven classes of language arts with thirty to thirty-five students in each class. Ninety-five percent were Yup'ik Eskimo with some Athabaskan, all from various Yukon-Kuskokwim Delta villages due to the boarding school in place at the time. The curriculum guide I was provided then, I believe, was from Minnesota or Wisconsin. It contained elaborate matrixes and an intricate scope and sequence with items such as all students will identify all prepositions by week five. I tossed this guide in the closet on top of a pile of brand new grade level English workbooks that the previous teacher had ordered for the next teacher in line: me.

My students were reluctant writers to say the least. I would do just about anything to get them to write. One day I had thirty-some seventh grade students in front of me and there were maybe fifteen minutes of class time left. I had a little magic show up my sleeve, so I stopped the class and showed them a preview, a teaser, to build some intrigue. They were definitely intrigued. I explained that I would continue with the rest of the performance if, and only if, each student in the class agreed to write a minimum of thirty words about anything, anything, he/she wanted to write about. I went around the room and each student nodded enthusiastically in agreement. I double-checked just to make sure each one bought into the deal.

The trick succeeded wonderfully. After the initial commotion and excitement died down, I reminded them of the bargain we made, and it seemed they all started to scribble away. When the bell rang they handed their piece of writing to me as they filed out the door.

Gary Pete, from Eek, tried to slip out of the room unnoticed. But he couldn't get by his teacher's eagle eye. I called him back, shook my head and said, "Uh uh Gary, c'mon, a deal's a deal. Thirty words, have a seat." He grinned and plopped down at a desk, ripped off a corner of a piece of paper and took out a chewed-up, stub of a pencil. I moved away to give him some space.

He looked up at the ceiling, pushed his taped-together glasses up on his nose, shook his long hair, thought a bit, and then hunched over his paper scrap with his tongue sticking out of the corner of his mouth. Maybe thirty seconds went by before Gary leaned back, stuffed his stubby pencil back into his shirt pocket, stood up, grabbed his books, clomped over to me with a huge smile and handed me his scrawl. Particles of snuff speckled his white teeth. He pushed his glasses back up on his nose and bustled off to his next class. This was quite a quick write. No rewriting or editing took place. The final stage of the writing process occurred when his creation appeared in the annual student writing publication. That less-than-thirty-second piece of writing by Gary is one of my all-time favorite pieces of poetry. It has hung on the wall near my desk in all the classrooms and offices I've occupied for the last three decades.

Once again, to honor the final stage of the writing process and to recall the kind of occurrence I was so fortunate to have experienced with my students, here is what came out of Gary's chewed-up pencil stub:

The Bluebird Singing

Where the dangerous fox stalks
Over the willow her magic stays
Sing no more, O bluebird! Go
to safer shade of green leaves

Sing, and set your little foot
on a blueberry bush.

Gary Pete, 1977

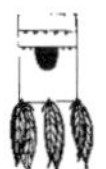

Then to Now and When

I recall that hike home from my Thinking Place that day thirty years ago when I pondered the logic, the rationale, and the irony, related to Kim-boy's situation; when I thought of similar tragedies in the making; and when I began considering how we could possibly change our schools so they would not continue to be revolving doors of ineffectiveness that so often negatively affect Alaska's indigenous children. There is comfort in imagining that the landscape for *The Bluebird Singing* is not too far from that Thinking Place near that pond I knew so well.

And there is comfort in believing that a critical mass of informed, concerned educators, policy makers, and individuals will be reached enabling definitive progress from the status quo in Alaska Native education (*Imagine*). Systemic change is extremely difficult to make happen. It will take more than concerned folk with misdirected emotions of anger and frustration echoing well intentioned but meaningless platitudes as solutions.

It begins with individuals seriously educating themselves on the subject and becoming informed, knowledgeable advocates with a positive, realistic vision that can be articulated. With enough similar minded people, the naysayers, those with limited vested interest who come and go, and those that perpetuate the system as it is and has been, can be negated.

Educators must escape the ingrained and comfortable beliefs as to how to hold school. We need an altered system manned by a higher percentage of Alaska Natives. Kim-boy's parents and grandparents experienced how it has been. Kim-boy and his brother experienced how it is. It is high time to renew and revitalize the dialogue and overcome whoever and whatever is preventing how it could be.

Clif Bates

IN CONCLUSION

The rather famously taciturn President Calvin Coolidge was asked what the sermon was about as he left church one Sunday morning. "Sin," Mr. Coolidge replied. What was the preacher's message on this topic? the reporter inquired. "He's against it," the President answered, and walked away.

Whenever educators have gathered over the last forty years to discuss issues in Alaskan Native education, they have inevitably dragged out the butcher paper and made lengthy wish lists, covering the walls of their meeting room with ideas and ideals that they collectively embrace as an ostensibly "concrete" blueprint for the future. But like President Coolidge's brief synopsis of his pastor's sermon, there is so little substance to these proposals, their content is so broad as to be meaningless. Who would vote against "dealing with or educating the whole child," or creating "culturally relevant and sensitive schools" and "appreciating and respecting different learning styles"? Of course! But the butcher paper of 1974 or of today contains identical lists. Nothing much has changed, not only because of institutional amnesia but also institutional and political inertia and resistance, and the lack of any concrete plan for discussing or implementing reform. Real change must challenge and even to some extent dismantle existing structures. Working within the system as it has been historically constituted will not suffice. It is the system itself that must change in very specific ways we have suggested here.

What would a "culturally sensitive classroom," look like in a particular community, incarnate in a particular culture, with real-life kids, in a particular school? Moving from the actual to the possible to the ideal requires a plan of implementation, a change in methods, new strategies and additional training. The "whole child" needs the community and the school to cooperate in harmony and mutual respect, not in conflict or opposition. The dissonance between them confuses, frustrates, and alienates, not only students, but parents, educators, and entire communities. It kills kids. The "whole, healthy" child deserves a "whole healthy" education, which only the school *with the community* can provide.

Our appeal here is rather simple. We are weary of the continuing deplorable situation, well-documented elsewhere. We have specifically omitted statistics on Native suicide, domestic violence, rates of fetal alcohol syndrome, substance abuse, homicide, accidental death and incarceration as both too depressing and readily available (Anyone who requires further data need only Google "Alaska Native Statistics"). We began instead by recounting our own experiences in rural Alaskan Native education and our research into its origins and history.

Our Part I basically declared: We have a problem here. We continued to suggest ways in which we can change things for the better. Just admitting the issues exist is a necessary first step. Knowing how the situation has deteriorated over the last half century is also helpful, at least insofar as it helps those struggling in today's schools to realize that it has taken a long time to mess things up as badly as they are and therefore it will take some time to reverse the current trends, break the old habits, procedures, reconsider the methods, rewrite the curricula and educate a new generation of energetic and committed teachers and administrators to creatively implement reform.

In Part II we offer some specific suggestions in teacher preparation and curriculum development so that we can begin to "educate the whole child" and create "culturally sensitive classrooms," with some genuine possibility for success, with some criteria for what success would look like.

There are no easy or quick solutions, but we can do better. Before we can move in that direction, we need to admit these problems exist, that addressing and solving them are critical to the very survival of Alaska Native communities, to the people, the children about whom we care specifically and deeply. It is our hope that each reader, as parent, as teacher, as school board member, as site or district administrator, as university professor, as commissioner, governor, secretary or president, will participate in this discussion and act, each in their own capacity, according to their position and power, to envision and implement positive change in curricula, teacher education, teaching methods, and the very structures of our school systems.

Alaskans possess, in our homes and communities, the resources and the talent to make schools welcoming and relevant to all our children including the "Kim-boys" and the "Slow Sams". The status quo, the schools as they continue to function today, are, without exaggeration, harming, wounding, damaging and ultimately destroying many Alaskan Native children. Parents, Elders, teachers, professors and politicians need to develop a common vision and commitment so that together we can become Real People, in the finest Alaskan tradition, building a healthier and more productive future for today's children and for generations to come.

We envision our State University emerging as the preeminent world-renown research, publishing, and training center, where curricula, methods, teacher education and support systems provide the best example of how the modern world and traditional societies cooperate, inform and enrich each other. In our personal experience, there have been several sporadic attempts to move in this direction. The most successful experiments have even won national recognition. Funded with "soft" grant money, however, these have been dismantled and abandoned as too costly or superfluous, rather than as central to the identity and mission of the school.

We foresee the day when teachers from all over the world flock to Alaska to experience firsthand the way we have brought together two worlds, the ancient wisdom of tribal Elders and the latest technologies, the knowledge of the modern age. We hope for the day when our rural Native graduates have assumed leadership positions in all professional fields, where, like the Aleuts nearly two centuries ago, they have, through education, reclaimed their self-identity, self-respect and sovereignty. We believe these possibilities are attainable and realistic. We need a common vision and commitment to move in this direction, to make the Great Land all that it can be, for ourselves, our children, and for generations yet unborn.

END
Michael J. Oleksa and Clifton Bates
2007

A Few Suggested Readings in 19th century Alaska Native History

• Black, Lydia T.
Good and Faithful Servant, UAF (1997)
Russians in Alaska 1732-1867, UAF Press (2004)
The Journals of Iakov Netsvetov: The Atka Years, Limestone Press, (1980)
The Journals of Iakov Netsvetov: The Yukon Years, Limestone Press, (1984)

• Dauenhauer, Richard
Conflicting Visions in Alaskan Education, UAF Press (2004)
The Spiritual Epiphany of Aleut, Orthodox Alaska, Kodiak,(1979)

• Garrett, Paul
St. Innocent, Apostle to America, SVS Press, (1979)

• Grinev, Andrei
The Tlingint Indians in Russian America 1741-1867, Univ. of Nebraska, (2005)

• Ivanov, Vyacheslav
Russian Orthodoxy in Alaska: an Attempt at a Multicultural Society, Library of Congress monograph

• Kan, Sergei
Symbolic Immortality, Smithsonian Institution, (1989)
Memory Eternal, University of Washington, (1999)

• Mitchell, Donald
Sold American, UAF, (2003)

• Mousalimas, Soterios
The Transition from Shamanism. Berghahn Books, (1995)

• Oleksa, Michael J.
Native Women Leaders: Pre-Statehood, Alaska State Department of Education
Alaskan Missionary Spirituality, Paulist Press (1987)
Orthodox Alaska, SVS Press (1994)

• Pierce, Richard, ed.
Proceedings of the Second International Conference on Russian America, Limestone Press, (1987)

• Riordan, Anne Fienup-
The Yup'ik Eskimo: John Kilbuck's Journals, Limestone Press (1988)
Wise Words, (2005)

• Solovyova, Katrina and Vovnyanko, Aleksandra
The Fur Rush, Phoenix Press (2002)

• Smith, Barbara S.
Russian Orthodoxy in Alaska
Russian America: the Forgotten Frontier, Washington State Historical Society, (1992)

• Vitt, Kurt, and Hinkelmann, John
Harmonious to Dwell, Bethel, (1987)
Varhola, Pirjo
The Etolin Collection, Finnish National Museum, Pirjo (1990)

• Veniaminov, Innocent
Notes on the Unalaska District, Limestone Press (1984)

• Andrei Znamenski UAF
Through Orthodox Eyes, (2003)

A Few Suggested Readings in Intercultural Communications and the Impact of Literacy on Oral Cultures

• Collier, James, and Blot, Richard
Literacy and Literacies: Texts, Power and Identity, Cambridge, (2003)

• Goody, John
The Interface Between the Written and the Oral, Cambridge, (1993)
The Logic of Writing and the Organization of Society, Cambridge,

• Heath, Shirely B.
Ways with Words, Cambridge, (1999)

•Oleksa, Michael J.
Communicating Across Cultures, KTOO-TV, (1994)
Another Culture/Another World, Alaska Association of School Boards, (2006)

• Olsen, David and Torrance, Nancy, eds.
Literacy and Orality, Cambridge, (1991)

• Ong, Walter
The Presence of the Word, (1981)
An Ong Reader, Hampton, (2002)
Orality and Literacy, Routledge, (2003)

• Scallon, Ron and Suzanne
Intercultural Communication: A Discourse Approach, Oxford, (1995)
Narrative, Literacy and Face in Interethnic Communication, Ablex (1981)
Interethnic Communication, UAF, (2004)

• Street, Brian, ed.
Cross-Cultural Approaches to Literacy, Cambridge, (1993)

• Tannen, Deborah
Exploring Orality and Literacy, Ablex, (1982)
Analyzing Discourse: Text and Talk, Ablex (1982)
Perspectives on Silence, Ablex (1985)
That's NOT What I Meant! Ballantine, (1986)
You Just Don't Understand, Quill, (2001)
Talking 9-5, Quill, (2001)
I Only Say This Because I Love You, Ballantine, (2002)
Conversational Style: Analyzing Talk Among Friends, Oxford, (2005)

APPENDIX 1

An Example of Using Context to Teach Concepts and Develop Oral Language Skills

The following activity involves using dictation to assist Native students by using context to teach decontextualized material as well as to help them develop oral language skills and a better understanding of the relationship between oral and written language. This technique illustrates how context can be used to assist Native students in learning decontextualized, abstract ideas, information, and concepts. This is a fairly innocuous example but it is effective and it may encourage teachers to transfer this principle to other areas of their teaching.

This is an excellent means to improve student listening and writing skills. Students get the opportunity to hear and pay attention to the rhythm of a sentence, to learn about writing conventions, to listen to ideas related to other disciplines and, as a by-product, to improve their handwriting and spelling.

Dictation also assists students who have not had exposure to reading and writing before school in knowing the "registers" of written language and in helping these students become familiar with what is involved in written language.

If writing is more than just regular speech written down, dictation models the features of written language but demonstrates the connection between oral and written language. An additional benefit of this exercise is its usefulness for students whose first language is not English; this is a valuable exercise for helping bilingual students learn to understand English speech and translate it into writing. The teacher chooses language appropriate to his/her students' levels. It is best to begin on a very easy level and then increase the difficulty over time.

Dictation can be done daily for about fifteen minutes, every other day, twice a week, or once a week depending on what the teacher decides. Dictation can be done in a special notebook that the students add to each session. This can be saved and periodically checked for improvement. As time goes by, students usually show a great deal of improvement in their ability to take dictation, and this carries over into improvement in listening to the teacher, in writing in sentences with proper conventions and more legible handwriting.

Process

1. No talking is allowed during dictation unless the teacher calls on a student at the appropriate time to speak or ask a question. Listening is the key. Though it can be difficult at first, no talking and the need to listen are crucial rules to establish.

2. At the beginning, students might be quite slow at dictation. They will display all kinds of frustration. As time goes by, the students will calm down and show great improvement if the teacher implements the rules.

3. Initially the teacher should compose about five highly contextualized sentences that are not complex. The sentences should be fairly simple and appropriate to the students' grade level. Using sentences that directly relate to the students in the classroom, (for example, using a student's name in an appropriate manner regarding her interest in basketball), and sometimes incorporating humor, allows for comprehension and causes high interest for the students in listening to the sentences about their lives and environment. Sentences can later be related to some other topic the class is dealing with such as literature being read, a content subject (sentences concerning social studies, science, health, etc.), or other appropriate topics of interest and relevance. The teacher can also ask the students for suggestions of topics they would like the sentences to concern. The intent is to move from very contextualized sentences to decontextualized information with increased comprehension.

4. The teacher should make sure the students are writing with a pencil, not pen, as erasing is often needed. The first time, the teacher reads the sentence in its entirety at a regular rate; students should just listen. There is no talking. Then the teacher repeats the sentence slowly while each student writes it down. The teacher moves around the room and observes each student's progress. Individual help can quickly be given. The sentence is slowly repeated until all students have the sentence written down. Assure the students that they do not need to panic; the teacher will read the sentence slowly until everyone has

written it down. Some may need a bit of special help at first. Students should spell the best they can. When the teacher is finished going over the different aspects of the sentence she determines are needed, then she asks the students to raise their hands and ask any questions or to get any clarification.

Sentence #1:

"Some students from Kavik will visit our school next Wednesday."

5. The teacher then helps to troubleshoot with the students, for example:

The teacher may ask, "Is the 'S', the first letter in the first word, capitalized? All sentences begin with a capital letter."

Or, "Look at the end of your sentence. Is there a period (or whatever proper end mark is needed)?"

If there is a word that the teacher sees from his/her observations that some students are having difficulty spelling: the teacher might say "Check and see if you spelled "Wednesday" correctly. It is spelled __________." It is capitalized because it is the name of a day of the week.

"The word Kavik is the name of a nearby village. That makes it a proper noun, the name of a particular place, so make sure it begins with a capital letter also."

"Does anyone have any questions? Does anyone need anything repeated?"

6. Over time as the sentences become more complex and more decontextualized, the teacher makes sure the students are informed as to the proper punctuation. The teacher can use this time to give very *brief* developmentally appropriate mini-lessons, explaining why certain things are capitalized, why a certain punctuation mark is needed, and even incorporate literary devices in the sentence, such as similes and metaphors, and discuss them. If these explanations are provided as a part of the dictation session, students are not necessarily aware that

they are receiving instruction in grammar or mechanics or content area concepts. It is just a relevant discussion. The degree of complexity is determined by what the teacher deems fitting for his/her students.

7. There are always students who zip along and write their sentences quickly. These students, while they are waiting, can be instructed to copy their sentences over a certain number of times, paying particular attention to whatever improvement is needed in their handwriting (slant, letter size, spacing, etc.); they can alter the sentence such as substituting the simile or metaphor given and provide one of their own, or they can even add or change adjectives and adverbs in the sentence. If the sentence includes content area ideas already being studied in class, students can provide additional information. Instructions and requests can be made one-to-one as the teacher maneuvers about the room.

8. Once the students get the hang of it, they can all start paying attention to the neatness of their writing. Various ways to improve their handwriting can be discussed and demonstrated. This is a good way to teach this skill since it is often not a part of today's curriculum.

These are just some examples of what can be done during dictation. Many other "mini-lessons" and bits of skill instruction can be incorporated as well. Dictation can be kept in individual student notebooks where progress can easily be observed. As the sessions continue, many students become quite proud of all the writing they have accomplished. They are able to see their improvement themselves as to the ease they gain with practice in listening and writing. Teachers will notice an increase in student comprehension of content area concepts presented during dictation, possibly an improvement in writing mechanics, in their handwriting, their overall language arts skills, as well as in their ability to listen and comprehend when the teacher talks to the class in other situations.

The main purpose for incorporating this technique relates to developing oral language proficiency as well as using highly contextualized content to teach concepts, abstracts, and decontextualized knowledge and skills.

APPENDIX 2

Using Context to Teach Test Taking Skills

As indicated previously, some Alaska Native students can demonstrate a certain proficiency on one-on-one diagnostic tests but often are not able to show the same proficiency on group tests (standardized or performanced-based). Three main factors (not related to a student's knowledge or abilities) can negatively affect the scores:

1. Testing conditions. Anything that contributes to testing conditions not being optimum can influence scores (e.g. substitute teachers, disruptions, lighting, proximity to a holiday or sporting event, etc.).

2. Attitudes of the test giver or the test taker. If the test giver does not present the test as a valuable activity and explain its purpose and that the students need to try and do their best. If a student does not see any purpose in doing well, is not motivated to try and do well on the test.

3. The degree to which the student possesses test-taking strategies including understanding the mechanics of test taking (filling in bubbles properly, ensuring correct alignment of answers, etc.).

There is a clear need to teach test taking skills in an appropriate, purposeful manner. There are many ways to do this. What follows is simply one example that incorporates the use of context directly related to a particular group of Native students

This is one procedure in developing a practice test designed for a particular class of third grade students. Initially it is highly contextualized and, thus, creates a high level of interest and familiarity. This helps remove one more obstacle in comprehending what is written by using known, recognizable information. Passage items relate to the students in the class and where they live. The students are taken by the hand and led slowly through the process repeatedly.

Procedure:

1. The teacher creates the test behind the scenes by listing the students in class and identifying known interests of each student.

2. Using the same format, reading level, and length as the actual test, the teacher writes passages which include the students' names and something related to their interests in the local setting using familiar places and landmarks. Two words are selected (in italics) as vocabulary words to be used in that portion of the test (This particular practice test is modeled after the Gates-McGinity Reading Test).

3. Friday: One test item is placed on an overhead and the teacher reads the passage aloud. The class choral reads the passage. The teacher reads the question. The class choral reads it. The teacher goes over each answer option and discusses how it does or doesn't make sense. The students and the teacher arrive at the correct answer and identify why it is correct. Strategies for selecting the answer are modeled.

4. Students mark the bubble on the answer sheet provided. The teacher makes sure this is correctly done.

5. Monday: A hard copy of Friday's test item is provided to each student. The one item test is given with a start and appropriate stop time.

6. The teacher collects the tests, and later counsels any student with an incorrect answer. He/she discusses individually with the student why he/she selected that answer, why it is incorrect and how the correct one can be chosen. Potentially difficult or new vocabulary is in italics. The words can be discussed and a short definition or synonym supplied. A separate vocabulary test can be devised similar to the format of whatever real test the students must take.

7. After three or four weeks, the teacher combines the previous test items and administers a longer test. The teacher reviews the questions and answers with the group. The teacher again reviews strategies with

each student with incorrect responses. As the weeks progress and the test gets more closely to the length of the real test, the teacher can start incorporating items that are less contextualized. Strategies for selecting answers are modeled the same way, preparing the students for the actual, decontextualized test.

Example (Grade Three, Age 8)

#1. Stephen wanted to go grouse hunting. "I know I can find one in the field near Brown's Store," he said. Stephen called Patrick and asked him if he wanted to go.

Patrick said, "I can't go. I am going moose hunting upriver near Kavik with my dad and uncle."

Stephen was sad. *Perhaps* Patrick could go grouse hunting the next day. Stephen decided to *remain* at home and play with his younger brother.

1. What did Stephen want to do?
   - O To go moose hunting
   - O To go grouse hunting
   - O To go see Patrick
   - O To go hunting with his dad
2. Where was Patrick going?
   - O Grouse hunting
   - O To visit Stephen's brother
   - O With his dad and uncle upriver
   - O He was staying at home
3. Stephen was sad because
   - O He could not find a grouse
   - O He didn't know a place to go grouse hunting
   - O Patrick couldn't go moose hunting
   - O Patrick couldn't go grouse hunting

APPENDIX 3

Alaska Native Students in Village Schools -Overview of Literacy Plan- An Example of a Structure To Be Imposed

This example plan is built on the premise that literacy (school language proficiency) is the centerpiece of school learning. Our school system rewards verbal ability. Students with inadequate listening, speaking, reading, and writing skills in the language of the school are at a clear disadvantage academically. The purpose of the plan is to act as a structure that remains as personnel come and go as well as provide a means of evaluating resources and methodologies over time. This example is not complete but provides a blueprint, a sketch of what can be done.

For the majority of rural Alaska Native students, school language proficiency is not their area of strength. This is not related to intelligence nor is it a criticism of Native students. This research-based proposal is in response to the literacy needs of these students that have not and are not being met in our village schools. A concerted effort must be implemented that addresses the characteristics of village students stemming from environmental and cultural traits (as discussed previously in this text).

Students proficient in school language establish positive self worth. It allows access to success in school (and on State tests), assists in developing problem solving skills and decision-making abilities as well allowing positive interaction with the society at large.

Examples of some of the components of this proposal are included. The intent of this overview is be concise, and not delve into lengthy explanations, be all-inclusive, provide reference sources concerning the various aspects of the plan or recommend specific instructional materials. This is by no means an entire working model. It is an example of how a school district's efforts in developing literacy can be articulated and used as a structure that remains in place and is adjusted on a continual basis. The costs and difficulties involved in implementing a complete plan to address literacy can be alleviated, for example, by emphasizing efforts in the K-2 program in year one, expand to grade eight the second year and then be all inclusive, school readiness efforts to grade twelve, in year three.

I. Articulate a Literacy Plan

All information including resources, assessments, certain specific methodologies and topics to be addressed and used throughout the preK-12 process are indicated in a written plan. This plan is monitored continually and adjusted based on assessment results and discussion among all participants. This plan enables staff development to be focused and coordinated. It assists in determining desirable skills and knowledge when seeking new staff members for hire.

The plan indicates the coordinated, sustained, progressive efforts this school district is implementing in order to address the literacy needs of all students as they move along the preK-12 continuum. By obtaining various assessment information and by monitoring individual and group growth over a long time period, informed decisions can be made on a continual basis regarding needs and the effectiveness or ineffectiveness of each component of the plan.

In order to maintain continuity and to acquire the necessary assessment data to make informed decisions and adjustments, it must be ensured that this plan exists over time and is not personnel dependent. A new superintendent or new principal must agree to continue with this plan and not start the district or school off into a new direction. The charge of new and all personnel is to carry out the goals of the plan according to whatever their role.

A school or a district's literacy plan can involve different resources and different approaches than those mentioned here, but certain tenets would likely be included in all plans.

Examples of basic tenets common to all plans:

- Oral language development is a definite, purposeful, progressive strand throughout the school day.

- All staff is committed to the literacy plan and emphasis on literacy development takes place throughout the school day.

• Multiple appropriate assessments are used. Education decisions are not made based on any one assessment.

• Assessments are used to diagnose individual strengths and weaknesses in literacy, to monitor individual and group progress, to determine reading proficiency in order to appropriately match reading materials, and to acquire miscues and other information to help guide instruction.

• Students are provided access to appropriate materials (fiction/nonfiction) that can be read at a 90% success rate.

• Each teacher of a student is informed as to that student's reading proficiency and adjusts student tasks accordingly.

• Content area teachers are provided with the resources and skills needed to assist students in comprehending decontextualized information.

• Training for all teachers and administrators regarding all aspects of the plan is available and provided on a continual basis.

For too long programs, assessments, efforts and energies have been uncoordinated, disjointed, fragmented, and short lived due to reliance on particular individuals in administrative positions or due to it being left up to individual classroom teachers operating in isolation with no connection to any unified effort or plan. Consistent efforts have not been sustained long enough to obtain meaningful assessment data over time in order to make informed decisions. For the most part, literacy instruction has not taken into consideration the needs particular to Alaska Native students. A literacy plan provides a common language allowing the participants to communicate about their efforts with each other, with parents, and with students.

The overall goal of this plan is to assist students in acquiring reading proficiency that is at or above their age level. Components of the plan are delineated in various ways to make the efforts, resources, and assessments visible and accessible.

Example
Delineating Assessments and Resources

Components of an Example Literacy Plan							
Assessment		**Age 5** **Kindergarten** •Concepts About Print •Letter/Sound Identification •Running Records to students who are reading	**Age 6-7** **Grades 1 and 2** •Running Records •Letter/Sound Identification •Woodcock Diagnostic Reading Battery	**Age 8-11** **Grades 3-5(6)** •Running Records •Qualitative Reading Inventory •Woodcock Diagnostic Reading Battery	**Age 11-13** **Grades (6)7-8** •Qualitative Reading Inventory •Woodcock Diagnostic Reading Battery	**Age 14-18** **Grades 9-12** •Qualitative Reading Inventory •Woodcock Diagnostic Reading Battery
	State Tests:	Dibbles	Benchmark Tests	Terra Nova		HSQE
Resources	**School Readiness Efforts** •School Readiness Coordinator •Resources to homes: KEEP books, Magazine for Parents (e.g. *Parent and Child, Let's Find Out*), Child desks for homes, Magnetic letters, crayons •Oral language activities •Modeling reading aloud to child	•Saxon Phonics •KEEP books •Houghton Mifflin Integrated Language Arts Program. •Benchmark Books •Rigby books •Media Center materials: class sets of leveled books, literacy kits	•Benchmark books •Saxon Phonics •Houghton Mifflin Integrated Language Arts Program •Asper Folta Kit •Daily Oral Language •Media Center materials; class sets level books, literacy kits	•Benchmark books •Saxon Phonics •Houghton Mifflin Integrated Language Arts Program •Daily Oral Language •Media Center materials; Class sets level books, literacy kits •ASG content texts	•Literature anthologies •Daily Oral Programs •High interest leveled books •Media Center materials; class sets leveled books, literacy kits •ASG content texts	•Literature anthologies •Daily Oral Programs •High interest leveled books •Media Center materials; class sets leveled books, literacy kits •ASG content texts

II. Assess Implementation of This Plan

An assessment rubric is used to determine to what degree the various components of the plan are being implemented by classroom teachers. By using the Literacy Plan Evaluation Rubric, knowledgeable administrators can assess a teacher's ability regarding each aspect of the plan and/or a teacher can self-assess his/her own knowledge and abilities. Any area that is scored less than proficient requires the teacher to attend the training center or spend time in another identified teacher's classroom to observe effective instruction or use of resources regarding that particular element.

Literacy Plan Evaluation Rubric

Criteria	Score
•Is there an interrupted block of time devoted to literacy instruction (minimum 90 minutes is recommended)?	
•During this block of time, are there opportunities for: -whole class instruction? -small group instruction? -one-on-one instruction? -teacher reading aloud to class?	
•Does each student have a literacy profile which is up-to-date, and has an explanation of that student's individual literacy needs? Are strengths and weaknesses identified? Are strategies, activities and appropriate comments written on the profile regarding that student and updated throughout the school year?	
•Are activities, strategies, and various means of instruction implemented on an ongoing basis to address the individual student's identified literacy needs?	
•Each student is assessed on a continual basis in order to: -ensure reading materials are at an appropriate level for that student -to monitor progress and effect of intervention strategies -to analyze miscues & other information to help guide instruction	
•Does the teacher understand how to interpret and utilize the various assessment results for each student and groups of students?	
•Is writing instruction based on the writing process and does writing assessment incorporate the analytical writing assessment rubric? Are the writing process model and assessment rubric on display for students to see?	
•Are the State reading and writing performance standards used as the basic plan as to what students need to know and be able to do?	
•Are advanced proficiency readers challenged with appropriate reading materials, critical thinking activities and standards-based tasks?	
•Are students being asked to read aloud only if it is for teacher assessment or only if the student has the opportunity to rehearse and practice reading the material before hand (or in such activities as paired reading)?	

•Are models which meet or surpass expectations of what the teacher is asking students to do available for students in order for them to see what the desired product looks like (e.g. writing samples, diagrams, explanations, etc.)?	
•Are there activities included in the literacy time which assist students in increasing oral language (listening and speaking) proficiencies?	
•Are students being taught test-taking strategies, motivated to try and do well on the various tests, and provided practice tests on an ongoing basis throughout the school year so that they are better able to demonstrate their true proficiency on group tests (e.g. Terra Nova, Benchmark Tests, HSQE)?	
•In kindergarten are concepts about print taught on a regular basis to ensure each child masters the fifteen basic concepts about print by the end of the school year?	
•In kindergarten is the alphabet taught on a regular basis so that students recognize letters and know their sounds?	
•Are materials and information being sent to parents at home to support our literacy efforts (e.g. KEEP books, *Parent and Child* magazine, *Let's Find Out,* ideas for parents to do at home with children)?	
•If learning centers/stations are set up in a classroom, are the necessary components evident? (Purpose? Means of Evaluation? Clear Instruction? Models of desired product? Expectations?	
•Are reading materials of appropriate levels available for students to select from and check out to read and take home?	
•Is there a variety of reading materials available: fiction, non-fiction, magazines, newspapers, manuals, etc.?	
•Are the designated assessments being administered according to the district Literacy Plan and are the required assessment results provided to the district literacy coordinator by the due dates?	
•Do secondary literacy teachers provide reading assessment information to content teachers so that individual reading proficiencies are known by each student's teacher and materials are matched?	
•Are content area teachers incorporating strategies to assist students with reading difficulties in reading for information and comprehending decontextualized material?	

Evaluator or teacher rates self between 1 and 4 based on the following criteria:

1= No Evidence/Unfamiliar Concept
2= Some Progress
3= Almost Achieved
4= Achieved

III. Individual Student Literacy Profiles

Each student will have a literacy profile that contains all assessment information related to literacy. Teachers indicate specific strategies used with this student that were effective or ineffective. A student's strengths and weaknesses, habits, his/her attitude toward reading/writing as well as his/her reading interests, likes and dislikes are noted.

This profile is designed to assist the teacher in monitoring this student's progress. It is designed to be useful when an instructional aide is involved in literacy instruction allowing communication between the aide and the teacher. This profile provides valuable information to content teachers, to the parent when conferencing as well as to every new teacher the child encounters from year to year. It is a working form, designed to be utilized by teachers and instructional aides and not for administrative purposes.

IV. Additional Personnel

The position of district Literacy Coordinator (often an itinerant position) is a crucial role for ensuring the success of a plan to address literacy. S/he must be exceptionally well trained and versed in all aspects of the articulated literacy plan. This person ties it all together from school readiness through high school by being responsible for the following:

- Providing or facilitating/arranging training for instructional aides, teachers, and administrators regarding all aspects of the Literacy Plan

- Acclimating new staff to the Literacy Plan

- Coordinating the administration of all literacy assessments

- Providing support in interpreting assessment results and diagnosing reading and writing difficulties

- Gathering and recording all assessment information to be housed in a central location for the purpose of evaluating all aspects of the district's literacy efforts

- Modeling reading and writing teaching strategies using district resources and for specific identified individual difficulties

- Ensuring the Literacy Plan is being carried out in all schools and classrooms

- Scheduling and facilitating ongoing formal discussions regarding the various aspects of the plan including assessments and resources in order to monitor effectiveness and make adjustments accordingly

- Monitoring availability of literacy resources so that all schools and classrooms have appropriate and adequate instructional materials

- Establishing and maintaining a teacher literacy resource library at each site

- Reporting regularly to the school board and the superintendent regarding the district's literacy efforts

A School Readiness Coordinator would also likely be an itinerant position. This person would be responsible for coordinating various activities to assist interested parents in preparing their children for entering school. This individual regularly contacts parents of children who have not entered school, visits their homes and works with those parents who would like to receive resources and information related to literacy. S/he models reading aloud to children and provides activities related to oral language development and concepts about print. This coordinator acts as a liaison to assist in bridging a child's initial attendance at school as well as in developing positive communication and relationships between the school and the home. In some situations it would be necessary for this person to be bilingual.

V. Resources

Strategies and activities to meet individual student and group needs are drawn from a variety of resources. They are not acquired in any one source or canned program. A site library, as well as classroom resources, provide effective reading teaching strategies and ideas.

A large quantity of leveled books of various genres and topics, fiction and nonfiction must be available for students to select from that are on their independent reading level. If a reading program exists in the district or school, teachers can draw from this resource for particular purposes. All available literacy resources for teachers and students are delineated in the plan.

VI. Use of Assessments

A variety of assessments are used with each student in addition to the State mandated tests. This is a critical component of the plan. This enables individual student needs to be met by design and not by chance.

Assessment results are reviewed continually in order to:

- Monitor individual and group strengths and weaknesses and progress

- Guide instruction to meet individual needs

- Determine student proficiency level to ensure tasks and materials are appropriate

- Determine effectiveness of resources and methodologies

One-on-one diagnostic tests are administered (by the classroom teacher and one test by an outside test giver), whole class tests (performance and standardized) are given, and other teacher tests and teacher observations are used. Assessments are a part of the written plan. It is indicated in the plan who administers the test, the purpose of the test, and when it is administered. Staff development is provided regarding interpreting and utilizing assessment results.

Currently the State requires that an eleven-year old student in grade 5 be given the Terra Nova, a group achievement test, as well as group standards-based assessments in math, reading and writing. The Literacy Plan indicates that if this student is below level in reading he would be given the one-on-one Woodcock Diagnostic Reading Battery by the district Literacy Coordinator in September to get base-line data and diagnostic information. Around this time the classroom teacher would administer the Qualitative Reading Inventory, a one-on-one informal reading assessment, to obtain a reading proficiency level as well as miscues to help guide instruction.

Based on the assessment results and the teacher and instructional aide's observations a plan or prescription would be devised in order to meet this student's needs by design and not by chance. Various specific strategies and activities would be identified to address these needs. This information is all placed on this student's Literacy Profile. The classroom teacher proceeds in teaching the various aspects of reading but also ensures the student receives this specific assistance.

The Qualitative Reading Inventory is administered periodically throughout the year to ensure the intervention efforts are successful, to determine if instructional strategies need to be altered, and to monitor this student's reading proficiency. The Woodcock Diagnostic Reading Battery is administered at the end of the school year to identify the student's growth, reading level, and to obtain diagnostic information.

Example
Delineating Assessment Information

LITERACY ASSESSMENT					
Test	**Type of test**	**Administered to**	**Administered by**	**Purpose**	**When**
Concepts About Print	One-on-one test. Abbreviated form of Clay's CAP test.	Kindergarten students, Grade 1 students by teacher observation.	District Literacy Coordinator	Gives indication of reading readiness	Pretest administered in fall, post- test in the spring.
K-2 Primary Reading Assessment	One-on-one test. Running record is performed.	Teachers determine which kindergarten students to administer this to. All students in grade 1-2. Some teachers can administer this to students in grades 3-5 as well instead of QRI.	Classroom teacher, instructional aide, Literacy Coordinator	Miscues can be analyzed to help guide instruction. Reading level is determined so appropriate reading material can be provided to student. Provides means of viewing	Running Records can be administered once a month if desired. Scores district records are first Benchmark level determined in fall & end Benchmark level noted in spring.
Woodcock Diagnostic Reading Battery	Diagnostic Test with up to ten subtests. Administered one-on-one. Subtests: L-W Identification Word Attack Reading Vocab. Passage Comp. Incomplete Words Sound Blending Oral Vocab. Listening Comp Memory Sentences Visual Matching	All ten subtests administered to students in grades 1-3. Four main subtests administered to students in grades 4-11 unless student maintains at or above age-level reading proficiency for two years.	District team, Literacy Coordinator. Not by classroom teacher.	Diagnose reading proficiency and related attributes to determine strengths and weaknesses. Results are used along with classroom teacher's observations & assessments to determine prescription of specific reading teaching strategies. Expected growth is number of months between pre and post tests.	Pretest administered in fall, post- test in the spring. Must be at least 6 months apart.

VII. Staff Development, Teacher Training Related to Literacy

Teacher training is continual, focused and determined by specific, identified needs. The contents of the literacy plan provide a basis and direction for staff development efforts and can assist in hiring educators with specific areas of expertise. All components of the articulated literacy plan are available (in district or in school) for teachers and principals to receive training year around (See Training Center). General topics for example:

- Literacy concerns particular to Alaska Native students
- Use of assessments, interpreting and utilizing results
- The use of specific resources such as an adopted phonics program
- Oral language instruction and assessment
- Whole class, small group, one-on-one instruction
- Establishing effective learning centers
- Effective use of an instructional aid during the literacy block
- Strategies for reading in the content areas
- Making useful observations regarding a student's literacy skills

VIII. Literacy Training Center

To address the issue of staff turn over and the difficulties in maintaining a sustained, progressive and focused means of training staff, a center is established in the district to which all educators (instructional aides and parents) have access to receive training in all aspects of the literacy plan including school readiness efforts. Often training is sequential by nature (beginning to advanced) and it is difficult to ensure all staff has the opportunity to receive professional development on all stages. A training center allows peers to train those teachers and principals who are new, those who were not able to attend a session, or those who did not comprehend a certain aspect. It is crucial that administrators, as instructional leaders, attend all training opportunities and have a working knowledge of all aspects of the literacy plan. How else can they assist, support, and evaluate teaching staff and instructional aides?

This center is equipped with the various resources available in the classrooms. Trainers are outside consultants, teachers and administrators proven to be effective regarding a certain aspect of the literacy plan. A well-equipped center will provide opportunities to demonstrate effective reading stations and learning centers, and to demonstrate teaching and tutoring techniques. Students can be available to assist as training subjects in order to model teaching strategies.

By using the Literacy Plan Evaluation Rubric, administrators can assess a teacher's skills regarding each aspect of the plan and/or a teacher can self-assess his/her own abilities. As stated earlier, any area that is scored as being less than proficient requires the teacher to attend the training center or spend time in another identified teacher's classroom to observe effective instruction regarding that particular element. The school or district provides a substitute teacher and transportation and lodging (if needed) for staff attending this center.

There are circumstances where it is more effective for the trainer from the center to travel, if necessary, and model practices in the teacher's classroom with students.

In some village schools substitute teachers are very difficult to come by, so it would be difficult for classroom teachers to attend the training center. This training center would likely be located in the hub or larger village where qualified substitutes are available. The substitute could be flown to the school and take over for the teacher that would take the same plane back to the training center.

IX. Emphasis at Age Levels (Brief Examples)

• *School Readiness Efforts*

Parents who are interested are able to take part in efforts in conjunction with school personnel in preparing students for entering school. Literacy behaviors, oral language development, access to print, reading aloud to children, school language materials are all a part of the literacy school readiness efforts. Ideally a school readiness coordinator visits homes and works directly with parents and their children.

• *Preschool/Kindergarten*

The main literacy-related goals at this age level (4-5) are to develop an oral language foundation in the school language, ensure students acquire basic concepts about print, gain abilities in letter/sound identification, and positive attitudes toward reading.

• *Elementary Ages 6-10*

Uninterrupted ninety-minute blocks of time each morning are devoted to literacy instruction. Whole class, small group, one-on-one instruction, and learning centers are incorporated. A literacy instructional aide works with the classroom teacher to ensure learning centers are functioning properly and allows the teacher to engage in one-on-one instruction to meet the diagnosed needs of individual students. Oral language instruction occurs as an integral part of the literacy block time..

• *Middle School/Secondary*

Students who are identified through various assessments as being less than proficient at their age level in reading and writing continue in a secondary 90 minute literacy block of time. Literacy classes focus on individual student needs in reading and writing as diagnosed by school/ district and State assessments and teacher observation. The teacher and instructional aide are trained in the teaching of reading. Traditionally secondary English/language arts teachers are not trained in diagnosing and addressing reading difficulties.

These classes have a different focus than the traditional secondary language arts/ English courses in that they are designed to assist each student in achieving a level of proficiency in reading and writing consistent with his/her age level. Reading instruction is generally not a part of the usual 6-12 English/language arts class and those teachers are usually not trained in the teaching of reading.

Middle school/secondary literacy classes include whole class, small group, one-on-one instruction as well as learning centers that address specific components of reading and writing. The curriculum is the State reading and writing performance standards for the particular age level of the student

At the onset of the school year and then again mid-year, the literacy teachers meet with each staff member and review the literacy profiles of each student in that teacher's class. Content teachers are provided with the knowledge of each student's reading proficiency and have available subject materials at various reading levels. It is assured that the reading tasks content teachers ask of each student are not at or above his/her frustration level. Content area teachers are trained in various pre-reading, vocabulary and guided reading strategies as well as in understanding the issues in assisting students in comprehending decontextualized lecture and text.

X. Example Instructional Concerns

• *Oral Language Proficiency*

An oral language curriculum must be implemented. Not just occasional oral language teaching activities but an organized, focused plan of objectives stating what we want students to know and be able to do, that is progressive in nature, and one that includes assessments.

There is a substantial amount of information available that indicates reading instruction will not be successful if the students do not possess an adequate oral language foundation. There is ample evidence available that the majority of village Native students do not possess oral language proficiency in school language to the degree needed to gain adequate proficiency in reading and, thus, function successfully in the school setting.

Like concepts about print and letter and sound identification, oral language ability is another attribute not sufficiently developed in many of these students. The school system, though, generally approaches reading instruction as if the students do possess these attributes.

• *Contextualized/Decontexualized Material*

The considerations concerning this instructional concern are previously addressed in this text.

• *Fiction to Nonfiction*

There are special considerations that need to be made around grade three (age eight). This is when students begin to be asked to read for information. They are asked to read text-type material whereas to this point they have only listened to and read narrative fiction. Teachers have told them stories or have read stories that entertain and have a plot. Native students who may still be learning to read may need assistance in understanding that reading for information requires different skills. A passage concerning hygiene in the third grade workbook does not have a plot, and it is not necessarily entertaining. This is another skill that is needed but too often assumed the child possesses.

• *Spatial/Perceptual Skills*

As stated earlier in this text, the school system rewards verbal ability and this is the weakest area for many Native students. Students strong in communication skills have a clear advantage in this system. This same system generally does not provide the opportunity for Alaska Native students to demonstrate the special strengths many of them do possess.

Spatial ability and perceptual skills can be included in the curriculum in a variety of ways: mapping, geometry, mechanics, drawing, carving, and model building are some examples. This cannot help but assist in developing positive self-esteem and a more favorable attitude toward school in students who are experiencing negative rewards in an academic verbal world. We cannot continue concentrating on the weaknesses of these students, expecting them to fit into this model and, at the same time, ignore their unique strengths. These strengths can be incorporated to assist in developing proficiency in verbal ability. A more complete plan could include a list of available teacher and student resources and examples of suggested activities.

• *Language Experience Approach (LEA)*

This is a methodology often used with limited English proficiency speakers. It became well known in the seventies as a successful way of teaching English as a second language. It is an approach to reading instruction based on activities and stories developed from the personal experiences of the student. In general, the personal experiences (individual or communal) are written down by the teacher. They are read together chorally, associating the written word with the spoken word and, by repetition, gaining automaticity. This practice leads to individual students gaining proficiency.

Why Include the Language Experience Approach?

- It assists in developing a stronger oral language foundation: increases listening skills, develops speaking skills.

- By using students' own language as the basis for activities, it is highly contextualized and, thus, very meaningful and motivational.

• A clear relationship is made between thought, oral language and writing.

• It shows thoughts and ideas can be spoken and written.

• It demonstrates that print conveys meaning.

• It contributes to concept development and vocabulary growth.

• It helps build a sense of community with the teacher and learners.

• It assists students in gaining fluency by repeated readings of passages consisting of familiar words they do not need to decode.

• Various State standards are addressed such as sequencing, restating, summarizing, supporting details, multi-step directions, etc.

REFERENCES

Blakesley, K. Zirkelbach, T. The Language Deficient Child, Academic Therapy/20:5May 1985

Bock, R. Feldman, C. Cognitive studies among residents of Wainright, Alaska, Arctic Anthropology, 1970, VII 1, 101-105

Braunger, J. Lewis, J. Building a Knowledge Base in Reading, NWRL, 1997

Brown, G. Reading and language arts curricula in elementary and secondary education for American Indian and Alaska Natives, Review Literature, 1991, 1-36

Buckley, M. What Basic Oral Language Strategies Need To Be Included In An Integrated English Language Arts Program, University of Alaska, Anchorage, 1993, 7

Coles, R. Eskimos, Chicanos, Indians, Children In Crisis. Boston, Toronto: Little, Brown and Co., 1977.

Collier, J. Jr. (1974). A Classroom is not a Fish Camp. In J. Orvik, & R. Barnhardt (Ed.), Cultural Influences in Alaska Native Education. Fairbanks, AK: Center for Northern Educational Research, University of Alaska Fairbanks.

Collier, John Jr. Alaskan Eskimo Education: A Film Analysis of Cultural Confrontation in the Schools. San Francisco, California, Holt, Rinehart and Winston, 1973

Duran, E. & Duran, B. (1995). Native American postcolonial psychology. New York: State University of New York Press.

Florey, J. Identification of gifted children among American Indian population, an inservice model, RIEJAN87, ED273399, May, 1986

Gillespie, L, Grant A. Joining the Circle A Practitioner's Guide to Responsive Education for Native Students, 1993

Kaulbeck, B. Style of learning among Native children: a review of the research, Review Literature, 1984, v11, 27-37

Kleinfeld, J. Effective Teachers of Indian and Eskimo High School Students. Alaska: Institute of Social, Economic and Government Research, 1972

Kleinfeld, J. Intellectual strengths in culturally different groups: an Eskimo illustration, Review of Educational Research, 3, 1973

Lipinski, T. Visiospatial and verbal-sequential performance of rural remote Alaskan Native, urban Alaskan Native, and urban Alaskan white male children, Research in Education, 1990, v6 n3, 43-47

More, A. Learning styles and Indian students: a review of research, Evaluative Report: Conference papers: Review Literature, 1984, 1-13

Moore, B. Living history: using role-playing in the classroom, Conference paper, 1976, 1-14

Olsen, J. The Verbal Ability of the Culturally Different, Teaching the Language Arts to Culturally Different Children, Editors: Joyce, Banks, Addison-Wesley, 1971, 68

Oswalt, W. Bashful No Longer, An Alaskan Eskimo Ethnohistory, 1778-1988, University of Oklahoma Press, Norman and London, 1990

Reyhner, J. Teaching Reading to American Indian/Alaska Native Students, ERIC 2001

Salisbury, L. Communication for survival, the COPAN program, Journal of English as a Second Language, 1969, vol. IV, 25-34

Sanders, B. A Is for Ox. New York. Vintage Books, 1995

Stodolsky, S. , Lesser, G. Learning patterns in the disadvantaged, Harvard Educational Review, 1967, 37, 22-69

Stewig, J. Oral Language: A Place in the Curriculum? The Clearinghouse, December 1988

Streiff, V. Reading Comprehension and Language Proficiency Among Eskimo Children, New York, Arno Press, 1980

Swisher, K. American Indian/Alaska Native learning styles: research and practice, ERIC, EDO-RC-91-4, 1991, 1-3

York, G. *(1989).* The Dispossessed: Life and death in Native Canada. Toronto: Lester and Orpen.